D0710658

RACE AND LABOR
◄ IN ►
WESTERN COPPER

The Fight for
Equality, 1896–1918

Philip J. Mellinger

THE UNIVERSITY OF ARIZONA PRESS

TUCSON AND LONDON

The University of Arizona Press
Copyright © 1995
Arizona Board of Regents
All rights reserved

♾ This book is printed on acid-free, archival-quality paper.
Manufactured in the United States of America

00 99 98 97 96 95   6 5 4 3 2 1

Library of Congress Cataloging-in-Publication Data

Mellinger, Philip J., 1940– .
    Race and labor in western copper : the fight for equality,
1896–1918 / Philip J. Mellinger.
        p.   cm.
    Includes bibliographical references and index.
    ISBN 0-8165-1477-1 (alk. paper)
    1. Copper miners—Southwestern States—Political activity—
History.   2. Trade-unions—Copper miners—Southwestern States—
History.   3. Strikes and lockouts—Copper mining—Southwestern
States—History.   4. Labor movement—Southwestern States—History.
I. Title.
HD8039.M72U66   1995   94-18730
331.89'2823431'0976—dc20   CIP

British Library Cataloguing-in-Publication Data
A catalogue record for this book is available from the British Library.

For Dad, Dan, Dave, and Bonnie

CONTENTS

ILLUSTRATIONS

ACKNOWLEDGMENTS

Because I am a native Chicagoan, western history didn't come naturally. I learned the West slowly, from many, many helpful people. This book began long ago, as both a master's thesis about Wyoming and a Ph.D. dissertation about Utah, Nevada, and the Southwest; but most of it developed more recently, and I can best remember, and thank, those who have helped bring it to fruition within the last few years.

James D. McBride accompanied me through recent years of verbal excursions in early Arizona history. Jim offered thoughtful discourse, frequent and careful correction, and he generously shared a wealth of ideas. For more than twenty years, Helen Zeese Papanikolas has been explaining Salt Lake County, Utah, history to me. Helen and her husband Nick practically created the modern academic basis for the study of Utah ethnic history, and her advice and encouragement have been immeasurably helpful.

Several people were especially generous with research assistance, reading of introductory sections, sympathetic comment, or translation suggestions. I'm very grateful to my father, Morris Mellinger, and to Bonnie McKinley, Sally M. Miller, James Foster, Chris Marin, Maria Orr, R. Emmett Melia, and Jean Nudd for their staunch and timely support. I also benefited from extensive discussions or assistance from Charles Ambler, Beatrice Arnold, Joseph Conlin, William Crough, Al Fernandez, Dan Georgakas, Bill Haak, Clinton Jencks, Vernon Jensen, Bill Kruthers, the late

xi

Edward Laustaunau, Joseph Park, Don Peterson, Marv Shady, Scott Sonne-born, Charles Spezia, Peter Steere, Greg Thompson, and Tom Vaughan. The excellent cartography was produced by Barbara Trapido-Lurie.

Library, museum, and archives staff at the following institutions pro-vided essential assistance: the Arizona Historical Foundation and Arizona Room of the Arizona State University Library, the Arizona Historical Society (in Tucson), the Arizona State Archives, the Bisbee Mining and Historical Museum, the Central Nevada Museum (in Tonopah), Cornell University's Catherwood Library, the Duke University Library, Eastern Washington State Historical Society's Cheney Cowles Museum (in Spo-kane), Jerome Historical Society Museum, Jerome State Park, Northern Arizona University's library, New Mexico State University's library, the U.S. National Archives, the libraries and archives of the universities of Ari-zona, Colorado at Boulder, Nevada at Reno, New Mexico, Texas at El Paso, and Utah, the Utah State Archives, the Utah State Historical Society, Wayne State University's Walter Reuther Library, the Wisconsin Historical Society Museum, and the Yuma Territorial Prison State Park. I'm grateful for the reliability, intelligence, and boosting of Marie Verheyen, who typed the manuscript.

I was inspired, in writing this book, by the dedication of the men and women who gave so much of themselves long ago, who suffered daily hardship, ingratitude, vilification, beating, jailing, shooting, and even mur-der because they wanted to help western workers. The faces of Weneslado Laustaunau, Juan de la O, Guy Miller, Charles Moyer, John Panczner, Lázaro Gutiérrez de Lara, and E. G. Locke look out at me from the other end of this century, reminding me that theirs was a noble effort, and that there is yet work to be done.

Race and Labor in Western Copper

INTRODUCTION

American history turned westward when Jim Marshall discovered gold near the American River at Sutter's Mill, in California. Beginning with the 1849 California placer camps, the search for gold and silver created thousands of small communities and dozens of big towns across the trans-Mississippi West. Since the 1849 rush to California, the mining of coal and metals, and especially copper, at one time or another has been the main industry and biggest employer in most states from the Rocky Mountains to the Sierra Nevadas. More than any other single industry, mining built far western communities during the late nineteenth and early twentieth centuries.

Nineteenth-century western hard-rock (metal) mining began with prospecting, rocker, pan, and sluice work on creeks and rivers, pick and shovel work, hand loading, and crude processing. The early demand for gold and silver was fairly constant, but everything else in the mining areas continually changed. In less than twenty years, new gold strikes in Colorado, Nevada, Idaho, Montana, and then in Dakota and Arizona dimmed the luster of the original California gold rush. Less than a generation later, most of the original placer and blanket-and-jackass prospectors of the earlier rushes who had filed on patches of rocky ground had sold or abandoned their claims. Small mining companies replaced them. Then, beginning as early as the 1860s, larger companies, managed by business executives and owned by wealthy stockholders in distant cities, began replacing the small mining companies. The new mine owners utilized modern, efficient extractive and processing techniques for ore production, as well as sophisticated managerial techniques for controlling large mining and processing work forces. By the end of the nineteenth century, the copper needed for the efficient production and transmission of electric power had become more important than gold or silver, and a newer, larger far western copper-mining boom had begun.

Copper was very unlike gold and silver. Precious metals are valuable even in small quantities, but "common" metals like copper are not. Before 1900, most of the big veins of gold and silver in the West had played out, and when the precious ores disappeared, the gold and silver camps went with them. But copper mining was a modern industrial proposition. Copper was mined by the ton, like iron or coal. The quest for shiny blue-green rock with 20 or even 30 percent copper content soon shifted to a search for lower-grade ore, in which less than 5 percent metal content was sufficient for profitability. Copper extraction had its own specialized technology, which corporations radically upgraded every few years during the late nineteenth and early twentieth centuries. Low-grade ore processing meant massive blasting, hauling, and loading, using complex road and rail systems and huge factory extraction operations. The newly created western copper-mining and processing operations had physical presence and economic power sufficient to dominate counties and entire subregions of the Southwest and intermountain West.

The miners, millworkers, and smelter workers, along with the many men who worked with steam-powered equipment, those who fabricated metal and wood, and the men and women who worked in mining-corporation offices and stores were a veritable industrial army. Many of them risked their lives and health in some of the most dangerous work available anywhere, for wages that ranged from above the national average for industrial work to considerably below it. Much of the mining work was generally understood to be impermanent: the gaudy careers of the early gold and silver camps had clearly established that pattern. Copper mines, too, had boom and bust cycles, during which companies added or eliminated work shifts. A basic cause of higher and lower pay was the daily copper price on the New York City wholesale market, over which no working miner had any control. Recurrent change, unsafe conditions, sudden surges in employment and pay rates, and equally sudden plunges were all part of a worker's life in the western copper communities. By the turn of the century, both the mine managers and the daily-wage workers generally understood the rules of the game.

But unlike the gold and silver camps of earlier years, the copper communities also offered stability and permanence. The copper towns, especially the larger ones, generally lasted longer than had the gold and silver camps, and some of them became small cities. By the early twentieth century, the copper companies were offering many people steady employment most of the time. Some of them still do.

America had once been a nation of farmers. By 1900, blue-collar workers had become the typical residents in many towns and cities. It appeared likely that sometime in the new century working-class people might become the most important social force in the nation. Their labor unions, hitherto generally unsuccessful, might be bigger and readier for struggles with management. Major strikes—against the railroad corporations, in the railway shops and out on the tracks, against Carnegie Steel at Homestead, Pennsylvania, against the Pennsylvania, West Virginia, Illinois, and Colorado coal companies, and against the large metal-mining corporations in Colorado and Idaho in the 1890s and again in 1903—were dramatic confrontations between giant corporations and large labor organizations at some of the nation's most important industrial facilities. Coal miners and hard-rock miners, affiliates in the American Federation of Labor in the middle 1890s, both played leading roles in the unfolding industrial drama. Many miners were Socialist Party members, using socialist politics to fight for political change, just as they utilized the union for economic warfare. At the turn of the century socialism was growing faster than any other national political movement.

Both the great corporations and the big unions moved west. In 1903, the United Mine Workers fought to organize District 15 in the Colorado coalfields, while the Western Federation of Miners, trying to incorporate Colorado smelter workers into the mining-union federation, fought the big metals companies at Cripple Creek and Telluride. Some of the United Mine Workers of America (UMWA) and WFM men who fought the mining companies had been skilled miners, pick-and-shovel men who knew how to set a charge and timber a room. But, especially after 1903, the organizers who worked the myriad mountain camps in the West and the men at union headquarters who directed them functioned as labor-union professionals. For the Western Federation of Miners, the only great national union of metal miners and concentrator and smelter workers, the newest and best opportunities for future growth lay in the new mining districts developing between Butte and the Mexican border in the early twentieth century. In the last years before the First World War, the Southwest, Utah, and Nevada copper regions had the newest mines and the fastest trains, included the last territories which would join the contiguous United States as states, and were regions of great opportunity for massive minerals investment by the Rockefeller, Guggenheim, and Phelps Dodge interests. The Western Federation of Miners would lead American labor into an epic confrontation with American mining corporations in the Far West.

The WFM split with the American Federation of Labor in 1897. Its leaders differed with AFL policy on two principal issues. Most of the WFM leaders, including Ed Boyce, the Federation's president, were enthusiastic socialists and wanted to promote socialism while furthering the cause of unionism. Although socialists were scattered among the American Federation of Labor's membership, neither Samuel Gompers (at the top of the AFL) nor John Mitchell (who led the United Mine Workers—the only other miner's union group within the AFL) favored socialist ideology.[1]

Industrial unionism was an even more important issue. Industrial unionism meant that all the men and women working in an industrial facility, skilled and unskilled, at all status levels, would be represented within the same union. Skilled-trades unionism, practically industrial unionism's diametric opposite, represented the interests of individual groups of craftsmen in a workplace. Industrial unionism was a recent and radical idea at the turn of the century. The only major western unions espousing it were the United Mine Workers and the Western Federation of Miners, and only the Western Federation actively proselytized for it. As an active exponent of socialist and politically radical causes and industrial unionism as well, the WFM was a nuisance to the relatively conservative leadership of the American Federation of Labor. After the WFM and AFL separated in 1897, the mantle of leadership for national labor reform and for organizing among the vast numbers of nonunion working people, especially in the West, fell, albeit briefly, upon the Western Federation of Miners.

Immediately after the WFM and AFL separated, the WFM created a stepchild, a regionally organized, industrial-union surrogate for the American Federation of Labor, and called it the Western Labor Union. In 1902, the WFM expanded, reorganized, and renamed the WLU. It became the nationally organized American Labor Union (ALU). Neither the WLU nor the ALU flourished, although both secured the adherence of some surviving remnants of the old 1880s Knights of Labor locals still struggling on in the West, and both enlisted some new recruits. In 1905, the WFM jettisoned its previous efforts and tried once again to establish a national, industrially based union confederation. The 1905 planning was far more comprehensive than anything that had previously been attempted.

The 1905 WFM plan called for the creation of a national organization built upon a network of alliances which would be capable of supporting great struggles against large corporations. The Western Federationists and the ALU sought and obtained allies among independent unions with radical leanings, among dissident and disaffiliated AFL leaders, and among elements of the American political Left in eastern cities. The result was the IWW, the Industrial Workers of the World. As the principal creator and sponsor of the IWW, the Western Federation of Miners had become the most important reformist labor union in the nation in 1905, a role that it would continue to play for only about two more years. Also, as the sponsor of the only great regionally organized union confederation in most of the far western states and territories, the WFM, in tandem with the IWW, was the most powerful organized working-class social movement in the West.

The Western Federation soon broke with part of the American political Left and abandoned its own creation, leaving the IWW as an independent union confederation in 1907. The Western Federation then moved toward reaffiliation with the AFL, while simultaneously trying to recruit nonunionized recent-immigrant mining workers, in order to regain both its strength and its sense of mission. Eventually, the WFM and the IWW were to compete with one another for the support of western mining workers, and both were to be nearly destroyed in the process.[2]

Consistently, from the time it created the Western Labor Union in 1898, the Western Federation tried to build a system of alliances for itself. WFM leaders believed their confederation to be not only a conventional labor organization, but also the epicenter of western working-class society and a future catalyst for a much larger working-class movement. But the Western Federation had never been really strong in any meaningful way. Its early leaders had been threatened with incarceration and mob violence. Beginning in the late 1890s, the WFM sought real strength: not only political and financial help, but the local support that could translate into physical control of western mining, processing, and smelting facilities in the event of labor conflict. The WFM badly needed local allies, especially among the working class of the hundreds of western mine and mill towns, and it needed national labor-union affiliates as well. Even in the worst of times, the WFM maintained its network of AFL and United Mine Workers connections, and in return, organized labor frequently offered a measure of financial and political help during the WFM's times of trouble. From 1898 to 1907, the WFM consistently tried to expand in order to protect its support systems for the unionized work forces in western mining communities. Expansion beyond this, in direct defiance of existing AFL unionism, was a vague possibility which many WFM men were willing to discuss, but upon which few were ready to act.

Politics and some aspects of social life in most of the copper areas south of Butte were dominated by persons of British (especially Cornish), Irish, or northwest European and other older-immigrant ancestry. Although British- and Irish-Americans were culturally distinct from one another, in the turn-of-the-century Southwest, Utah, and Nevada, they generally blended into an English-speaking segment of the working-class community. In this book, English, Welsh, Scotch, and Irish are variously described as "Anglo-Irish," "English and Irish," "English-speaking men," and "Anglo- and Irish-Americans." But the numerical majorities in the copper communities between Butte and the Mexican border were the multiethnic populations whom the Irish, English and other older-immigrant groups called "the foreigners" and "the Mexicans." Recent European immigrants, Mexican immigrants, and U.S.-born Hispanics outnumbered Anglo-American and other northwest-European-ancestry groups at every large copper mine, mill, and smelter in the Southwest, Utah, and Nevada.[3] Most of the recent immigrants in both Utah and Nevada were Greeks (and Cretans), Italians, Finns, South Slavs, and Japanese. In Arizona, there were Italians in Clifton-Morenci and Globe (and later, Miami), South Slavs in Globe-Miami and Bisbee, and Spaniards (immigrants from Spain, rather than from Mexico), in Ray, Clifton-Morenci, and Jerome. Both Mexican immigrants and U.S.-born Hispanics (all of whom were called Mexicans by members of other ethnic groups) lived in all of the Arizona communities, in El Paso, Texas, and in Hurley-Santa Rita, New Mexico.

No two mining areas were quite alike, and none was typical. Each camp had a unique ethnic-racial mix, including, in some camps, smaller numbers of Swedes, Navajos, Yaquis (from Mexico), Papagos, African Americans, French, Germans, and Albanians. In several places like Bingham Canyon, Utah, where Serbians, Croatians, Slovenes, and a smaller number of Montenegrins worked near one another, or Clifton-Morenci, where Italians worked next to Mexicans, the mining companies deliberately juxtaposed antagonistic national groups in order to "mix" their work forces. "The mixing of nationalities," one coal-mining company executive told a journalist, was "the secret of his company in downing the Unions . . . [because] the Unions cannot hold peoples from different countries together into a solid mass."[4] A 1912 mining engineer explained that lead smelting required mixing nationalities, too. "A rotation of duty may be resorted to," he said, "and

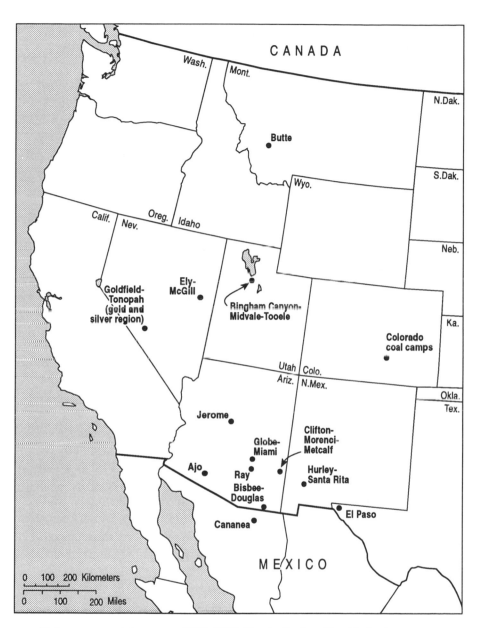

Major western mining areas, 1896–1918. Map by Barbara Trapido Lurie.

pains will be taken that different nationalities are well represented among the laborers. As long as little dissensions and rivalries keep the men busy, they are fairly amenable."[5]

Immigrants and U.S.-born Hispanics had had jobs in western mines and mills since the California gold rush. Gold-rush photos show Chinese working close to white miners in the 1860s. Men of Spanish and Native American descent dug copper near Hurley and Santa Rita, New Mexico, long before the English and Irish arrived there, and many Spanish Americans continued to work in New Mexico and West Texas throughout the late nineteenth century. Italians and South Slavs were being employed in Utah by the mid-1890s, and Italians, South Slavs, and Spaniards had begun working in Arizona at least that early. The Europeans, Asians, Mexicans, and Americans of Spanish and Mexican descent generally lived in separate communities, segregated either voluntarily or involuntarily both from the Anglos and Irish and from one another. Nearly all the mining-company employees among them were unskilled or semiskilled workers.

The several large ethnic groups were culturally different from one another. Mexican Americans and native-born Spanish Americans were culturally separate, and neither was directly connected to Spanish immigrants. Europeans obviously had distinct cultural identities. Although most of these groups were ethnically segregated into separate residential communities, their efforts at ameliorating working conditions sometimes united them.

At the start of the great copper boom, most of the WFM's western members had been skilled gold and silver miners, with the sole, significant exception of the men in the Butte, Montana, local.[6] But few skilled men were needed to work the newly expanded nonselective mining operations south of Butte, especially after 1900.[7] Instead, the newcomers from Europe, Mexico, Japan, and the rural Southwest were hired for a variety of jobs in the mines, mills, and smelters. Whether they were designated pitmen, dumpmen, charge wheelers, or even miners, they were paid at unskilled labor rates, which were generally well under $3.00 a day through 1912. Many of them found dismal working and living conditions in the copper communities, and some of them grew to hate company housing and company stores. In thousands of major and minor incidents, angry copper-company employees, fed up with what they perceived as mistreatment and inequitable wages, threatened their bosses and sometimes attacked them, destroyed company property, or dropped their tools and walked off their jobs. Some men quit and never came back. Less frequently, semiorganized groups walked out and some even declared strikes, with listed demands, attempts at nego-

tiation, picketing, and organized efforts at assertion of workplace control—
all of which had begun before there were unions for the workers to join.

Many of the labor actions in early copper communities were conceived
and effectuated by ethnically based groups. Some South Slavs, Italians,
Mexican Americans, and Spanish Americans belonged to *mutualistas* and
other sickness-and-death-benefit societies. In Arizona, ethnic social clubs
sometimes temporarily functioned as labor unions in disguise. Some Mexican mining workers planned labor action as members of politically connected groups, and some organized temporary *uniones de obreros* to fight
against copper-company management for just a few months at a time, at
specific moments of labor conflict. In each of the big western copper districts the major ethnic groups organized locally before engaging in large-
scale conflict. But the clubs, societies, mutualistas, and uniones de obreros
were inherently limited by the size of their local ethnic bases. There were
no instances of national ethnic societies offering assistance in local labor
disputes in the copper region until 1914, and the national ethnic organizations played no significant role in copper-country labor disputes through
1918. Only a real labor-union organization, with considerable expertise and
a reasonably strong set of political and social connections, could plan and
carry through a major strike in the Southwest and Utah and Nevada copper
regions with some likelihood of success. Gradually, the immigrants and
rural southwesterners and members of the Western Federation of Miners
came to realize that they needed one another.

Most of the new or expanded copper operations were intended to utilize
low-wage, unskilled workers to mine and process low-grade ore. At most of
the new copper areas the new men quickly sought institutional defenses
against the least bearable aspects of management-imposed work routines.
Labor trouble occurred in many places where copper mining, concentrating, smelting, and road and railway facilities had been recently expanded,
and the trouble generally began soon after the arrival of large new populations of immigrants or U.S.-born Hispanic workers.

Ethnic-racial conflict fueled by intolerance had a long history in the
United States, from early colonial mistreatment and enslavement of Indians
and enslavement of Africans, through mid-nineteenth-century racist notions of Manifest Destiny and Indian cultural inferiority. This intolerance
was made explicit in California's Foreign Miner's Tax, the anti-Catholic
American Party (the Know Nothings), the Chinese Exclusion Act, and the
hundreds of books and pamphlets which railed against "nunneries," the
"Yellow Peril," and "the Pope's legions." Immigrants—African, European,

Asian, and Mexican—and Native Americans were seldom welcome in communities in which descendants of northern and western Europeans were the majority.

Partway into the twentieth century, America's racial-ethnic climate began to moderate. Native Americans became eligible to vote in national elections in 1924, the Democratic Party offered immigrant Catholic voters Al Smith's presidential candidacy in 1928, Marian Anderson sang at the Lincoln Memorial in Washington, D.C., in 1939, and two years later A. Philip Randolph helped push Franklin Roosevelt into signing fair employment practices legislation. Racially segregated Mexican American, Japanese American, and Navajo troops returned heavily decorated from the Second World War and soon afterward President Truman began the desegregation of the U.S. armed forces.

Even as the early-twentieth-century United States moved toward immigration restriction, as the number of lynchings increased and the Ku Klux Klan reappeared, racism and ethnic intolerance were diminishing in many parts of the mining West. Despite continuing general Progressive Era intolerance, a measure of egalitarianism was beginning among working people, at least in the Southwest, Utah, and Nevada, during 1896–1918.

This book is a history of significant social change among a region of working people. It is about more than 25,000 copper miners, muckers, mill workers, and smelter employees in the western copper-mining areas south of Montana, a region which includes large parts of Arizona, New Mexico, Nevada, Utah, and El Paso, Texas. Copper-industry and railroad work predominated there, and most of the communities were industrial rather than rural. The process of on-the-job change described in this book is called *inclusion,* which means lowering the barriers to joint ethnic-racial cooperation and cooperative labor action. The process of inclusion in the West was complex and may have been unique; but there are, at this writing, no comparable regional studies of early-twentieth-century American inclusion. When comparable studies are done, the Southwest, Utah, and Nevada copper region may prove to be typical, rather than unique.

At the turn of the century, most of western industrial labor was bifurcated. Men of northern and western European antecedents, including Irish as well as English, Welsh, Swedes, and Germans too, were a labor elite. Their jobs, their wages, their status on the job and their community status were all better than the jobs, wages, and community status of the more numerous group of men from Mexico, central, eastern, and southern Europe, Asia, and the men from Hispanic towns in the western United States.[8] Many of the relatively privileged men relished their superior status and jealously guarded it against encroachment by their non-Anglo-Irish coworkers. The privileged northwest European unionists carefully delineated and reinforced status markers which effectively excluded recent immigrants and nonwhites. Other northwest European unionists strove for workplace equality by lowering the exclusionary barriers to better-paying and higher-status jobs, and by trying to recruit the minority group men into industrial union locals. Both the anti- and pro-immigrant unionists used complex strategies to achieve their purposes; their goals, too, were complex. Western unionists who favored ethnic-racial inclusion, more often than not, were motivated by a blend of nonaltruistic and fraternal purposes which varied according to place, time, and circumstance. But during the approximately two decades described in this book, the philosophy of ethnic-racial inclusion scored some notable successes.

The miners, concentrator hands, and smeltermen of the vast western copper region south of Butte were anonymous: the scant historical record of their working lives offers only minimal insights into their individual motives, actions, and affiliations. However, most historians have chosen to study the western mining workers of the early twentieth century as if they were collective entities, investing them with special group personalities. Much recently published mining-labor history discusses collective entities such as the "Butte Irish," the "Arizona Mexicans," and the "Greeks of Bingham, Utah."[9] Such group designations tell us little about individual workingmen. Until about 1910, most mining workers in most western communities retained their jobs for two years or less before seeking work elsewhere.[10] From 1910 to 1918, job-retention rates in at least one major western copper district rose somewhat, but even during 1910–18, most men (and, in many instances, their families) moved on within five years or less.[11] These men typically worked in many places for short periods of time, not long enough to become Butte, Arizona, or Bingham entities; and it is only when they are studied as individuals, rather than as hypothetical, geographically defined ethnic collectivities, that their biographies can become meaningful.[12]

This book is about actual people—a great many of them, in fact; rather than about towns, mines, companies, labor unions, or ethnic groups in the abstract. But the people who lived in the turn-of-the-century western mining camps moved from place to place so often that they are difficult to find and to remember, all of these years later. Each chapter in this book represents only a momentary snapshot of their mining-community lives. The people in each chapter lived where they lived and worked where they worked only during the several-year period included within each chapter. Viewed together in rapid sequence, the series of snapshots will, I hope, resemble a turn-of-the-century, nickelodeon version of a moving picture. But the people in each snapshot *change* as the show moves along.

Think of Dodge City in the days of the great cattle drives. Many contemporary historians treat western mining areas as the radio and television industry treated Dodge—the same old familiar marshall, deputy, town doctor, and the same Miss Kitty, scarcely aging over the decades. But *real* western mining communities resembled the *real* Dodge City. The real community residents were not the same steady, reliable cast of Matt, Chester, Doc, and Kitty but an ever-changing multitude of recent-immigrant mining workers, like the changing cast of law officers, deputies, doctors, and Long Branch Ladies seen over the years in the real Dodge City. However, most of their names and stories are unknown.[13]

Some mining workers did retain their jobs far longer. Some men bought property, raised families, joined organized societies, voted for local political candidates, and participated in the settled institutional life of the mining communities. These men became, in effect, the Arizona Italians or Utah Croatians. But settled workers and their community institutions were exceptions in an era of pervasive industrial transiency.

The early-twentieth-century western working class's frequent change of occupation and residence suggests that Arizona Mexicans and Utah Greeks are stereotypes, created for historians' and readers' convenience, and historically static. Descriptions of historical change within these hypothetical Mexican, Irish, Serbian, and other communities do not refer to the actual individuals living in the communities, who were a variable, rather than a constant factor. Conventional community histories which discuss Mexicans or Greeks, and include a place, like Bingham Canyon or Bisbee, describe ethnic-racial populations as "growing," "changing," "politicizing," or "becoming increasingly militant" within particular communities; but most of the individuals in the communities never experienced these changes. The western mining community and its institutions were a constantly shifting population base which could change over time. But before many changes could take place, most of the constituent populations would depart. Increments of community politicization, institutional diversity, or economic development represented not *changing* levels of social activism, but *differing* levels of social activism among different populations, even when the different populations seemed to be Arizona Mexicans or Utah Greeks.

Leaders, of course, were often visible even when their followers were not. The individual careers of a few ethnic and union activists in the Southwest, Utah, and Nevada are visible in this account. But these chapters are only incidentally about the history of particular ethnic groups or communities. There was a *regional,* multiethnic working class which shifted residence from job to job and from town to town. Over time, this working-class group changed significantly. Ethnic-racial barriers gradually lowered, and a sense of common purpose developed, in many places. This is a study of a single, regional entity (Arizona, New Mexico, Utah, Nevada, and El Paso, Texas) and the recent immigrants, Hispanic Americans, and Irish Americans and longer-resident Anglicized groups who were associated with it.

Some recent U.S. working-class histories proclaim that their subject matter is race, class, or both. The parameters of American race and class defy definition, which offers some historians license to create "vital connections," "inter-penetrations," and other arcane categories of description. American ethnicities and races included both the poor (especially the working class) and the better-off; and the working and upper classes included various ethnicities and races. Historical interpretations which juxtapose and compare abstract descriptive social categories with one another tend to create masses of murky jargon.

Regional working-class activism ("class"), rather than ethnic activism ("race"), catalyzed social change in early-twentieth-century Utah, Nevada, and the Southwest. This book, written from a local and regional rather than a national perspective, discusses the related experiences of several ethnic groups of working people. Also, labor unions, especially the Western Federation of Miners, tried to connect themselves to immigrant and minority-group workingmen in a series of incidents. Labor unions were always there, always trying, sometimes successful, and a constant explanatory factor in this book.

In addition to ethnicity, class, and the activities of labor unions, a concern for the pattern of chronological change is another constant in this study. Consistent chronological sequence is absent from much current working-class and western historical writing. The topical-essay format favored by some current historians blurs essential cause-and-effect relationships.[14] Transitional developments—highly significant changes in ethnic institutions and workplace behavior, in union organizing techniques, and in employer-employee relations—occurred very frequently. This book's chapters describe several-year-long sequences of significant events. The copper camps, towns, and small cities and the unskilled and semiskilled employees of this study are treated as variable factors, as the scene shifts from Arizona during 1896–1907 to Utah and Nevada, briefly to El Paso, Texas, and then back to Arizona and New Mexico during 1914–18.

Most recent studies of working-class social change maintain that change began in working-class communities, rather than at workers' jobs in factories, railroads, and mines. Ira Katznelson's 1981 book, *City Trenches,* for instance, argues for the preeminence of community-based change in his description of highly politicized nineteenth- and early-twentieth-century eastern urban areas in which the power exercised by urban institutions overwhelmed urban labor groups. David M. Emmons portrays Butte, Montana, Irish copper-industry employees as men whose first concern was the maintenance of stable community life. According to Emmons, the deliberate exclusion of recently arrived immigrants from jobs in Butte was necessary because the "new men" threatened Butte Irish community stability. Charles Stephenson and Robert Asher use the same notion of a quest for security in a "family-centered world" to explain workplace behavior in their book *Life and Labor* (1986). Stephenson and Asher also quote John Bodnar, whose research demonstrates that a group of early-twentieth-century Polish millworkers in Pittsburgh chose the kind of stable community life provided by steady work, rather than fighting to improve their status in the workplace.[15]

Locating the origins of social change in the community rather than at work can facilitate "gendering," the process of incorporating women's history into the history of (in this case) male-predominant industrial communities. Gendering in early-twentieth-century western mining areas practically requires a community, rather than a workplace approach. Recent articles by Vincent DiGirolamo and Colleen O'Neill gender the accounts of two early-twentieth-century western labor conflicts in which all the major participants were men. But their gendering is accomplished by minimizing men's roles, and by insisting on the improbable proposition that these all-male labor-management conflicts originated in the community rather than on the job.[16]

Though mining-camp *community* gendering is highly desirable, the gendering of all-male workplaces is not. This book describes social change that began at *work,* rather than in the community. Workplace emphasis is not new. Over twenty years ago, sociologist William Kornblum studied social stratification in the South Chicago and Gary, Indiana, steel mills and demonstrated that the vehicle for social change was the development of the interracial primary groups which first appeared at the workplace and in local labor union activities, and which were only later established in the nearby residential communities.[17] More recently, James R. Barrett has connected Anglo and Irish trade unionists to acculturation and institutional development in European immigrant working-class communities. Similarly, Emilio Zamora has shown that industrialization (but not necessarily unionization) "was the single most important development that shaped the condition of the Mexican community [in South and East Texas] . . . during the early 1900s."[18] This book demonstrates that industrialization *and unionization* catalyzed social action in Mexican and other Hispanic, Greek, Italian, and South Slavic industrial communities across a large part of the early-twentieth-century West.

Working-class organizing evinces an interconnected pattern of western social change, whereas studies of individual racial and ethnic groups tend to be somewhat parochial. Beginning at least as early as the Mexican, Hispanic, and Italian immigrant mining industry strike at Clifton-Morenci, Arizona, in 1903, both the origins and the developmental phases of western working-class activism were ethnically interconnected. With one exception, all major early-twentieth-century southwestern and intermountain working-class activism resulted from ethnically combined initiatives, and had ethnically complex results.[19] Monographic individuation of western ethnic groups and the simplification of ethnically complex labor actions can create extraordinarily distorted historiographical interpretation. Individuation and simplification are currently accomplished in two principal ways.

Complex interrelationships can be made simple by defining away their complexities. The Spanish-speaking and culturally Hispanic people of U.S. origin, Mexican immigrants, linguistically and culturally Hispanic people of European and African coastal origins, and Yaqui Indians from Mexico (who formed a distinct group in at least one major southwestern mining area), are sometimes agglomerated into a single, manageable category. In most agglomerated accounts, these groups become Mexicans or Mexican Americans. Croatians, Serbians, and Slovenes become European immigrants.[20] If, of course, these variegated ethnic groups actually functioned monolithically, then the avoidance or ignorance of the real differences among them would be functionally efficient. But, in fact, there were no monolithic masses of Mexican or immigrant workers. The agents of southwestern and intermountain working-class social change were activist factional ethnic subgroups which combined and recombined with one another during episodes of labor conflict.

Neither Hispanics nor non-Hispanic European immigrants ever presented a united front against management in early-twentieth-century workplace disputes in the intermountain West or Southwest. Ethnic internal differences were partly ideological, but they were also related to social class and region-of-origin subgroup characteristics. There were no consistent activist groups of Greeks or Mexicans in the mines, mills, and smelters of early-twentieth-century Arizona, New Mexico, Utah, or Nevada. Neither were there consistent conservative and radical subdivisions of Mexicans or Greeks. Instead, there was a constant process of ethnic factional combination and recombination.

Some historians blur or omit information about ethnic interconnections in order to enhance the distinctiveness of their preferred subject matter. The presence and significance of South Slavs, Spaniards, or Italians in some early-twentieth-century mining areas presents difficulties for some recent western historians, so they ignore these ethnic groups. Historians who are determined to present simple, sharply focused portraits of their ethnic favorites, free of the real complexities of ethnic interaction, avoid discussion of other relevant ethnic groups whenever it seems most convenient to do so.[21]

Social change in the early-twentieth-century Southwest, Utah, and Nevada had no simple racial-ethnic or class causation. Subgroups—factions—a variety of separate component elements, were the real determinants of western working-class social change. This book emphasizes racial-ethnic and pro- and anti-unionist factions. Small factional groups, described here as pro-inclusion and pro-exclusion factions, are the relevant building blocks in explaining western working-class history.

This story begins in Arizona, where a sudden influx of Mexican workers at a recently modernized copper mine linked the union movement to a redefinition of local Hispanic-Anglo relations. southwestern Mexicans, Italians, and Spanish Americans, and Anglo- and Irish-American unionists divided over the issue of ethnic-racial exclusion and inclusion during the first decade of this century. The newly developed group of pro-inclusion unionists joined forces with burgeoning Greek and South Slavic ethnic-activist movements in Utah and Nevada in 1912. Finally, an even greater mass of coalescing Mexican and Hispanic working-class activism connected to the Anglo and Irish western mining-union movement between 1913 and 1917. The story ends with a survey of the massive, ethnically conjoint copper-industry strikes, sitdowns, walkouts, and the several "deportations" of 1917–18.

Coordinated labor action led inevitably to social change. Fairness, a semblance of equality, and a measure of ethnic-racial toleration, achieved on the job for the first time in the Southwest, Utah, and Nevada, created a necessary precondition for the increased community-wide social and political change that occurred later. This is the history of the beginnings of major social change in the western copper regions; of how labor conflict brought the earliest beginnings of ethnic-racial toleration to one region of the United States.

◄ 1 ►

WESTERN FEDERATION OF MINERS UNIONISM BEGINS IN THE SOUTHWEST, 1896–1903

The West was settled in population waves, and the Indians preceded all others. Apaches were the first residents of most southwestern mining areas. Utes, Shoshones, Gosiutes, and Paiutes were the original claimants of the Nevada and Utah copper lands. The Apaches were particularly effective in making their presence felt. Because of the Apaches, Anglo-Americans, Mexican Americans, Chinese, Cornish, and Irish were forced to delay their collective entry into parts of the Southwest for at least an extra decade.

Non-Native Americans first settled most of the southwestern copper regions in the 1860s and 1870s. The Europeans, Asians, and Mexicans built small settlements of shacks and stores, and prospected for gold and silver, and some of these gold and silver camps and stagecoach stops would become copper communities by the end of the century. But the little wood, adobe, and stone villages and towns were twenty to thirty years old before the copper boom began, and they earned their Indian-fighting, pioneering, and Wild West credentials during the gold-camp years. By the 1890s and early 1900s, when the original frontier days were several years gone, Phelps Dodge and Company bought the Old Dominion claims at Globe, Arizona, the Arizona Copper Mining Company at Morenci, and the Copper Queen at Bisbee. The Guggenheim brothers of New York City selected management for their newly acquired Utah Copper Company in Bingham Canyon and for their huge smelter complex in El Paso, Texas. W. A. Clark of Montana also built his United Verde mine and mill operation at Jerome during the late 1880s and 1890s. Ray Consolidated Copper Mining Company at Ray, Arizona, and Nevada Consolidated at Ely and McGill, both created by the Guggenheim syndicate, opened during the first decade of the twentieth century. The Guggenheims' Chino Mines at Hurley and Santa Rita, New Mexico, the Miami area near Globe, and the Ajo mining complex in Pima County, Arizona, all began large-scale operations between 1910 and 1920.

Late-nineteenth-century copper miners and processing workers were Cornish in some parts of the southwestern and intermountain regions, and Spanish American, Irish, or Chinese in others. These men were hard at work with picks and shovels in the late 1870s and 1880s, before the advent of the big corporations. Few men of the next generation of miners had worked during the pick-and-shovel era. The men of the new generation came from Europe and Mexico, the rural Southwest, and less frequently, from Japan, to work for the great corporations at newly created unskilled and semiskilled jobs that paid much less than the $3.00, $3.50, and $4.00 a day that were traditional, respectable wage rates in the mines. The European and Mexican immigrants began arriving in the southwestern and lower intermountain area in the middle 1890s.

Cornish-Irish antagonism was a legendary Protestant-Catholic antagonism in the Old Country, and the two groups contested the ground upon which they met in the late-nineteenth-century United States. But hostilities soon ceased: cooperation between the Cornish and Irish began remarkably early. Ralph Mann's study of the California gold fields refers to the beginning of Cornish-Irish cooperation there in 1869, and Arthur Cecil Todd's book about Cornish miners in the United States dates the end of Cornish-Irish antagonism from the early 1890s. Cornish-Irish cooperation has been described as a "nativist" alliance, formed to create an effective joint opposition to Chinese, and then to central European and Italian immigrants at the mines.[1]

Cornishmen and Irishmen began to look alike to their employers after 1900. Out in the community, after work, one man would still walk back to the Irish section of town and drink in an Irish tavern, while the other would return to "Cornish Hill" or its equivalent. But mine work sped along their Americanization more rapidly than did their community experience. By the turn of the century, Phelps Dodge treated the Cornish and Irish as "Americans," along with other second-, third-, and fourth-generation men of northwest European descent. At work, the Cornish and Irish immigrants, and the descendants of the Scotch, English, Welsh, Scotch-Irish, Dutch, and sometimes the Germans, Rhenish, Flemish, and Scandinavians, Americans all, had the white-collar jobs, the security and staff jobs, the administrative and supervisory work, and also the mine and mill work with the highest skill requirements, highest wage rates, and highest ascribed status. Men whom the copper companies defined as Americans had a powerful inducement to accept the companies' definition.[2]

The copper companies treated immigrants and U.S.-born workers very differently from one another. Some copper companies treated Mexican immigrants and Spanish-surnamed, U.S.-born men of long-time U.S. residence as virtually the same ethnic group. Some employers offered their Spanish immigrant employees the same unskilled jobs and wages that they offered their Mexican immigrant and Mexican American employees, some included Italian workers in the same category, and some lumped all of the non-Anglo-Irish together. Eventually, because they shared a common workplace life, many of these men would organize and strike together. From an employer's point of view, the only significant ethnic-racial division in the work force was the gap between the so called Americans and the group characterized as either Mexicans or European immigrants.

The gulf between the two company-defined ethnic groups in the workplace was matched by a similar division in the copper communities. The communities were further divided: the Americans, Europeans, Japanese, and Mexicans were segregated into distinctly separate ethnic communities within the camps, towns, and cities near the mines and mills. But the Protestant Anglo-Irish commingled, and to a limited extent, they were socially connected to the Catholic Anglo-Irish, while the non-Anglo-Irish were both physically and socially separated from both of the other groups. As explained in the introductory pages, the gulf between Mexicans and recent European immigrants on one hand, and the men who were called Americans on the other, was first bridged at the workplace, not in the community.

The first group of Greeks and Cretans that came to Utah was brought to help break a coal strike there in 1903.[3] Some of the Italians, Mexicans, and Mexican Americans in the Southwest had originally been brought to Colorado in the same year to break a Colorado coal strike.[4]

Another reason for hiring new immigrants as unskilled copper-industry workers was simply that immigrants lowered the companies' wage bill. The demand for labor varied with demand for the mines' product, and copper fluctuated in the international commodities market. The copper corporations were sometimes forced to offer high wages in order to attract men away from local railroads and mines, or away from distant factories and farms in response to increases in copper demand. Since the corporations were unable to force stability upon the wholesale copper price (although they had attempted to do so),[5] they tried to stabilize wage rates at low levels, in keeping with their large investments in land and heavy machinery. The copper companies also wanted a large surplus labor pool in case they had a chance to produce copper for a profitable fifteen-cent-a-pound wholesale market.

During the 1890s, the mining areas were riven with ethnic-racial hostilities. Recent-immigrant and native Hispanic workers came to represent a threat to the Anglo and Irish work force already employed in the southwestern copper industry. During the earlier, high-grade-ore era, industrial employers had employed Anglos and Irish and the other Europeans, Mexicans, and U.S.-born Hispanics at such completely different jobs as to make direct ethnic replacement impossible.

Mexicans, Mexican Americans, and Spanish Americans tangled with the Anglo-Irish before the recent European immigrants did. Victor Clark, in his extensive study of Mexican labor in the Southwest, interviewed many Anglo-American and Irish American workers and their employers. He was told that Mexicans and northwest Europeans were different from one another because "they [the Mexican workers] do not do as much work as a white man." Clark wrote that "North of the border White miners are everywhere preferred on machines," partly because "Mexicans are careless," and "the Mexican is not socially or industrially ambitious . . . which counts very much in his favor with White workers." Clark concluded that "They compete little, if at all, with what is called 'white labor' in the Southwest."[6] Many employers despised Mexican workers and valued them only as cheap and pliable unskilled labor. When employers placed Hispanic men and non-Hispanic men in different kinds of jobs, no competition between the two groups was possible.

But there *was* ethnic replacement. It was in no sense unique to the Southwest, of course. In the 1860s and 1870s, Arizona and Nevada Irish Americans and Anglo-Americans were anti-Chinese, even before they were anti-Mexican.[7] Mexican-against-Anglo labor trouble came next, beginning in the Southwest at least as early as 1892, when Mexican workers replaced non-Mexicans at a relatively small smelter strike in Jerome, Arizona.[8]

In 1895, the Old Dominion copper mine at Globe, Arizona, came under new ownership and new management. The new superintendent, S. A. Parnall, set policy. He reduced pay for part of the work force from $3.00 daily to $2.50 in September 1895, and then reduced it to $2.25 in May 1896. Hispanic workers were brought in, too, and they began to replace some of the Irish and Anglo-American workers at the Old Dominion mine.[9]

The precise nature of the newly augmented work force is not known. The new men were either locally resident Mexican Americans and Spanish Americans, Hispanics brought to Globe from the Clifton-Morenci mining district ninety miles away, men brought from some more remote location or even from Mexico itself, or some combination of these elements.[10] In light of the explosive reaction that the management move engendered, it seems probable that the new Hispanic workers were not local men, but that they were, in some sense, imported.

The English-speaking workingmen were alarmed by the threat of ethnic replacement. They quickly arranged a public meeting, marched to the mine superintendent's house, and threatened to injure or kill him. Parnall conceded to the mob's demands. Subsequently, his concessions were retracted and many of the workers went on strike. Old Dominion mine management responded by suspending operations at the mine. The strike-and-lockout ended on July 3, 1896, with a partial restoration of 1895 pay rates and a re-hiring of the primarily American, English, and Irish work force. The striking workers won, the Old Dominion Company lost.[11]

No effort was made during the strike to eliminate Hispanics from the Globe area, and some Hispanics were apparently rehired along with the Anglo-Irish in the settlement reached on July 3. Years later, one Anglo-Irish observer claimed that "the opposition of the miners to Mexicans was directed at those born in Mexico, and not against those who were born in the United States of Mexican ancestry."[12] Newspaper accounts of the strike definitely refer to an extant group of Mexican and/or Spanish American employees who lived in Globe *before* the strike and who were "able, reliable and steady workers" including "family men with responsibilities who did their work in a most satisfactory and quiet fashion."[13] The job status of these workers was different from that of the Anglo-Irish workers, and they were not seen as a replacement threat because they were doing rock-quarry and surface-mining work that

> white men will not perform save under stress of necessity, and then only temporarily[,] and during the summer working under the full glare of the sun is intolerable to a white man, while the Mexican, accustomed to such exposure, performs the labor without apparent distress. Neither are they more objectionable as a class than some other aliens and the discrimination is not just.[14]

Unionization was an unforeseen result of the Globe 1896 strike. The mob that threatened Parnall made itself into a temporary miner's union of 125 members. The Old Dominion Company did not recognize this union group in the July 3 strike settlement, but the pro-union men remained organized and requested assistance from the recently created Western Federation of Miners.[15]

The white man's camp or white man's town issue surfaced at Globe. A white man's camp, in turn-of-the-century parlance, was a predominantly or completely Anglo- and northwest European-American mining or milling community, a community that would allow few or no perceived members of nonwhite ethnic groups to either reside, or to obtain industrial employment within its bounds. Its extreme opposite in the Southwest was sometimes labeled a Mexican camp, although non-Mexican, non-Anglo-Irish employees were sometimes subjected to the same kind of discriminatory treatment. At Globe, the leaders of the new Anglo-Irish labor group said that whites *could* replace the Hispanic men in the rock quarry, and that

> any person familiar with this country knows that where Mexicans attain a foothold the white man is soon ousted, or working starvation wages. [The situation amounted to] whether the residents of the locality, who have made their homes here, are to be allowed to earn a decent living or whether they must give way to undesirable aliens who do not . . . speak the English language.[16]

The organized Globe men explicitly demanded a white man's town after the strike was over.[17] After 1896, Globe became, in essence, a white man's town.

Ed Boyce, the president of the Western Federation of Miners, traveled incessantly to promote miners' unionism. Most of Boyce's railroad tours circled through the western gold-camp regions, from California to the Dakotas, with detours up to the Butte, Montana, copper area. But in October 1896, Boyce made a long, carefully planned trip by train and stage-coach to Arizona Territory. Boyce had been invited to Globe, and he spent almost a week there. He began by speaking about the WFM to a meeting of English-speaking miners. The day after the meeting he organized them as WFM Number 60, the Globe Miners' Union. For several more days, Boyce spoke to union men and addressed a series of mass meetings in Globe. Then he boarded a westbound stagecoach. Boyce organized at several Arizona gold camps and at the Jerome copper area. He traveled through Arizona Territory for another week before finally heading west into California.[18]

Ed Boyce and the men and women of Globe had had almost a week to exchange opinions. They probably understood one another pretty well by the time Boyce left. Globe's English-speaking union men were anti-

Edward Boyce, Western Federation of Miners president, 1896–1902. Photo taken at Cliff House, San Francisco, California, 1900. Courtesy of Eastern Washington State Historical Society.

Mexican. What, then, were they trying to create—a labor union or a racially exclusive community civic club? Whatever the actual intentions of the Globe townspeople, the WFM's national leadership believed that a conventional WFM labor union local had been started in Globe. Race and social class issues were to haunt the Globe Miners' Union.

In 1900, miners' unionism began to spread across Arizona Territory, and the Globe local was its partial prophet and messenger. A Globe organizer helped create the Jerome, Arizona, local in 1900. The Jerome Miners' Union, in turn, proselytized unionism enthusiastically and helped to build several more locals. Boyce himself always kept a hand in. He made several more carefully planned speaking and organizing trips to Arizona. He probably helped create the Jerome Miners' Union and personally organized the local at the small Helvetia, Arizona, gold camp. From 1896 to 1902, when he left the WFM, Boyce consistently maintained contact with the Arizona miners. By 1905, Arizona and Nevada had become the two fastest-growing regions in the WFM's jurisdiction.[19]

Did the Globe organizers also spread their special variety of racism across Arizona? Curiously enough, they did not, or at least, they did not do so consistently. Although racial-ethnic hostility played a part in much of Arizona's early-twentieth-century labor-management trouble, the race-and-ethnicity issue sometimes assumed unexpected forms.

A series of labor-management conflicts began in February 1901, with a strike at Ray in Pinal County, about forty road miles south of Globe. Management at a copper mine there was paying miners $2.00 a day in 1900, when shift time was suddenly cut from ten hours down to eight. Then, just as unexpectedly, management announced the sudden resumption of ten-hour shifts. The Ray miners struck for eight hours and a $3.00 daily rate. They were reportedly Mexican, likely including both immigrants and U.S.-born Hispanics. Three dollars and eight hours were, by no coincidence, standard southwestern wages and hours at many of the mines that employed primarily Anglo and Irish labor.[20] The strikers' complaints were most probably not only about wage rates, but about the ethnic-racial discrimination that was reinforced by wage rates.

"The Mexicans declare they have provisions for two months and will not allow other miners to work in the mine," reported the *Arizona Daily Citizen*.[21] The Hispanic workers' action was the flip side of that taken by the 1896 Globe Anglo-Irish. The Mexican and/or Spanish American miners were aiming at the elimination of the wage-and-hour differential that separated them from the Americans. As long as the wage-and-hour differential was operant, of course, the Spanish-surnamed workers were "different": they were not directly comparable with Anglo-Irish-surnamed workers on a man-to-man, job-by-job basis.

In a sense, the elimination of the Anglo-Hispanic wage-and-hour differential, or what has sometimes been termed the dual wage system, was a real declaration of war upon early-twentieth-century mining employers' industrial arrangements. Given the either-or set of practices prevailing among mining-industry employers at that time, the demand for wage-and-hour equality threatened to convert every southwestern mining camp into an Anglo-versus-immigrant or Anglo-versus-Hispanic battleground. The Mexicans at Ray, because they were unable to attain ethnic inclusion, were demanding equality. Equality threatened Anglo-Irish prerogatives.

The company fired the Spanish-surnamed miners, approximately two dozen of them, and closed the mine. What appeared to have been a strike became a lockout, and most of the miners left the community during the next several days. A newspaper report explained Ray Company's new racial policy: "Hereafter all work in the mine will be done by contract and it is said that white miners will be employed exclusively."[22] Exclusively contract labor was nonsensical. Such a policy was suited only to a small, old-fashioned mine, and Ray was soon to expand into a huge, low-grade mining facility. A much larger, predominantly Hispanic work force was soon hired. Ray quieted, but only temporarily. There was more ethnically driven labor trouble there later.

At Pearce in Cochise County, Arizona, in late October of 1901, a small group of Anglo-Irish workers formed a miners' union, and were promptly told that "if the union was not disbanded at once the works would be closed down." Neither side conceded anything to the other, and all of the men of at least one shift, every one of them a union member, were fired.[23] After the Pearce strike, a newspaper correspondent reported that mining-company management was making the same kind of mean-spirited threat that Ray management had made a year earlier; in the future, they would "probably make a Mexican camp of" Pearce, and perhaps other parts of Cochise County too.[24] Although the threat of ethnic replacement had one standard form, either ethnic group could be used against the other.

Again at Jerome, in Yavapai County, ten months later, ethnic replacement became the ultimate threat in a simmering labor dispute. Because of a mine-shaft fire, the work force was cut back at the United Verde mine. Because of the fire and the low copper wholesale price, work on a new smelter was delayed. The pay at W. A. Clark's Montana mining property was higher than that at his Jerome mine, and WFM men in the Jerome Miners' Union had been complaining about that fact for two years.[25]

Then, according to the *Jerome Mining News,* came ethnic replacement.

> Superintendent Giroux imported a carload of Mexican miners and they were en route to Jerome when the train reached a bridge underneath which had been placed a charge of dynamite, and but for a premature explosion the entire train would have been blown to atoms.
>
> The car was backed down to Jerome Junction and that train with the Mexicans never came into the camp.[26]

The Jerome newspaper was ultimately proven wrong. Mexicans *did* come into the camp, and they came soon afterwards. By 1903, men described as Jerome Miners' Union radicals were recruiting Italians and Mexicans into the JMU. The chief recruiter was Albert A. Ryan, a tall, thin miner who was a dedicated Socialist Party proselytizer and unionist. Al Ryan had previously been an officer in tiny Chloride, Arizona, Local 77. Ryan had been brought to Jerome to reorganize the Jerome local and to begin Hispanic recruiting there. He recruited at the hot, dusty 500-foot level of United Verde's main shaft, where most of the men were ethnic immigrants; and he also met incoming new hires as they arrived at the railway station. Ryan intended to take every man in the mine into the JMU, "and if . . . [a man] did not join the union they would put him on the 'bum' [force him to leave the area]." He amazed the United Verde Copper Company's undercover detective, who was routinely spying on union activists like Ryan, with his eagerness to recruit Mexicans and Italians. The company spy, in fact, was worried by the JMU's ethnic-recruitment successes.[27]

Ryan's most genuine, heartfelt motives may never be known, but his practical purposes were explicit enough.

> He said that it was difficult to get the Mexicans into a Union and was of the opinion that some steps ought to be taken in that direction so that if the other men made any demands on the Company and went out on strike, that the Mexicans would go out with them.[28]

The recruitment of recent immigrants may have been a matter of cold, hard necessity, but there were other relevant circumstances. Ryan's private sentiments were in perfect harmony with his public activism. He combined fraternal loyalty with class ideology, and he was ready to accept the United Verde Company's Mexican and Italian employees as brother unionists, and to put even nonunion fellow Irishmen "on the bum." Also, Ryan and his supporters exhibited at least a modicum of decency toward non-Anglo-Irish workers. On one occasion, a Mexican worker who had been recently fired by United Verde told a JMU meeting that he had been cheated, that his family was destitute, and that he was trying to travel to his brother's home to obtain help. The discharged miner was not a union member, but the JMU men voted to give him ten dollars anyway.[29]

Albert A. Ryan and those who had dynamited the Jerome Junction bridge represented juxtaposed ideologies within the same union local.[30] Most probably, at least a plurality of JMU members supported Ryan; and given the JMU's original Globe connection, the dynamiter(s) probably also represented a group of Jerome unionists. Ryan represented men who were sometimes called radicals, although their union local opponents were not necessarily moderates or conservatives.[31] The content of WFM radicalism varied with time and circumstance, and other men may have had entirely different motives for supporting Ryan's recruitment initiatives. But this much is certain: there were, at least in Jerome, Irish and probably Anglo-American unionists who favored Italian and Mexican inclusion, and Anglos and Irishmen who wanted to exclude men of other ethnicities. Precisely what it was that divided the men of the Jerome Miners' Union—ideology, fraternal feeling, or a combination of both—cannot be determined with certainty; but the fact that they were divided is clear enough. The JMU's 1902–3 intramural factional struggle and a similar struggle in Globe over ethnic recruitment would be replicated by other western mine and mill union locals during the years that followed.

At the same moment in August 1902 that the dynamiters were preparing to blow up the Jerome Junction railroad bridge, another labor war was beginning at the smelter in Globe. Fifteen hundred smelter and mining workers walked off their jobs in a big wildcat strike. The Old Dominion Company responded to the walkout with a lockout at both the mines and smelter. Unionized miners, in turn, organized a boycott of the company store and also boycotted the *Silver Delt* newspaper and two other businesses that sided with management. The miners were fighting against wage-scale reductions and the Old Dominion's practice of denying employment to outspoken union men—essentially, the blacklist. Especially because of the blacklist issue, messages of support for the Globe strike action poured in from unionized Jerome, Ray, and the little Yavapai County gold camp of Octave.[32]

Globe's late-summer strike was formally settled in October. Globe Miners' Union officers signed a detailed contract with representatives of all the major companies operating in the Globe Mining District. But the union officers who signed the October contract were not the men who had begun the labor trouble during the summer. A faction favoring the recruitment of recent-immigrant unionists struggled against an antirecruitment faction. The prorecruitment men predominated at the onset of the strike. The antirecruitment men controlled the GMU in October.

The establishment of formal contractual relations with mining-company management was forbidden by Western Federation of Miners rules. Contracts froze wages and conditions of employment, tended to force out itinerant miners (of whom there were many), and eliminated the strike weapon as a means for redress of grievances. The Globe contract froze wages and hours that were still arguably inequitable for some of the mine laborers and mill and smelter workers employed around Globe; and it ignored the question of an eight-hour day, the WFM's hottest single western ideological issue during 1902–4. But the contract did not ignore blacklisting: it *approved* it. Blacklisting was to be permitted via a contractual stipulation. Either a company or an individual member of that company would have the "right . . . to discharge an employee whenever he sees fit."[33] This was the contract that the anti-immigrant men wanted.

To permit blacklisting was practically to encourage it in the give-no-quarter atmosphere of early-twentieth-century copper-camp labor relations. Moreover, blacklisting had already begun. A group of miners at the Silver Queen Mine near Queen Creek, a few miles west of Globe, had gone on strike for the Globe area's standard wage scale and had been fired and blacklisted just a few weeks earlier, as had forty-two members of the Globe local itself.

The use of a contract also encouraged the exclusion of racial-ethnic groups. In a separate incident occurring at the same time, the Globe Miners' Union had refused a request for help from thirty or forty mostly Mexican American smelter-excavation laborers who were being paid substandard wages and who had struck for Globe-area standard pay. The Hispanic laborers wanted to join Globe Local 60, but the GMU "refused them membership in Globe Union on account of their nationality, they being mostly Mexicans, but nearly all of them were born and raised in the country"— meaning that nearly all of them were U.S.-born Mexican Americans and/or Spanish Americans, rather than Mexican immigrants. For all of these violations of the letter and spirit of WFM unionism, the 1903 WFM national convention censured the Globe local.[34]

Local 60's late-autumn 1902 policies were the essence of 1902 conservative unionism. The local's countenancing of the blacklist guaranteed some union men protection at the expense of nonprotection for other workingmen in the Globe district. The non-Hispanic men who were being blacklisted and excluded from union protection were being treated as the conservative unionists' enemies. They were the "radical elements," "disturbers," and "agitators" according to the GMU's new leaders and their town-businessmen allies. Thus GMU conservatives were excluding a group of conventional union men from their midst—radicals perhaps, but also men whose unionism was in the mainstream tradition of the 1903 WFM. The WFM was itself fighting against contractual relations, the blacklist, and the undercutting of standard wage rates.[35]

In shunning the Mexican American smelter-excavation strikers, the Globe Union majority faction was making race a primary criterion for recruitment of union members. Few of the excluded men were Mexican nationals, and they had not been brought to the Globe area to replace other workers by working for lower pay. But they were ethnically Hispanic, and their ethnicity—their race rather than their country of origin—was the actual basis for their exclusion. The excluded men (even the miners at Queen Creek, who were probably Anglo or Irish) were fighting for standard wage rates. If they had won, they would not have been able to steal anyone's job, because they would have been working no more cheaply than any of the other men in the Globe district. By forcing them to continue working at inequitably low pay, the union's new conservative majority was deliberately condemning them to a continued cheap-labor, job-stealing status.

There were two separate aspects to 1902 Globe conservative unionism. First, the Globe majority was either opposed to, or uninterested in, the fight against the blacklist or the fight for the eight-hour workday and related issues. The second item was racial-ethnic exclusionism. The Globe majority wanted to exclude Hispanics, at least as much as the Globe Miners' Union's founding fathers had wanted to exclude them six years earlier.

But the GMU contained a large minority faction as well. The size of the minority faction is not known, although it was certainly large enough to have led the union into the wildcat strike and boycott activity during the summer months.[36] The minority included "disturbers," "agitators," and "radical elements" in the union, but it also included J. Tom Lewis. Lewis was a powerful and popular WFM national Executive Board member elected from Globe, and was either part of the minority faction, or was sympathetic to its point of view.[37] Although racial-ethnic inclusionism was an entirely separate issue and not connected to blacklisting, the eight-hour day, or wage levels, many of the radicals also promoted a policy of racial-ethnic inclusion.

Dissimilar sets of circumstances had produced similar factional division at Jerome and Globe. By early 1903, the majority in Jerome's Local 101 had decided that their union would recruit recent immigrants. Globe Local 60's majority had decided that theirs would not.

The Globe Miners' Union had already changed direction at least twice in its seven-year history. During the brief ascendancy of the GMU's pro-immigrant faction, J. Tom Lewis, acting as a roving WFM organizer, had helped create a pro-Mexican union local at Kofa (an acronym for "King of Arizona"), a small gold-mining community near Yuma; and Lewis had brought Albert Ryan from Chloride to Jerome to recruit Mexican workers.[38] Frequent changes and internal factional power struggles often centering around the question of recent-immigrant inclusion were characteristic of the political behavior of southwestern and intermountain WFM local unions during the early twentieth century.

Pro-inclusion men were among the leaders of the Arizona WFM movement from 1901 through 1907. In addition to Tom Lewis and Albert Ryan, there were W. M. Murphy, a delegate to the 1903 WFM national convention, from Troy, Arizona, Local 102; Alfred John Bennett, who became president of the Globe Miners' Union several years later; and J. P. Ryan, a delegate from the Walker, Arizona, local. All of them spoke in favor of recruiting Mexican workers into Arizona WFM locals during 1901–3.[39]

Inclusion in turn-of-the-century Arizona was partly a tactic, a means to an end, rather than an ideology. Tom Lewis, who was Arizona's leading WFM unionist, explained on one occasion that he had chosen to support Mexican participation in Arizona unions despite "the indisputable fact that they were direct competitors in the field of labor." "I took the position that it was for the best interests of the Federation to take them into the local union and, therefore, instructed this Union to work along those lines," he said.[40] Lewis expressed no interest in racial-ethnic equality, only in inclusive unionism. The same was true of the other Anglo-Irish WFM men. J. P. Ryan, the Walker delegate, who was also president of the Arizona Labor Federation and connected to the Trades Assembly of Tucson, called the organizing of Mexican workers "my scheme, especially in our part of the country."[41] There was no place in this scheme for Mexican American or Spanish American union-local officers or even for Hispanic organizers. The plan was to increase the size of union-local membership rolls and treasuries and to eliminate the ethnic-replacement strikebreaking threat by including Mexicans and other Hispanics. Ethnic inclusion would make the WFM locals richer and stronger, but the Arizona Anglos and Irish who concocted the plan had not planned to advocate equality in jobs and wages for Mexican or other Hispanic workers.

But principle did play a role in the early Arizona WFM inclusion struggle. The general principle was that of augmenting the power and status of the unionized labor movement, a goal that was also pursued through the Democratic and Socialist political parties. Organized labor in Arizona, and especially the WFM men who were a part of it, had a long shopping list of prolabor legislation that they hoped to have enacted, and which they continued to pursue through the Arizona Constitutional Convention in 1910 and through the first few years of statehood.[42] The eight-hour principle, which was a partial cause of the contemporaneous Colorado labor-management wars of 1903–4, was the most important item of all. Organized labor succeeded in putting an eight-hour law on the books in Arizona Territory, and it was to take effect on June 1, 1903, as explained in chapter 2. But the union men knew that passing the law was not enough. Arizona mining companies were powerful enough to evade the eight-hour rule, whether it was law or not. The union men wanted to force the mining companies to reduce ten-hour shifts to eight hours without reducing wages. The WFM's 1903 convention resolved, by passing a motion introduced by Albert Ryan, to help all Arizona locals fight wage reductions associated with the newly legislated eight-hour work shifts.[43] Lewis, Al Ryan, J. P. Ryan, Bennett, and other pro-inclusion men hoped to utilize the enhanced power of ethnically conjoint unions to fight for these radical goals.

Not all southwestern copper labor trouble was about race and ethnicity. There were many small copper-industry strikes, some of which were unconnected to ethnic issues. The pot boiled continually at Jerome. In April, 1902, five hundred smelter and converter workers struck there because of the "reduction or attempted reduction of the work force." There was a strike at the Green Cananea Copper Company's works in Sonora, just south of the Arizona border, also in the spring of 1902. The trouble "grew out of the discharging of one of the men by the foreman."[44] A few weeks later, Cananea concentrator mechanics struck for higher pay and better living conditions. Ray was struck again and was closed down during May 1902.[45] The smallest of the three principal copper companies operating at Clifton-Morenci in Graham County was struck "by mechanics at the mine and smelter" at the same time that Ray was struck. The main issues at Clifton-Morenci were hospital fees and hospital administration.[46]

The Western Federation of Miners' agenda and the decline in wholesale copper prices caused by manipulation in the world market brought about much of the labor trouble.[47] The miners intended to make basic improvements in their conditions of work. In Jerome, the "Democratic Platform of Yavapai County" issued in September 1902 listed, with special emphasis, an "anti-blacklisting" bill, a bill to mandate territorial safety inspection of mines, and a bill to establish an eight-hour workday in underground mines.[48]

WFM strike action continued unabated into 1903 in Arizona and elsewhere in the southwestern and central western copper areas. In early May 1903, in Jerome, a group of Mexicans encountered a group of Anglos after work at some distance from the mines. They began throwing stones at one another. Then there was a hail of bullets.[49] At Cananea, Sonora, there was an even bigger Mexican-against-Anglo rock fight, albeit without bullets. "Eighteen Anglo-American miners and 200 Mexicans" threw rocks at one another.[50] Cananea had just undergone an ethnic replacement in its work force. In 1902, the *Arizona Silver Belt* reported that the Greene Consolidated Copper Company was "eagerly seeking all the American white labor that the law allows, which is 40 percent of the work force, and there are now 2,500 or more Americans on the payroll." Six months later, after a strike by some of the Americans, the *Silver Belt* announced that "For some time the company has been pursuing a policy that is intended to replace white labor with Mexican help."[51] Thus, most likely, the 1903 rock fight. There was also another small strike at Globe in the spring of 1903, in which the inclusion issue again played a role.[52] In the newly expanded copper camp at Ely, Nevada, men struck "in order to retain their scale of wages." It was a "severe" strike, and there were probably both Greek immigrant and Anglo-Irish strikers.[53] By May 1903, there were rumors of strikes to come and small strikes beginning in several places in the Southwest.[54] Most of the strikes in 1901, 1902, and the first few months of 1903 were small ones, except for the summer 1902 strike at Globe. Some were about conventional issues of wages, hours, and working conditions. The issue of ethnic inclusion and exclusion had been raised repeatedly, and had become an especially inflammatory component in locals' internal power struggles. But something much bigger was coming. In retrospect, most of the 1901–3 strikes would appear to have been curtain-raisers for the great conflict that was about to erupt in June 1903 in eastern Arizona.

◀ 2 ▶

THE FIRST BIG
STRIKE IN THE SOUTHWEST:
CLIFTON-MORENCI, 1903

Within this town up in the pines
Two thousand workmen closed the mines,
By striking for a raise in pay
And took to arms the second day.[1]

The Arizona territorial legislature's 1903 Eight Hour Law began the trouble at Clifton, Morenci, and Metcalf in eastern Arizona. Eight-hour legislation had become a hot issue across the mining West, and Arizona Territory was thoroughly embroiled in it. WFM unionists, some local AFL men, and the territorial Democratic Party had combined to pass the bill in Arizona. The new law stipulated eight hours as maximum allowable shift time for underground mining workers, beginning on June 1, 1903.[2]

The eight-hour question, however, was only a part of the trouble underlying the great western mine-and-mill strike wave of 1903–4. A related series of power struggles in Colorado (which had begun as wage and hour demands, evolving into a duel to the death between national WFM leaders and Colorado mine operators combined with their business and political allies) culminated in unionist defeats, arrests, deportations, and the ultimate decimation of the WFM's Colorado gold-mine and smelter-union locals. George C. Suggs, Jr.'s book, *Colorado's War on Militant Unionism,* explains how Colorado companies, with the help of small businessmen, Governor James Peabody, and the state's militia, fought Colorado unionists in 1903–4. But, as indicated above, 1903 was also a tumultuous year south and west of Colorado. Mining labor fought management in the copper-mining regions of Arizona and Nevada, although the copper conflicts were brief, scattered, and small. While Coloradans fought a full-scale war, labor and management skirmished in Nevada and Arizona, and a sense of class warfare pervaded the western mining regions.[3]

Most Arizona mining camps had no need for eight-hour legislation. The small Troy-Manhattan copper mine in Pinal County had eliminated the ten-hour day by early 1902 and was paying miners $3.00 for eight-hour shifts. The Phelps Dodge Copper Queen mine in Bisbee had begun eight-hour shifts early in 1902, and the United Verde Company in Jerome began an eight-hour schedule in early 1903. Globe's Anglo and Irish miners, heralded as "the best paid labor in Arizona," were earning $3.50 for eight hours in 1903, as were the Anglos and Irish working at large U.S.-owned Cananea, Sonora, copper mines a little below the border.[4]

Anglo and Irish miners earned $3.00 for eight-hour shifts at the Clifton mining district in Graham County, too, but few of the miners working there were Anglo or Irish. The Clifton district had employed both Anglo- and Irish-Americans and non-Anglo-or-Irish since the 1870s.[5] The Clifton-Morenci wage pattern indicated future trends in southwestern copper. In the 1870s, the Anglos and Irish working near Clifton had been earning an estimated $3.00 or $4.00 a day, and Mexicans and Spanish Americans had been making $1.50 or $2.00.[6] Most, and perhaps all of the Spanish-surnamed men working near Clifton in the 1870s had been New Mexico-, Arizona-, or Texas-born Hispanics, rather than Mexican immigrants. In 1901, the Anglo and Irish miners at Clifton-Morenci were still making $3.00 a day, but the new industrial labor pattern was already emerging. Many of the men called Mexicans *were* Mexican immigrants by 1901, and they were earning $2.25 and $2.50 daily. Also, Mexican immigrants and native-born Hispanics together had become the majority of the work force in the Clifton district.[7] The Mexican immigrant workers were part of the large population movement from Jalisco, Michoacán, Guanajuato, Aguascalientes, and Zacatecas which had come through Sonora and Chihuahua and then El Paso, and thence into Arizona and New Mexico.[8] Smaller numbers of Italian immigrants, Spanish immigrants, and black Americans also arrived in Clifton, Morenci, and Metcalf at some time before 1903.[9] With few exceptions, these men were hired at lower wage rates than those paid to the English- and Irish-ancestry mining and smelter workers.

Clifton, about 120 miles north of the Mexican border in eastern Arizona, smelted most of the ore which came 7 or 8 road miles down the mountain from the Morenci mines above. Miners and their families lived both on and near mining-company property both at the Morenci mines and at Metcalf, which was an agglomeration of shacks and small houses north of Morenci. The two big copper operations at Clifton-Morenci-Metcalf

Downtown Clifton, ca. 1903. Courtesy of Arizona Historical Society, Tucson (#20780).

were the Arizona Company and the Detroit Company, both Phelps Dodge Corporation affiliates. Both the Arizona Company and the Detroit Company were managed by the several generations of the Douglas family— James, James S. ("Rawhide Jimmy"), Walter, and later, Lewis Douglas.

The Arizona and Detroit company mines were the only big extractive operations in all of Arizona which employed large numbers of European and Mexican immigrants underground on ten-hour shifts in 1903. The territorial Eight Hour Law was deliberately designed to apply to only one set of mines in all of Arizona, the Phelps Dodge interests in Graham County, and the law was also an indirect attack on the immigrant work force in Clifton, Morenci, and Metcalf. Joseph Park, in his important study of territorial-era Arizona labor, concluded that the Eight Hour Law was intended to be "an effective blow delivered to mine operators who sought to employ alien Mexicans whenever possible because they would submit to working ten to twelve hours a day at a wage that undercut the union scale by about fifty percent."[10]

The Phelps Dodge companies prepared to obey the letter of the new law while defying the Western Federation of Miners. Just before June 1, they offered "to pay underground men nine hours pay for eight hours work."[11] Wages mattered far more than working hours to the poorly paid Clifton-Morenci workingmen. Nine hours' pay for eight hours' work was, in effect, a 10 percent wage reduction; the Mexican, Spanish, Hispanic, and Italian workers had been earning *ten* hours' pay, and after the first of June, they were to be cut to nine. Both the WFM and the copper corporations were more than willing to treat the non-Anglo, non-Irish copper work force as cannon fodder in their own struggle. The underground men struck against the 10 percent wage cut. The 1903 Clifton-Morenci strike began on June 1.

There were between 2,000 and 3,500 picketing strikers. According to one Anglo Clifton resident, there was "a pretty big crowd—mostly Mexicans, but a lot of Dagoes, Bohunks, and foreigners of different kinds . . . no whites at all."[12] The strikers congregated near mine shafts, storage sheds, railroad tracks, and all over company property. They were more of a crowd than a picket line, including not only men but women and perhaps some children. The thousands of strikers and strike supporters maintained an intimidating presence throughout the strike. Some of them were armed.[13]

Although the Mexicans, U.S.-born and other Hispanics, and Italians were being mercilessly squeezed between organized labor and company management, their strike was far from inevitable. It was, in fact, somewhat unexpected. No large group of recent-immigrant European, Mexican, or native Hispanic working people had ever struck before anywhere in the Southwest, Utah, or Nevada. More than that: the Clifton-Morenci strike was the first really large Mexican and Hispanic strike anywhere in the United States.

Dissatisfied men frequently quit their jobs and left Clifton-Morenci. The WFM and copper-company management both expected extensive employee turnover. During the seventeen months prior to the strike, most of the Spanish-surnamed, unskilled mine, mill, and smelter work force had been quitting Phelps Dodge employment three to six months after their initial hire. More than a third of the Italian-surnamed employees quit in less than six months too. Most of the Clifton-Morenci working people had probably never struck before. Yet this time they did not quit. The huge crowds persisted throughout the two-week-long strike. The Mexicans and recent immigrants had chosen to fight management rather than seek work elsewhere.[14]

Itinerancy was the rule, rather than the exception, at early-twentieth-century western mines and metal-processing plants. Studies of early 1900s "tramp miners" suggest that Anglo and Irish low-wage men, too, were at least as ready to quit their jobs as were the Mexicans, U.S.-born Hispanics, and Italians.[15]

But two or three thousand strikers and their families were staying put this time. Who were these men, collectively, and how many of them decided to strike rather than quit? Precise answers are unavailable. But 1900

Street scene in Morenci, 1903. The women, girl, and young man in the foreground are probably Mexican immigrants. Courtesy of Arizona Historical Society, Tucson (#74468).

statistics suggest that a significant proportion of these men were settled Clifton district homeowners.

In 1900, a definable group of relatively long-resident, married home-owners lived in Clifton, Morenci, and Metcalf and worked at unskilled and semiskilled jobs in the mines. In a work-force sample, more than half of the Mexicans and half of the Italians who had lived in the United States for at least six years were married, as were more than half of the U.S.-born Hispanics. Many unskilled and semiskilled workers owned their own homes (see Table 2.1).

More than half of the Mexican mining workers included in the 1900 census sample owned the homes in which they lived, free of mortgage obligations, as did one-third of the native-born Hispanics and half of the Italians.[16] Many of the homes owned were one-, two-, or three-room frame or adobe owner-built structures with improvised roofs, without foundations or utility connections. Many of them had a taxable value of $100 or less,

Table 2.1 Demography of the 1900 Clifton-Morenci-Metcalf Unskilled Mining Population

	Age			Marital status	
Ethnicity	25 & under	26–40	41 & over	Single[a]	Married
Mexican	17	44	11	24	48
Hispanic American (U.S.-born)	10	9	2	9	12
Italians	12	12	6	15	15

Source: U.S. Bureau of the Census, Manuscript returns for 1900.
[a]Includes the census categories of "Widowed" and "Divorced."

and many of the homes were apparently unmarketable. Small adobe dwellings were easy to build, and probably easy to give away but hard to sell, since they changed hands frequently without benefit of officially recorded transactions.[17] But the little homes were improvable. Old photographs of some small wood and adobe working-class homes in Morenci and Metcalf indicate various possibilities. The Morenci dwellings shown on page 40 are shacks, some of them slightly more elaborate, neat, and well-appointed than others, but shacks, nonetheless. The dwelling shown in the bottom photo on page 40 had probably begun as a shack, but it had been extensively improved. It had been converted into more of a house than a shack, and it would have offered relatively attractive living space. Photograph collection files include other photos of relatively fixed-up homes, which had apparent worth as real estate, even though they were located on copper-company land. These homes, too, indicate the presence of a population potentially interested in improving its residential status in Clifton-Morenci, apparently a stable group of homeowning mining workers.[18]

The copper companies helped create the racial definitions used throughout the mining West, and in the process, helped unify the copper workers. Histories of individual ethnic and racial groups fail to explain strikers like these adequately because theirs was a highly significant, ethnically *combined* job action. Job status, wage rates, and opportunities for job-status improvement offered to non-Anglo, non-Irish employees were substantially the same, regardless of their specific ethnicities. As strikers, they were still considered "foreigners" and "Mexicans." Local Anglo and Irish labor played practically no role in the 1903 Clifton-Morenci strike.

Years of U.S. residency				
2 or less	3–5	6–10	11 or more	Sample size
10	13	23	26	72
—	—	—	—	21
14	1	7	8	30

Although the corporations recognized no significant differences between foreign and Mexican labor at Clifton-Morenci, the companies *did* create a huge gap between the two non-Anglo-or-Irish groups and the Anglo and Irish worker population. Job-by-job comparisons illustrate the extent of difference.

Laborer, the job held by the largest number of Mexicans and Hispanic Americans, was the job least commonly held by the Anglo- and Irish-Americans. Non-Anglo-or-Irish laborers earned $2.00 a day, and Anglo-Irish earned $2.50. The job of miner was both better paid and more desirable than that of laborer. Non-Anglo-or-Irish miners were paid $2.50 a day in early 1903, and Anglo and Irish miners were paid $3.00. Mexicans and Hispanic Americans, Italians, and Anglos and Irish were employed as miners at Clifton-Morenci-Metcalf in numbers approximately proportionate to their respective populations at the Detroit Copper Company's mines in 1902–3. In most mines, the majority of miners were Mexicans and Mexican Americans, several miners were Anglo- and Irish-Americans, and a few were Italians. Timberman, the best semiskilled job classification available in the mines, paid $3.00 a day regardless of ethnicity. Anglo and Irish, Italian, and Spanish-surnamed timbermen were employed by the Detroit Company in 1902–3, but there were proportionately fewer Spanish-surnamed timbermen, in respect to their total populations at the Detroit mines, than there were Anglo, Irish, and Italian timbermen.[19]

There were a few relatively well-paid Spanish-surnamed men and Italians who were doing skilled work at several Detroit Company departments in 1902. A few Spanish-surnamed employees occasionally earned $3.50 at specialized furnace work, although they seldom worked enough $3.50 days

Homes of Morenci mining workers, ca. 1903–5. Houses were built with scraps of scavenged material, mud and branches, processed lumber, and roof shingles, and sometimes with rock. With the addition of sheeting, fencing, and windows, substantial improvement was possible. Courtesy of Arizona Historical Society, Tucson (#47511, #47514).

to significantly improve their biweekly pay. A Spanish-surnamed employee earned $3.00 for a day's work at the sawmill, and in November 1902 another earned $3.50 at the blacksmith shop. One Italian, working at "New Buildings" earned $3.50 a day regularly. However, Anglos and Irish had all of the other jobs paying $3.00 or more at New Buildings. The machine shop, which employed only Anglos and Irish in 1902, paid a typical daily wage of $4.00. All of the carpenters were Anglo or Irish, and they earned $3.50 and $4.00. At the blacksmith shop, several Anglo- and Irish-Americans made $4.00, some made $3.50, and most made at least $3.00.[20] Wages paid to the unskilled and semiskilled men at the Detroit Company mines show the same tendencies.

Immigrants just arrived from Mexico, men newly arrived from Spain, second- and third-generation Mexican Americans, and Spanish Americans from northern New Mexico were practically indistinguishable from one another in company records. Their company-designated ethnicity, "Mexican," was occasionally even noted on payroll sheets, apparently to insure that they would be paid lower wages.[21] Hindsight can offer hypothetical reasons for a "Mexican wage." English-language fluency may have mattered in some job situations. Spanish-surnamed workers may have lacked relevant industrial experience or specific job skills. Anglo and Irish workers may have been generally longer-resident, and so they would have been generally more likely to have acquired advantageous job status.

Demographic information about the several Spanish-surnamed populations working in the Clifton district negates all of these hypotheses. Some of the U.S.-born mining-company employees with Spanish surnames were fluent in English. Similarly, some of the large Mexican-immigrant population with more than ten years' U.S. residency (as indicated in Table 2.1), spoke fluent English. Also, some Spanish-surnamed workers, whether from Zacatecas, northern New Mexico, El Paso, or even Spain must have had previous mining or metal-processing experience.[22] Further, as indicated in chapter 11, young Anglo and Irish ranch hands and other rural Southwesterners *without* previous mine, mill, or smelter work experience were given entry-level jobs and rapid promotions associated with trust and experience in a similar copper-mining and processing area at Hurley-Santa Rita, New Mexico, beginning about a decade later, while Spanish-surnamed workers were not offered those jobs and promotions. There were the above-listed exceptions: a very few Spanish-surnamed employees working at higher levels than their fellows. *Enganchadores* or *padrones,* that is, labor agents, were sometimes hired as supervisory personnel, crew bosses, translators,

Table 2.2   Unskilled and Semiskilled Wages at All Detroit Copper Mining Company Mines, May 1903

	Under 30¢ hourly	30–39¹/₂¢ hourly	Over 39¹/₂¢ hourly	Sample size
Mexicans and Hispanic Americans	246 (64%)	135 (35%)	3 (0.8%)	384
Italians	11 (20%)	42 (78%)	1 (2%)	54
Anglos and Irish	1 (1%)	34 (43%)	44 (56%)	79

Source: DCC "Payroll" and "Time Book" records, May 1903.

and company informers, or spies, and the placement of names and occasional cryptic notations on old Phelps Dodge records indicate the probability that some of the Spanish-surnamed exceptions were privileged for these reasons.[23]

The collective wages and job status of the Italians positioned them roughly between the Anglos and Irish and the Spanish-surnamed men, and the Italians could perhaps have chosen to disassociate themselves from the strike. But 20 percent of the Italians were paid at the lowest levels of the Mexican scale, and practically all the rest were paid at the upper end of the Mexican wage scale, significantly below the wage scale for most Anglos and Irish (see Table 2.2). Both Italians and Spanish-surnamed workers were almost totally excluded from the jobs paying over 40¢ an hour, while the majority of the Anglos and Irish had those jobs. The Italians' job titles were also generally similar to those of the Spanish-surnamed workers, and inferior to those of the Anglos and Irish. The same set of hypothetical reasons for their management-inspired on-the-job inferiority—those related to language, experience, and length of U.S. residence—are similarly inapplicable. The homeowning and marital status of Italian and Spanish-surnamed workers were similar.

The copper corporations which united men from old Spanish-surnamed New Mexican families, Mexican immigrants, second- and third-generation Mexican Americans, and even immigrants from Spain with one another, and all of them with Italian immigrants, were redefining western U.S. ethnicity.[24] Almost all of the men who earned the Mexican wage and the somewhat less explicit Italian wage were made equals by company fiat. Mexicans were not the sole organizers or participants in the Clifton district's 1903 labor troubles, contrary to interpretations expressed in virtually all current historiography. Combined *working-class* activism was very different from ethnic community activism, which often had community rather

42

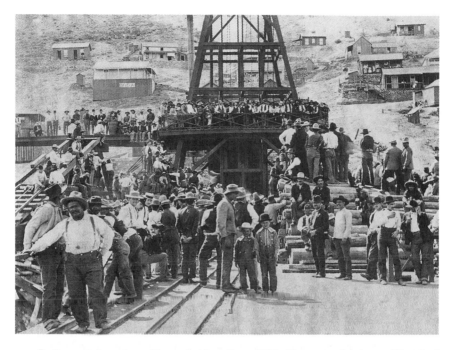

Strikers at the mines, Morenci, May–June 1903. Courtesy of Arizona Historical Society, Tucson (#59415).

than workplace origins. Western mining-camp labor history is generally working-class history, rather than ethnic history.[25]

The strike wore on, and the Italians were adjudged "the most dangerous element involved in the strike" and its probable chief instigators, and it was said that once the trouble was over, the copper companies would probably never hire Italians again.[26] Contemporary observers saw no visible organizational structure behind the strike. No list of demands was posted on the morning of June 1, and no union organizer or recognizable labor leader called the men off the job. The Clifton-Morenci strike, as Joseph Park described it, "in all of its outward aspects . . . [was] a paradox that caught the whole territory by surprise."[27]

The best known of the strike's leaders was Weneslado H. Laustaunau, the vice-president of a "Mexican and Italian organized local labor organization" at Morenci in early 1903. Laustaunau was probably a Morenci mines blacksmith in 1903.[28]

Mystery seemed to shroud Laustaunau, and by extension, the strike itself. Strike reportage made him into a grand schemer and mover of men.

Weneslado Laustaunau, the man whom hostile reporters called "Three Fingered Jack," and the principal leader of the 1903 strike at Morenci. This photo and the Salcido, de la O, and Salerni photos (pp. 48–50) were taken at Yuma Prison. Laustaunau's $2,000 fine and two-year sentence were the most severe punishment meted out to any of the Clifton-Morenci strikers, and his sentence was subsequently extended. He died in prison in 1906. Courtesy of Yuma Territorial Prison State Historic Park.

The Adjutant General of Arizona believed that Laustaunau was "an agitator sent into Morenci from Chicago."[29] Strike accounts dubbed him "Three Fingered Jack," a name created either by hostile local nonstriking Anglo-Irish, or else by newspaper reporters. Laustaunau hated the nickname.[30] In contemporary reportage, "Jack" was everywhere, organizing, scheming, and exhorting. He was believed to be Romanian, and was believed to have had something to do with the assassination of President William McKinley in 1901.[31] He made good copy.

Why was "Jack" mysterious, and why did the strike, as Joseph Park wrote, catch the whole territory by surprise? Was the strike so improbable an event, so difficult to plan and lead?

Its spontaneous aspect provided some degree of surprise, and its spontaneity probably made some of its participants mysterious. But in some respects, this was a conventional early-twentieth-century strike. What could have been more obvious than an angry crowd of two or three thousand workingmen communicating openly, for weeks? In a geographically isolated, densely populated mining area with few telephones, there must have been plenty of ordinary, face-to-face contact. Surprise labor action under these conditions would have been impossible. The Mexican and Italian organization which was to play an important role in the strike was anything but secretive. It was registered, with its officers' names listed in Graham County public records, as were the names of the officers of several other, similar organizations.

"The Mexicans belong to numerous societies and through these exert some sort of organization to stand together," observed an *Arizona Republican* reporter in 1903.[32] Three Hispanic-sponsored organizations were legally incorporated at Clifton during the several years prior to the 1903 strike. These organizations were certainly visible in 1903, and were probably not designed for plotting labor action. One, the Sociedad Progresista Auxilios Mutuos (Progressive Mutual Assistance Society) was incorporated as a sickness-and-death-benefit group.[33] Another actually called itself the Unión de Obreros (Union of Workers), but also described itself as a sickness-and-benefit society.[34] The third was Lodge Number 2 of the Alianza Hispano Americana (Spanish American Alliance). In 1903, the Clifton Alianza was nominally a social group, although five years later, Mexican government officials residing at Clifton were labeling it a seditious, revolutionary organization.[35] A fourth Mexican organization, the Sociedad Juarez Protectora, does not appear to have been legally incorporated in Clifton, but was nevertheless flourishing there until at least 1908, when it too was proscribed as a secret revolutionary society by Mexican officials.[36] Extant records indicate at least one similar Italian organization, the Società Fratellanza Italiana di Mutuo Soccorso, existing in 1903.[37]

Mutualistas, the social organizations that Mexican immigrants, Mexican Americans, and Spanish Americans first developed in the southwestern United States in the 1870s, served many purposes. Recent studies delineate several varieties of mutualista social and political activism, and indicate that individual mutualista groups in southwestern communities may have coalesced around factional subgroups representing particular social classes. During the most active phases of the Mexican Revolution, some mutualistas may have been connected to factional subgroups emanating from the Revolution itself.[38] But the mutualistas studied in east and south Texas were part of a well-developed pattern of Mexican immigrant and Mexican American community institutions, and ministered to social concerns in communities, rather than to workplace problems. The Hispanic communities of 1903 Graham County, Arizona, were newer and less institutionally diverse than those in Texas, and as a consequence, the mutualistas in them may have been less socially active. South and East Texas *labor unions,* in fact, sometimes functioned as mutualistas, but the reverse situation was practically unknown there.[39] Current research indicates that mutualistas were not labor-union surrogates on a regular basis, although they were sporadically concerned with workplace issues.[40]

But some mutualistas bridged the social gap between Mexican immigrants, native-born Americans of Mexican descent, and Spanish Americans.[41] Early mutualistas which abjured ethnic subgroup exclusivity helped create environments in which several Hispanic subgroups could sit together and plan joint action. Some portion of the Clifton-Morenci strike, in fact, was probably planned in local mutualista meetings. Some studies of contemporaneous non-Mexican ethnic societies have established clearly defined connections with specific labor-organizing activity. In Sunnyside, Utah, in 1902, an Italian coal-camp mutual society lodge, the Fratellanza Minatori, "functioned as a labor union, expelling . . . its members for scabbing." An early-twentieth-century Slovak Mutual Society based in the East, the National Slovak Society, did the same thing, albeit briefly.[42] Since there were at least four legally incorporated Mexican and/or Spanish American and Italian organizations at Clifton-Morenci, and since there may have been additional mutual-benefit societies which did not appear in 1903 county incorporation records, there were opportunities for plenty of well-planned labor organizing in Graham County before the 1903 strike started. But it is also likely that Morenci-area workingmen planned and effectuated at least a portion of their strike by means of the clandestine societies called "clubs" or "unions" that were sometimes created on the spur of the moment, just before strikes began; and which helped facilitate the Clifton-Morenci and Ray-area strikes a dozen years later.[43]

Two of the known founding members and known officers of Clifton-Morenci mutualistas were leaders of the strike. Abrán (or Abraham) Salcido was described as the "president of the local Mexican society", and Juan B. de la O owned the house in Metcalf at which the Sociedad Juarez Protectora's meetings were held several years later, in 1908.[44] There was, as previously mentioned, a Mexican and Italian labor organization which was *not* listed as a mutual-benefit society in incorporation records.[45] It was probably the same "local Mexican society" mentioned in other accounts, because Abrán Salcido was *its* president, too. Its vice-president was Weneslado Laustaunau.[46] Laustaunau, Salcido, Frank Colombo (whom journalists called "the Italian leader"), and several other men appeared to be essential to the strike effort. It is probable that, just as the mutualistas themselves facilitated the connection between immigrant Mexicans and native-born Hispanics, the Mexican and Italian workers' group bridged the Italian-Hispanic gap and further unified the Clifton-Morenci work force as the strike began. After Weneslado Laustaunau, Abrán Salcido, and Frank Colombo were arrested, the mass of strikers became "perfectly docile."[47]

The 1903 Clifton-Morenci-Metcalf labor action was a big, turn-of-the-century American strike, and no mystery to its participants. In fact, ethnic groups began organizing at least two months before the strike began. The Detroit Copper Mining Company reacted to the ethnic organizing by hiring Italian and Mexican operatives from the Theil Detective Agency and infiltrating them into the Morenci work force as company spies. This was the first known instance of utilization of detectives by the Detroit Company.[48] The copper company knew that trouble was coming.

Fifteen men were described as the leaders of the strike. One report refused to credit Mexicans or other Hispanics with leadership, but it implicitly included "Jack," and other Mexicans, under a different rubric. The leaders, it said, were "the Italians and the labor agitators." Three of the fifteen leaders were Italians.[49] All of the best-known strikers, and in fact, all of the men who were sentenced to the Arizona Territorial Prison for strike-related offenses at the conclusion of the strike, had either Spanish or Italian surnames except Weneslado Laustaunau, who was, nonetheless, an immigrant from Mexico.[50] Two men, Abrán Salcido and Juan de la O, were definitely Mexican immigrants, and one, Severo Montez, was born in Texas.[51]

Weneslado Laustaunau, the best known of the strike leaders, was part-French, part-Spanish, and half-Mexican, and in 1903, he was a recent arrival in Clifton-Morenci from Mexico. To his family, he was El Negro, a little darker than his siblings. As a child, he had been overly venturesome; and one day blasting powder with which he had been playing exploded, and he lost three fingers of his left hand.[52]

Laustaunau's name does not appear on the 1900 census rolls for Graham County. He probably arrived in Graham County less than three years before the 1903 strike. He was a well-proportioned man of average height, and a widower with two children. By the time he had become the vice-president of the "Mexican and Italian organized local labor organization,"

47

Abrán ("Abraham") F. Salcido, another important Clifton-Morenci strike leader. Salcido's punishment, a $1,000 fine and two-year sentence, was second only to Laustaunau's in severity. Courtesy of Yuma Territorial Prison State Historic Park.

he was known by another nickname, no more of his own choosing than the first one had been. He was, according to newspaper reports, El Mojo, "The Crippled Hand" to some of the Mexican and Hispanic people who knew him.[53]

Abrán Salcido was an unskilled or semiskilled smelter worker, living in a rented house in Clifton in 1900. He was single, he could read and write in English, and he had been living in the United States for four years. He was twenty-six years old. At the time of the strike, Salcido owned no taxable property around Clifton.[54]

Severo Montez was probably a miner in 1900. He may have been the "Seledo Montez" who owned a quarter interest in a mining claim, worth about $250, in 1900, but he did not own property in Clifton itself. In 1900, Montez was forty-six, married, and living in a rented house in Morenci. He was also literate in English.[55]

Juan de la O was a long-time Arizona resident, but he had only recently arrived at Clifton-Morenci at the time of the 1903 strike. He was married, and in 1903 he owned a Clifton-area lot with an improvement on it which had a total assessed value of $450. None of the other eight Mexican or Hispanic strike leaders appears to have owned property in the Clifton area during 1903, nor do the Italian strike leaders appear to have owned any. Most of the other leaders arrived at Clifton-Morenci-Metcalf between late 1900 and the end of May, 1903.[56]

Juan de la O, another of the eight men convicted of "riot" during the 1903 Clifton-Morenci strike. De la O was subsequently associated with Partido Liberal Mexicano activity in and around Morenci after 1907. Courtesy of Yuma Territorial Prison State Historic Park.

Francisco ("Frank") Salerni was among the best-known of the Italian strikers at Clifton-Morenci in 1903. Salerni was sentenced to two years at Yuma Prison for "rioting." Courtesy of Yuma Territorial Prison State Historic Park.

The leadership elite which managed the 1903 Clifton-Morenci strike was large. Late in the strike, an injunction listing over two hundred men by name prohibited them from "persuading or addressing a public meeting in the effort to prevent men from entering employment of the company."[57] Perhaps all two hundred were seen as leaders by mining company officials. In another account, just the fifteen men previously described were considered strike leaders. Ten men, four of them immigrant Italians and six immigrant Mexicans, were sent to the territorial prison at Yuma on trumped-up charges of "riot."[58]

As a group, the known strike leaders were men neither of the bottom nor of the top. They were semiskilled workers, and were thus perhaps a bit more fortunate than were most of their countrymen. Some apparently had a moderate amount of property interest in the Clifton area; others had none. Collectively they were neither a long-settled, propertied, or exceptionally stable group, nor were they, on the other hand, ten-day tramp miners. Most of the men who received prison sentences could read and write and probably were literate in English, and none of them was known to have had a previous prison record. Laustaunau was thirty-four years old in 1903, Salcido was twenty-nine, and the Italian leader was twenty-six. Half of the Clifton-Morenci prisoners were in their twenties, but their ages ranged from nineteen to forty-eight.[59]

The completely separate major ethnic groups of workingmen, the immigrant and native-born Mexicans, Hispanic Americans and Spanish and Italian immigrants, had begun a huge strike together, without assistance from organized labor, against a powerful set of mining employers in 1903. The combined effort was facilitated by the common language of their leaders—English. Ethnic issues had not divided them, and instead their primary workplace concerns had bound them together.

Their strike demands were specific and rather conventional. The Clifton-Morenci strikers' organization wanted some form of union shop. The strikers wanted prices at the Detroit Copper Mining Company store (the only big store at Morenci) kept low. They asked that "If a man is discharged a good reason must be given or the man must be restored to his job." They wanted to eliminate mandatory paycheck deductions for company hospital and insurance fees. They wanted change rooms provided so that men could change clothes when going off shift.[60] The general complaint which originally inspired the strike was the wages-and-hours grievance. The Mexican, Hispanic, and Italian miners who struck on June 1 to retain their $2.50 daily wage were demanding $3.00 on June 9.[61] Three dollars was, of course, the Anglo and Irish miners' pre-June daily wage. As one newspaper described it, "the wage grievance was a cover for race grievance or quickly became so after the trouble began." It was a duplicate of the Ray troubles of 1900, except that both the Spanish-surnamed and immigrant Italian communities were demanding on-the-job equality this time.

The Mexicans gathered "two or three times a day in Morenci . . . [to] listen to speeches from the leaders who are very industrious [and] have used harsh language concerning the 'gringos.' "[62] There was a constant awareness of the ethnic problem at the center of the strike. The strikers had severed the tenuous connection to contemporaneous events in Colorado.

Although the trouble had begun in the Morenci mines, it quickly spread to the mill employees and to the contract miners at the Coronado (Arizona

Copper Company) mine, none of whom was directly affected by the eight-hour problem. The much smaller Shannon Copper Mining Company's work force also struck, even though they were offered their old daily wage for eight hours' work. Management shut down the mines and mills on the same afternoon that the strike began.[63] There were no formal negotiations during the strike, probably because management refused to negotiate, although there were informal discussions on at least one occasion.[64] Sheriff's deputies, most of whom were probably Anglo and Irish, tried to act as intermediaries between the strikers and the Detroit Company's superintendent early in the strike, but the superintendent refused to discuss the strikers' demands. Explanatory notices and written announcements were posted by both sides during the strike, instead.[65]

Little violence actually occurred, but the possibility of it was often mentioned. On June 6, the Mexicans and Italians were "unruly," and Arizona Rangers were brought to town. They came to "assist in preserving order, the idea being to quietly arrest the agitating leaders." There was an "immediate need of a large force to quell riots that were impending . . . [because] the strikers were fully armed."[66] On June 10, "All is excitement and fifty extra police are on guard, heavily armed. Nearly 2,000 men are marching around town today. All saloons are closed and heavily guarded." On June 11, copper-company officials let it be known that they were afraid that their big company store would be looted.[67] The *Arizona Republican*'s reporter sent word of a growing panic among the company's partisans:

> The strike situation is growing more alarming hour by hour and violence is expected to break out in full force any minute. The first demonstration occurred this afternoon in the capture of the mill of the Detroit Copper Company at Morenci by a strong and well armed force of strikers, who disarmed the guard. Made bolder by their success and realizing that what is to be done must be done before the arrival of the military, it is reported that they are intending to make themselves complete masters of the town. They are also threatening the lives of prominent citizens, most of whom are officers of or managers of departments of the copper company. Reports of further violence at Morenci reach this place every few minutes, but beyond the fact of the capture of the mill nothing has been verified at this instant.[68]

The scene on June 11 was worthy of a John Wayne film:

> The miners had been wrought up to a frenzy of excitement by their leaders. . . . More than a thousand of them were armed and marching. They captured the works and held all of the commanding positions in the hills

surrounding the town. They had cut all of the telegraph and telephone lines, and they were ready to fight.[69]

But the cavalry was on the way. The acting territorial governor had solicited President Theodore Roosevelt's help, and Roosevelt called out the army to break the Clifton-Morenci strike.

On June 11, it appeared that the cavalry might not get to Clifton in time to stop the impending bloodbath.[70] But, as the two sides faced one another that afternoon, storm clouds gathered overhead. Rain began to fall, and then suddenly the rain became a deluge. Rainwater poured down the cliffs near the creek, which flooded down through the main canyon and into town. Bridges and transportation and communication facilities were all washed away. The impending armed confrontation was averted.[71]

About 50 sheriff's deputies, the entire force of Arizona Rangers, the whole 230-man Arizona National Guard, and a unit of the United States Cavalry, totaling perhaps 800 men in all, began working together against the strikers on the next day, June 12.[72] The Mexican consul had been sent by the Mexican government to "use his influence with the strikers."[73] Strikebreaking began. The lawmen and soldiers "kept the strikers in motion," "kept them from holding meetings at which a great deal of devilment would probably been hatched," used "the bayonet in a number of instances on unruly subjects" and arrested the men considered to be the strike's leaders.[74] On the following day there was a newspaper report that "Superintendent Mills of the Detroit Company says that there will be no compromise with the strikers. The works will start tomorrow. Those who have not made themselves objectionable may return to work."[75]

Many of the men did not immediately return to work. In fact, the strike dragged on for about two more weeks, but its main force had been broken on June 12 and 13.[76] A group of arrested strikers was held for trial, and the ten men mentioned above went to the territorial prison at Yuma.[77] The wages for underground work were set at the old nine-hour rate for an eight-hour day, just as the companies had offered in May—that is, the underground men's daily pay was cut by 10 percent.[78] The Western Federation of Miners voted a belated resolution of support for the Clifton-Morenci strikers, and denounced President Roosevelt for having used the cavalry for strikebreaking.[79]

Many American miners left Clifton-Morenci-Metcalf during the strike.[80] Some Mexicans and Spanish Americans, who were reportedly "sulky," prepared to sell their houses and leave the area afterward. Some Italians were also leaving.[81] During normal periods of 1902–4, as indicated above, almost half of the men in various Morenci and Clifton work crews left their jobs within six months or less. Usually, at year's end, only about 25 to 35 percent of the work crews that had begun the year remained.[82] The end of this strike apparently accelerated the normally high job turnover rate at Clifton-Morenci.

Men deprived of work because of a strike frequently quit rather than striking.[83] Many miners and muckers could not afford protracted unemployment, and chose traveling over picketing. The American miners who left Clifton-Morenci would not have picketed for the strikers in any event, and they probably left town in the usual manner, seeking work. But it is significant that the Mexicans, Hispanics, Italians, and perhaps some Anglos and Irish generally did *not* leave during the strike. They left afterward, and those who left after the strike ended were not tramps, drifting aimlessly down the tracks, but included homeowners who deliberately disposed of their houses and left as a group. Theirs had been an organized, concerted action by unskilled labor, without union assistance, and they maintained unity even in defeat.

The failure of the strike did not materially affect the situations of the Mexicans, Spanish Americans, and Italians at Clifton-Morenci-Metcalf. The unskilled and semiskilled labor force there still included the same groups after the strike.[84] The Alianza Hispano Americana, the Unión de Obreros, and an apparently new organization—a local Club Liberal Mexicano—were functioning normally there after the strike, too.[85] At least one of the July 1903 officers of the Unión de Obreros, in particular, was identified by Mexican government officials as a radical revolutionary several years later.[86]

The six Mexicans and four Italians convicted of riot in the autumn of 1903 received one-year and two-year prison sentences. In addition, Weneslado Laustaunau was fined $2,000 and Abrán Salcido $1,000. Laustaunau was "Confined in solitary cell for assaulting Supt. and Ass't Supt. and attempting to escape" on April 28, 1904, with "all good time earned to this date forfeited." His sentence was extended an extra ten years in mid-1905 for "assault with a deadly weapon." His own personal correspondence and family memories of him indicate a sensitive, intense man who may have been easily provoked to hostility.[87] Yuma prison legend has it that he was repeatedly confined to "solitary," the "dark cell," or the "incorrigible ward." Confinement at Yuma sometimes meant being thrust into an iron cage built inside of a dark chamber cut into solid rock. Summer days in Yuma are among the hottest anywhere in the Western Hemisphere, and some of the punishment cells were exceptionally hot. In summer, rattle-snakes sometimes crawled into the dark cell seeking shade. Prison records show that Weneslado Laustaunau suffered "heat prostration" there in the summer of 1906. The prison personnel may have been the direct cause of his suffering. He died in the prison hospital during the predawn hours of August 20, 1906.[88]

Abrán Salcido returned to Metcalf after serving his two-year peniten-tiary sentence "for being one of the leaders in the Morenci riots."[89] He had become an anti-Díaz Partido Liberal Mexicano (PLM) revolutionary: his political education was probably acquired within the walls of Yuma Prison. On May 5, 1906, at the annual Cinco de Mayo celebration, Salcido spoke before a crowd of more than 2,000 people in Morenci. His speech "greatly shocked all present." "Pointing his finger at the portrait of President Diaz [the president of Mexico] he exclaimed: 'Down with Diaz! Cursed be Diaz! Traitor! Tyrant of the republic! Imposter! Thief!' etc., etc." The audience went wild.[90]

Local Anglo- and Irish-Americans were outraged, as were some influ-ential local Mexican Americans. In front of the crowd, conservatives, including the Mexican consul resident at Clifton "secured a resolution . . . ordering all members of the anti-Diaz club to at once leave the country, and by the following day they had all disappeared." Salcido had probably gone to join the Mexican revolutionary precursor movement.[91]

The Mexican Revolution and its precursor events and organizations were contemporary with early-twentieth-century southwestern labor activ-ity at the copper mines and mills. Abrán Salcido was a part of both, but not concurrently. He did not reappear during subsequent organizational activity at the copper mines and smelter in Graham County, so far as is known. Most probably, he could not have safely done so.

Possible connections between the 1903 labor activity and the precursor revolutionary activity in the Southwest have only been demonstrated infer-entially, and have never been conclusively proven. Juan Gómez-Quiñiones and W. Dirk Raat, in particular, have developed coincident examples of la-bor and political activism into conclusions. Gómez-Quiñiones, in his *Sem-bradores: Ricardo Flores Magón and the Partido Liberal Mexicano,* posits a relationship between labor organizational activity and radical Mexican Liberal Party politics. Gómez-Quiñiones includes the Clifton-Morenci strike in his analysis, endeavoring to explain the hypothesized relationship between the strike and revolutionary politics.[92] Similarly W. Dirk Raat, in his *Revoltosos,* a study of U.S.-based Mexican political activists during this period, connects the 1903 strike with both Mexican Liberal activism and Western Federation of Miners radical organizing. Using information about the 1903 WFM national convention drawn from published sources, Raat claims that 1903 was a kind of turnaround year for the WFM; a year in which the national leadership "urged [convention delegates] to change past practices and pay special attention to organizing immigrant workers."[93] Although those sentiments were, in fact, expressed at the 1903 WFM convention, they were volunteered by individual members, and were completely unconnected to any WFM organizing campaign or to any measure of WFM responsibility for the Clifton-Morenci strike. Also, there is no evidence that the presence of men like Abrán Salcido, who became a revolutionary, or *revoltoso*, three years later, made the 1903 strike in any way a revolutionary precursor event. The organized portion of the Mexican, Hispanic American, and Italian communities was certainly crucial to the strike; but similarly, there is no indication that any of it was influenced by Mexican pre-revolutionary politics in 1903. The Clifton-area Club Liberal Mexicano may have become a constituent part of the Partido Liberal Mexicano several years later; but in 1903, its officers' names were being voluntarily published in a Clifton-Morenci newspaper advertisement a week before the strike began. This was surely an unlikely practice for a revolutionary organization. Furthermore, the 1903 strike was nearly as much an Italian-immigrant strike as it was a Mexican-immigrant strike, and the Clifton-Morenci Italians were highly improbable Mexican revolutionary precursors.

However, the 1903 Clifton-Morenci-Metcalf strike may have helped initiate political activism. It may have been the greatest single catalyst for Mexican, Spanish American, and other Hispanic political and social activism in the Southwest.[94] Several years after the 1903 strike, Salcido and other former Clifton-Morenci area strikers, and also newer area residents who may have associated with them, were being listed as Partido Liberal Mexicano adherents and as revolutionary activists. Other future labor action by immigrant European and Mexican workers in Arizona was connected, at least peripherally, with residents and former residents of the Clifton mining district. When Mexicans and other Hispanics joined the established Arizona organized labor movement during the First World War, the first Hispanic representatives to the State Federation of Labor and to the International Pan-American Labor Congress included former strike participants and former residents of the Clifton mining district. This suggests a reversal of conventional historiographic interpretation. It suggests that labor activism and particularly the 1903 strike experience itself should be credited with giving birth to future political activism, rather than crediting nonexistent political activists with having made Arizona Mexicans, other Hispanics, and Italians politically conscious.

A wire from Arizona told Big Bill Haywood, then the WFM's secretary-treasurer, about the strike. "Mostly Italians and Mexicans" on strike, it said. "Good chance to organize." Someone in Morenci itself asked Haywood and national WFM headquarters to send an organizer.[95]

Two Arizona supporters of immigrant inclusion explained to WFM members at the national convention, then meeting in Denver, why they ought to support the Clifton-Morenci strike:

> We believe that the conditions are such as would warrant and justify the Western Federation of Miners in taking immediate steps to organize this camp. There has always been a peculiar condition existing in this camp, which up to the present has made it particularly difficult for the Western Federation of Miners to get a foothold, these conditions being that the company makes a distinction between the wage of its different employees on account of nationality. Therefore, we believe that these men, unorganized as they are, coming out as they have, shows to us that if the Western Federation of Miners takes advantage of the present conditions and sends a representative or representatives to this locality, the result will be beneficial, not only to our unorganized brothers, who are struggling for the principles we contend for, but also will redound to the advancement and upbuilding of the Western Federation of Miners.[96]

The WFM had not yet made up its mind about whether or not to actively recruit "Mexicans and foreigners." There was the contract-labor issue. *Miners' Magazine* had been ruminating about "idle men of nations of Europe [who] are a grave menace to the working class of this country." But the Western Federation already included some non-Anglo-Irish members, and its Executive Board had recently voted to translate the union ritual and constitution into "Italian, Slavish, and Finnish."[97]

The WFM sent an organizer to the Clifton district. He arrived too late, when the strike was nearly over. But the Clifton-Morenci strike pushed the Western Federation into tentatively deciding in favor of the Mexicans and foreigners, which in turn helped predispose the WFM's partial creation, the Industrial Workers of the World, to recruit immigrants and Spanish Americans several years later. One after the other, 1903 convention delegates rose to announce their support for Mexican and recent-immigrant recruitment. One man urged an organizing drive in Arizona, "especially of the Mexicans." Another suggested "organizing the foreigners by hiring their own people as organizers." Former WFM president Ed Boyce asked the delegates to "Discourage talk about scabs and foreigners. Foreigners are leaders in labor movements." An Arizona delegate simply said, "Organize the Mexicans."[98] An important part of the American labor movement had decided, in principle, to accept recent-immigrant inclusion in mid-1903, and neither WFM nor IWW national leadership was ever to support exclusionist principles again thereafter.

◄ 3 ►

JUSTICIA, IGUALDAD, AND UNIONISM
IN CLIFTON-MORENCI, 1904–1907

The early years of the twentieth century were generally years of prosperity for the U.S. copper industry. Between 1904 and 1907, copper prices were high, production soared, and more men were hired at the western mines, mills, and smelters.[1]

Arizona's Mexicans and other Hispanics, Italians, and South Slavs, the growing Greek, South Slavic, and Italian work-force populations of the White Pine County, Nevada, and western Salt Lake County, Utah, copper mines and mills; and the Mexican immigrants at the American Smelting and Refining Company (ASARCO) smelter in El Paso were all quiescent. No major work-force initiatives were launched from within the intermountain or southwestern recent-immigrant copper communities for several years after the 1903 Clifton-Morenci strike.

Western Federation of Miners' influence increased in Arizona, Nevada, and Utah during these years of nonconfrontation and high production. At first, there was no WFM plan for unionizing the western recent-immigrant hinterlands. But defeated Colorado miners began finding work south and west of the Colorado gold camps, and in 1905, the WFM helped create what at first seemed to be a like-minded young giant of a labor confederation, the new Industrial Workers of the World. Hope was reborn, albeit for a brief time, at WFM headquarters.

The WFM had been engaged in a succession of confrontations with powerful employers since its inception in 1893. The miners' unions fought at Coeur d'Alene in 1893, Cripple Creek in 1894, Leadville in 1896–97, Salt Lake and Coeur d'Alene in 1899, Telluride in 1901, and they marched into the near-fatal Colorado labor war in 1903 and 1904.[2] Some of the pre-1903 warfare had been successful, and through 1903, the WFM was the lone great force pushing the eight-hour day and the $3.00 daily wage in western mining states and territories.[3]

Ed Boyce had retired from the WFM's presidency in 1902 and Charles H. Moyer was elected president just as the Colorado labor cataclysm began. The WFM was never to win another major battle thereafter. Moyer was to lead it through twenty years of defeats and disasters, punctuated by brief, temporary intervals of stability and hope. After 1903, the WFM was struggling for survival even as it struggled to organize.

The WFM proclaimed itself eager to organize the unskilled. In 1897, Ed Boyce had said: "Open our portals to every workingman, whether engineer, blacksmith, smelterman, or millman. . . . The mantle of fraternity is sufficient for all." Three years later, Boyce said that the WFM would "at all times and under all conditions espouse the cause of the producing masses, regardless of religion, nationality or race." Charles Moyer also reminded WFM members of their duty and interest in strengthening unskilled labor, the "weakest link in the chain of the labor movement." Bill Haywood, the union's secretary-treasurer, restated the same general policy at the 1903 WFM national convention.[4] In quantity of verbiage devoted to the virtues of organizing the unskilled, WFM leaders were probably far ahead of the United Mine Workers of America (UMWA), the only other big western union which was organizing among non-Anglo, non-Irish workers. Although the UMWA lacked ideological interest in organizing among the unskilled, as John Laslett's study of radical labor points out, in practice, eastern coal miners' locals included African American and Slavic miners even before 1900. "The English-speaking miners did not exclude the Slavs from their unions because of the danger of their being used against them during strikes. For the same reason they also accepted Negroes."[5] Italian strikebreakers first appeared in the Colorado coalfields in about 1903. By 1904, the UMWA apparently had taken over an Italian immigrant organization in Colorado which included a newspaper with a two-thousand-name subscription list, and the coal-miners' union had transformed the ethnically organized Italians into UMWA District Number 15.[6] West of Denver, the UMWA was practicing what the WFM preached.

Despite its radical pronouncements, the WFM was not yet adequately

Charles H. Moyer, WFM president 1902–26. Photo taken about 1902. Courtesy of Archives, University of Colorado at Boulder Libraries (General #2319).

prepared to organize immigrants. Almost all of its national organizers were Anglo and Irish until 1904, when two organizers with Serbian surnames began working at the metals smelters in Pueblo, Colorado.[7] The officers of WFM locals and the delegates they sent to the convention were almost all Anglo and Irish, with only one likely exception, in 1903.[8] By 1904 and 1905, the preponderant majority was still Anglo and Irish but delegates from five locals, including Denver and Pueblo, had non-Anglo and non-Irish surnames.[9] There were, of course, several WFM locals in southwestern copper areas and in Utah and Nevada as well by 1905, but most union members in those locals were semiskilled and skilled Anglos and Irish.

The WFM really began broadening its base in 1906. The Colorado coal miners who had been "deserted" by the UMWA could be organized, some

WFM men suggested.[10] There were more non-Anglo, non-Irish officers of local unions in 1906. Most of them were Italian, and an Italian organizer was working (along with at least two English-speaking organizers) at the Mesabi iron range in Minnesota.[11] A group of men connected to both the Western Federation and the IWW was tentatively planning to organize in southwestern copper areas. Fernando Velarde, who belonged to a new IWW industrial union formed at Phoenix, Arizona, was "preparing a manifesto to be circulated among the Mexicans of Arizona, New Mexico, and Mexico." He was to be assisted "in every way possible as his services will be of exceptional value as an educator and organizer of his countrymen."[12] At the 1907 WFM convention, the delegates again specifically rejected nativism, and generally agreed to increase the number of immigrant organizers.[13] Men contemporaneously designated as Austrians, most of whom were probably Serbians, Croatians, and Slovenes, were joining the WFM in Montana, and WFM resolutions were to be published in English, "Austrian," and Spanish at Jerome, Arizona.[14]

Three WFM men, including two of the Federation's leaders, Charles Moyer and Bill Haywood, were railroaded to temporary imprisonment and eventual trial in Idaho during February, 1906. Moyer and Haywood remained incarcerated while the newly formed Industrial Workers of the World, and then the WFM itself, fought internecine battles and split into irreconcilable factions.[15] As its annual 1907 convention drew to a close, the Western Federation was losing some of its own members to the IWW and some of its connections to the American Federation of Labor's left wing.[16] The major struggles in the 1907 convention were won by WFM moderates, who adopted a new charter preamble continuing support for class struggle and implying continued support for political socialism. But in 1908, after Charles Moyer's return from Idaho and his resumption of the union's presidency, Moyer himself began to argue against the industrial form of union organization and in favor of ideologically conservative unionism.[17] An economic collapse, the Panic of 1907, had struck the mining West in October of that year. The Panic's effects continued into 1908, resulting in forced wage and hour reductions and massive layoffs. Union organizing became more difficult under these conditions, and strikes seemed less likely.

The Western Federation of Miners had once found a temporary home in the American Federation of Labor, had later helped create potentially broad-based affiliation through the Western Labor Union and the American Labor Union, and then had tried again with the IWW. Except for brief moments, the WFM had always been affiliated with other segments of organized American labor. After the WFM-IWW split, and in the midst of the defeat and depression of 1907–8, the WFM was facing the real possibility of total destruction, either through attrition or at the hands of the mining corporations. The WFM would have to either grow or die. More members and more money were badly needed, and necessity pushed the WFM into beginning new organizing initiatives.

Organizing south of Utah meant organizing in Clifton-Morenci and in Bisbee and nearby Douglas, Arizona. The Southwest's large Phelps Dodge-connected mines and mills, employing thousands of unskilled and unorganized workers, were located in those two mining areas. The Clifton district had had its strike, the strike had been crushed, and Bisbee did not look promising. The Bisbee-Warren district and the Douglas smelter area were situated at the Mexican border, which meant that strikebreaking and labor replacement were an ever-present possibility, and unionization prospects were dismal. Later, the copper areas at Jerome, Hayden and Ray, Ajo, and Globe-Miami-Superior in Arizona, and at Hurley-Santa Rita and Tyrone in New Mexico would expand and begin to employ many unskilled copper workers. But between 1904 and 1907, the largest Arizona copper camps were at Clifton-Morenci and at Bisbee.

A transition period had begun for the southwestern Anglo-versus-Hispanic labor organizing problem. In two small strikes soon after the Clifton-Morenci debacle, the problem began to assume a more complex form. There was a WFM smelterman's local at the American Smelting and Refining Company's Durango, Colorado smelter; and in September, 1903, the smeltermen struck for the eight-hour day. ASARCO used strikebreakers, some of whom were Navajo Indians and many of whom were men recently arrived from Mexico. But some Mexican smelter workers became strikers, and according to the WFM report, they "struck better than the Americans," although "only six [joined] the union, as most . . . contemplated leaving the camp if the strike continued any length of time."[18] The WFM organizer's report described non-English-speaking men as both potential ethnic replacements and potentially loyal union recruits. According to the organizer, the local Anglo-American and Irish-American smelter workers were mostly opponents of WFM national organizing objectives, just as they had been at Globe, in 1903.

Another Anglo-American organizer explained that he had failed at a small Arizona mine in 1905 because "it was useless to attempt to reorganize the union, as fully seventy-five percent of the one hundred and twenty employees are Mexicans." But then he went on to suggest that union headquarters send an organizer who could speak the "Mexican and Italian" languages to work in Arizona and Southern California because, "if the benefits of organization could be properly shown to these people, they would join with us by hundreds and make good members."[19]

When Edward Crough traveled through Arizona for the WFM during 1907, he organized and collected dues. Crough helped sign men into the union at Bisbee, and eventually helped direct a 1907 strike there. His notebooks indicate his satisfaction at the progress of ethnic, and particularly Mexican recruitment at Bisbee. Yet, at Helvetia, Silver Bell, and Dos Cabezas, Arizona, he saw Mexican miners at work, and did not try to recruit them. Crough was able to communicate in Spanish, but he was not fluent. The ambiguity evident in his approach to Mexican recruitment was probably related to difficulties in communication, but may have been connected to an unwillingness to tackle the more difficult discussions about unionism, race, and money which Mexican recruitment required. When Crough was in Bisbee, he had had assistance from a Mexican organizer. Operating alone, he was less than eager to recruit Mexican and Spanish-surnamed Arizona miners. Crough's approach to Mexican recruitment may have been typical of Anglo and Irish WFM organizers in 1907.[20]

The second great strike in the modern southwestern copper industry began at Cananea, Sonora, near the U.S. border, in 1906. The Cananea strike has been thoroughly explained as part of the Mexican Revolution's history. But the Cananea strike was, in fact, both revolutionary history and a part of the history of modern southwestern and near-southwestern industrial unionism.

A demand for *justicia* or ethnic fairness was a partial cause of both the Clifton-Morenci strike and the Cananea strike. Mexican and Spanish immigrants, Spanish Americans, and Italian immigrants were being treated as the ethnic inferiors of English-speaking workers, and they resented it. *Igualdad* and justicia, of course, were not conventional labor-union demands.[21] But, as Rodney D. Anderson explained it in 1976, "the fact that American miners received double the pay that their Mexican comrades collected for the same work" was the most important issue at Cananea, and "bread and butter issues" were less important. Anderson wrote that Cananea sparked further labor action, including the boilermakers' strike on the Mexican Central Railroad in June, 1907, which was also caused by "the preference shown to foreign employees of the railroad over Mexican workers."[22]

The Partido Liberal Mexicano (PLM), functioning in both Mexico and the United States, was definitely organizing for both political and labor action shortly before the Cananea strike. One of the strike leaders had been discussing the formation of a Liga Minera de los Estados Unidos Mexicanos just two months before the Cananea strike began.[23] The PLM was also an important presence in the southwestern United States, and immigrant Mexican and Hispanic workers could not have been unaware of it. In addition, north of Cananea, there were men who had struck in 1903, and who had become revolutionary activists by 1906. Abrán Salcido, Juan B. de la O, and Luis Mata were Clifton-Morenci activists in both 1903 and 1906–8.[24] But in Clifton-Morenci, politics and labor were not directly connected. Salcido, de la O, and Mata were not leaders in 1906–8 Clifton-Morenci *labor*. Arizona's 1906–8 strike activity was not comparable to that of 1903. Two of the three Clifton-area 1903 leaders lived there in 1908, but they had become politically, and only politically, active.[25] The Western Federation of Miners sent nationally known radical luminaries and organizers to Clifton-Morenci during 1906–8 too, and they actively recruited unionists and made occasional political statements. But the proximity of labor leadership and political activism during this campaign did not mutually reinforce either one. No conjoint action involving revolutionary Mexicanos and their radical Anglo and Irish unionist sympathizers ever took place in the southwestern copper areas during those years.

In its own way, the Western Federation of Miners did support both the workingmen and the revolutionaries, both north and south of the U.S. border. The WFM played the role of sympathetic outsider during the Cananea strike. The union confederation pronounced in favor of the Cananea revolutionaries:

> Whereas, the Western Federation of Miners recognize the class struggle throughout the world, and know no race or creed in the battle for industrial freedom; therefore be it Resolved, That the Western Federation of Miners in convention assembled sends greetings to the Mexicans, trusting that their efforts for a higher standard of living will be crowned with success.[26]

But no sum of money for Cananea accompanied that message, nor did the WFM organize a national campaign to help the Cananea strikers. The WFM had taken measures like these on other occasions, notably at Clifton-Morenci in 1903. Cananea was familiar terrain for the WFM and many of its members. In 1905, some Cananea foreman positions were held by former Cripple Creek miners, and about 1,500 sometime WFM members (of a total of 5,500 mining workers) were being employed at Cananea.[27] There was frequent travel and correspondence between Cananea and places nearby in Sonora and the U.S. Southwest. A former organizer and member of the WFM Executive Board went to Cananea to organize before the strike, in January 1906. Many individual WFM members contributed money to the Cananea strike effort, both before and during the strike.[28]

The WFM, or at least some of its membership, was clearly interested in Cananea even before it became an object of special interest to the PLM. Still, the official level of response to the strike was most similar to the response to the Clifton-Morenci strike three years earlier. There was a greater degree of publicity and interest at Cananea, but that was because of Cananea's political implications, its somewhat greater size, and because there was major violence there. The national WFM's response to Cananea does not indicate any change in the union leadership's policies in 1906. WFM headquarters offered sincere, verbal, nonrenumerative, and basically ineffectual support for strikes initiated by non-Anglo-Irish, and also for joint action with the PLM.[29]

In Cananea, Clifton-Morenci, and in Globe too, it seemed possible to organize combined Anglo-Irish and Hispanic locals. Labor conflicts offered tangible opportunities for creating them. But the organizing opportunities became a series of failures as it became increasingly clear that exclusionist Anglo and Irish miners, not Hispanics and Europeans, were at the heart of the WFM's major southwestern organizing problem.

Cananea's Anglo-against-Mexican racial climate was typical of some other camps in the Southwest during 1904–11. Overt racial violence appeared soon after Cananea in Christmas, Arizona—a tiny Gila County camp near Winkelman. "Race War" had begun at Christmas, according to a newspaper headline. On the night of Tuesday, April 9, 1907, a Mexican employee of the Saddle Mountain Copper Company was shot dead by an Anglo deputy sheriff for apparently insubstantial reasons.

> As soon as the Mexican miners, who number fully 300 in the Christmas camp learned of the killing by Pemberton of one of their number they organized into a mob and attempted to lynch the officer, who held them at bay during the greater part of Tuesday night with the assistance of the white miners, who are greatly in the minority.
>
> The Mexicans and whites in the Christmas camp have all armed themselves as far as guns and revolvers or knives can be secured, and all it will take to precipitate a bloody race war is for some one to fire a shot.[30]

Early-twentieth-century Anglo-against-Mexican violence, including incidents like the one at Christmas, were synchronous with the developing Mexican Revolution. Because of this association with epochal upheaval, early anti-Hispanic race hatred and its twin, Hispanic hatred of Anglos, are fairly well understood. But there were analogous situations nearby. Anglo-

Irish and Greek mutual hatred, for instance, flared in White Pine County, Nevada, in 1908, when a White Pine County deputy sheriff named Sam Davis was wounded during an apparently unnecessary altercation involving Greek copper-mining workers.

> The incident triggered a volley of hate. Retaliatory action drove the "white" dissidents to band together. In the inevitable clash, a Greek— Diamantes Kalampokas—was martyred through death from a gunshot wound.
>
> There was no immediate arrest. Instead, virtually all of the unemployed Greek men in McGill were rounded up as if they were cattle by a posse of self-righteous, excitement-hunting citizens, prodded on by a gun-slinging lawman from the county seat.
>
> The January 22, 1908, *White Pine News* reported that more than 100 of the Greeks—supposedly bad apples—from the helpless gathering of human victims were unceremoniously marched up the hill to a pair of waiting boxcars, commandeered for the occasion, and locked into the mobile prison for shipment out of the district. [They were later released.][31]

Cananea's violent strike and the race hatred evinced at Christmas, Arizona, and White Pine County, Nevada, illustrate the extent and intensity of ethnic-racial antagonism among the mining area work forces in the early-twentieth-century Central West and Southwest. Still, the WFM continued simultaneously organizing among both the recent immigrants and Spanish Americans, and among the English-speaking miners.

Small-scale labor trouble at Clifton-Morenci was continual. "Another walk-out took place yesterday," a reporter wrote in the late spring of 1906. The issue at Clifton-Morenci in 1906 was still the eight-hour day, and the company response was unyielding. Now Arizona Copper Company offered its concentrator employees an eight-hour day combined with a 20 percent pay cut. Three years earlier, the companies' "deal" had been an eight-hour day with nine hours' pay: in essence, a 10 percent pay cut. Twenty-three of the twenty-five concentrator employees walked off the job and were fired.[32]

Organized labor was no longer actively interested in the eight-hour issue, but eight hours had become a symbol for ethnic equality; and by 1906, the symbol was being used by *unorganized* labor. The demand for justicia and igualdad was being promoted to primacy above wage or working conditions complaints at Clifton-Morenci. It was being expressed as a demand for an eight-hour day *with equal wages*. The ACC concentrator work force said that it wanted "to be placed upon the same footing with the other great camps of the territory."[33]

During 1906 and 1907, as mentioned above, Clifton, Morenci, and Metcalf were visited by several prominent members of the North American Left. At various times during the year, Praxedis Guerrero, a leading Mexican revolutionary activist; Mother Jones, the famous speechmaker and organizer; Joe Cannon, of the new Arizona state IWW local; Frank Little, the WFM organizer who was later to be lynched during an IWW campaign in Montana; and Fernando Velarde, who was also organizing for the WFM, all spent some time in the Clifton-Morenci area.[34] They were collecting money for radical causes, including the Mexican Revolution, and they were organizing for both the WFM and IWW.

An Anglo-American organizer visited Clifton-Morenci-Metcalf in October 1906 and began organizing there, reporting that "The conditions of the workers is deplorable as the mining companies have absolute control, owning everything, and with the aid of all Government officials and militia have so far been able to dictate [conditions] under which the slaves shall work."[35] The organizer arranged to have Frank Little and Fernando Velarde sent from the Phoenix IWW industrial local to the Clifton-Morenci district. Little and Velarde arrived late in 1906, and submitted a charter for a Clifton local to WFM headquarters for approval promptly thereafter. By mid-1907, the WFM listed a Mill and Smelterman's Union at Clifton, and a Miner's Union at Metcalf: Frank Little was the national convention delegate for both.[36] The local officers for the two unions were listed in 1908 as H. F. Kane and William D. Steward for Clifton, and Carmen Acosta for Metcalf.[37] Carmen Acosta was a local mining worker, and was the only WFM functionary who actually represented the ethnic majorities working at Clifton and Metcalf.[38] (More than half of the mill and smelter workers below supervisory level at Clifton were Spanish-surnamed in 1908, and more than 80 percent of the Metcalf mining workers were also Spanish-surnamed.)[39]

In March of 1907, Clifton, Morenci, and Metcalf miners were petitioning all three local copper companies about a 50¢ wage increase and a sliding wage scale, pegged to the wholesale price of copper. The March wage petition was a careful effort at combining Anglo-Irish and Hispanic interests in the Clifton district. Such well-balanced planning suggested the fine hand of a WFM national organizer, again trying to bridge the yawning gap between the two principal groups at the big southwestern mines. Wage increases were specified as intended for both Spanish-speaking men and Americans. Also, higher pay was appropriate "because of the great increase of wages in other Arizona mining camps. In the event of a reduction in wages in a majority of other mining camps, we will most willingly accept the present wage scale again."[40]

In mid-May 1907, a large meeting was held in Morenci to arouse support for Charles Moyer, George Pettibone, and Bill Haywood, on trial for the murder of Governor Steunenberg in Idaho. Joe Cannon, of the WFM and Arizona territorial WFM headquarters, planned the meeting. It was "attended by a number of Mexican laborers of the camp who listened to a speech delivered in Spanish by Carmen Acosta." The founding of union locals at Clifton, Morenci, and Metcalf was also discussed at the meeting.[41] Number 158, the Clifton local, and 159, the Metcalf Miners' Union, existed on paper but were shakily established, and the Morenci miners were as yet unrepresented. Most of the Mexican and other Hispanic men worked and lived in Morenci and Metcalf.[42]

When the strikers walked out on July 22, 1907, they left the Western Federation with its carefully modulated, slow-developing tactics far behind. Nonunion Hispanic men at the Arizona Copper Company's smelter in Clifton struck for the 50¢ wage increase.[43]

The men who struck were Mexicans and Spanish Americans who were impervious to the blandishments of WFM organizers. They were not hotheaded radicals, spoiling for action and heedless of the consequences inherent in a premature confrontation with the copper companies, but were actually some of the better-paid Mexican and other Hispanic employees, including some men who were already earning over $3.00 for an eight-hour day.[44] They struck as an organized group, in disregard, although not necessarily in defiance, of WFM-proffered Anglo-Irish leadership:

> It was at first surmised that Little, the organizer who has spent much time in this district, had something to do with the strike, but an incident took place Tuesday evening that does not make it appear that way. The Mexicans, among whom are some whom have worked in this district for years, called a meeting Tuesday evening to which they invited local officers in order that they might see that the meeting was conducted in an orderly manner. Mr. Little thought that he could give them some fatherly advice and made an effort to attend the meeting. He attempted to take the floor, but the chairman asked him to shut up and withdraw from the room. This Mr. Little refused to do and he was then approached and assisted to the open air. The Mexicans announced that they knew what they were doing and considered themselves capable of conducting their own business. They are making what they consider a clean fight and are not ready to receive information from outsiders.[45]

The brand new Clifton WFM local (Number 158), which had English-speaking officers (including Frank Little), did not want the strike. The WFM men may have preferred to organize and to increase local union membership before fighting the copper company. But the WFM did cooperate with the strike, albeit reluctantly.[46] Striking continued into August, and was totally ineffectual.[47] Instead of the demanded 50¢ wage hike, their wages were cut 25¢ to 50¢ in November, because the 1907 Panic was under way. Many of the strikers left the Clifton-Morenci area as the strike was failing.[48] Local Number 158 disintegrated.[49]

The 1907 Clifton-Morenci strike was a small labor conflict directed at a limited goal, higher wages, and it was generally devoid of overt ethnic rancor. However, fairness, justice, and equality were again important issues. The wage increase for the Mexican and Hispanic smelter workers would have put them practically on a par with the Anglo-Irish-American smelter workers, many of whom were holding better-paying jobs.[50]

Although the strike had been preceded by WFM activity, it certainly was not a WFM-sponsored strike, as the Western Federation made clear later.[51] Did the Mexican and Spanish American smelter workers deliberately bypass an opportunity to function as equals within a WFM cooperative effort? Actually, no such opportunity was ever offered. Because Anglo-Irish-American officials predominated in Clifton Number 158, the Spanish-surnamed workers would have been subordinate, rather than equal, if they had chosen to join the local. Again, as in 1903, Hispanic ethnic societies already existed which enabled the smeltermen to conduct competently led, disciplined labor action without direct WFM assistance.

The economic and class characteristics of the 1907 Clifton-Morenci strikers and their leaders indicate that they were not men of the poorest, most disadvantaged, or the most rootless working-class strata. The 1907 strike was similar to the 1903 strike in this respect. The newest, lowest-paid, and most rootless element had been a *minority* of the Spanish-surnamed work force in 1903, when practically the *entire* Spanish-surnamed work force had struck. In 1907, the same lower-income element, again a minority, was best represented by the residents of Metcalf, who did not strike at all. Some of the leaders of the 1903 strike, and some of the strikers of 1907 were men with relatively good jobs and better pay than most Spanish-surnamed workers earned, and as we saw in chapter 2, some of the 1903 leaders had owned property.

Praxedis Guerrero was one of the Left's important visitors at Clifton-Morenci in 1907. As a major PLM organizer, he was apparently in contact with the PLM leadership in Los Angeles.[52] During the time that he resided at Clifton-Morenci-Metcalf, Mexican revolutionary activity began to smolder there.

During 1908, Spanish-surnamed residents of the Clifton-Morenci area helped in the planning of several armed attacks on Mexican cities and towns near the Mexican-American border, including one against Ciudad Juarez, Chihuahua. Some of the plots were actually carried out, and they were related to important prerevolutionary activities. Also, Praxedis Guerrero, Manuel Sarabia, and others traveled on revolutionary business between Clifton-Morenci and Globe, Douglas, Bisbee, El Paso, Los Angeles, Cananea, and several other towns in Mexico. The revolutionaries functioned through at least three of the Mexican social organizations at Clifton-Morenci-Metcalf in 1908—the Sociedad Juarez Protectora, the Sociedad Zaragoza, and on this occasion, the Alianza Hispano Americano.[53]

Luis Mata bridges the gap between the 1903 strike and the revolutionary activities of 1908. Mata was an officer in the Unión de Obreros in July 1903, and he was also described as the "chief of Morenci sedition" five years later.[54] Juan B. de la O, as previously mentioned, was one of the principal Hispanic strike leaders in 1903, and revolutionary members of the Juarez Society were meeting at his home in 1908.

Abrán F. Salcido, as mentioned in the last chapter, returned from prison to denounce the Díaz government at the 1906 Cinco de Mayo celebration, after which he was forced to leave Clifton. Salcido crossed the international border immediately, and became a major participant in the upheaval at Cananea, suffering arrest and imprisonment there. When Salcido was being forced out of Clifton-Morenci, an estimated "seventy five or one hundred Mexicans . . . left this district" with him, carrying guns, apparently heading for Mexico to join in the local revolutionary activity.[55]

At Clifton-Morenci in 1906–8 it is possible to distinguish the outlines of several factions, albeit through a glass, darkly. First, Abrán Salcido, Juan B. de la O, and Luis Mata were leaders in the labor movement of 1903, but they were political revolutionaries and *not* labor leaders during 1906–7. They had apparently become more radical. Yet this radical activism clearly was not channeled into the Clifton-Morenci labor struggle.

Also uninvolved, or unwilling to become involved, were the majority of Mexicans, Mexican Americans, and other Spanish-surnamed workers in the Clifton district. They continued working throughout the strike. Only the smelter was struck. The eight-hour issue had little meaning. The feeders, tappers, skimmers, and wheelers at the smelter were already earning from $2.25 to $3.25 for an eight-hour workday during July 1907; levels of pay that, while not on a par with typical Anglo-Irish-American wage levels, were reasonably close to them.[56] The strikers were a group of comparatively well-paid Hispanic workers, some of whom avoided associating with Anglo-Irish-American unionism as represented by the Western Federation of Miners.

Another Hispanic faction at Clifton-Morenci in 1906–8 opposed radical activity, unionism, and probably opposed mutualista-sponsored activity as well. The Spanish-surnamed men who arranged the ejection of Salcido and the other revolutionaries may have included Clifton-area businessmen with attitudes best described by Thomas Sheridan in his 1986 book *Los Tucsonenses*. In Tucson, and probably in Clifton and Morenci, the Mexican middle class generally opposed organized labor, according to Sheridan.[57] There were also Hispanic employees, probably few in number, who supported the copper companies and who worked diligently against both organized labor and political revolutionaries. One such person was Agustín Pacheco, who was a married, middle-aged Mexican American mine timberman during 1906–8. At various times, he was the secretary of the Unión de Obreros at Morenci, a secret informant working for the Mexican government, and a Detroit Copper Company spy.[58]

Finally, there were Fernando Velarde, Carmen Acosta, and those who gave both men a sympathetic hearing, some of whom joined the local union movement at Metcalf and Clifton. There were, at least at Metcalf, some mining workers, most of whom were probably near the low end of the wage scale, who were supporters of Western Federation of Miners-sponsored organized labor in the Clifton mining district in 1907. All of these factional elements together made up the Hispanic portion of the Clifton-Morenci work force which the WFM sought to organize. Mexican immigrants and other Hispanics had become politically and socially restive and there was labor-union activity as well, but ethnic divisiveness was pervasive. There was not the slightest hint of work-force unity as Panic-induced unemployment spread across the Clifton district late in 1907.

◄ 4 ►

UNION RADICALS RECRUIT MEXICANS, SPANIARDS, AND SOUTH SLAVS: BISBEE, JEROME, AND GLOBE, 1907–1910

Bisbee

Bisbee was the hard nut for the WFM to crack in 1907. The Phoenix Industrial local sent the WFM's Joe Cannon to the Bisbee-Warren district early in 1907 to try to develop a new local there.[1] The Copper Queen mine had never been struck successfully since Phelps Dodge management had begun operating it in 1884. The "Queen" was a big mine, in a big Arizona industrial town. Bisbee had 6,000 people in 1900 and more in 1907.[2]

Phelps Dodge dominated Bisbee. An older, settled population of mine workers lived in town, and they had an understanding with Phelps Dodge. The vehicle for that understanding was a company-sponsored arrangement called the Bisbee Industrial Association which claimed to have made Bisbee the best-paying camp in Arizona. The Copper Queen had maintained, almost constantly, $3.00 and $3.50 daily base wages for more than twenty years. Muckers, whose status and skill levels were below those of miners, received the miners' wage; and Bisbee had been converted into an eight-hour camp painlessly, without union pressure, a year before the other Arizona camps changed to eight hours. A 1906 WFM effort at organizing a Bisbee local failed. In a referendum meeting at which paid-up WFM members, former members, and many nonmembers all cast ballots, the proposition lost by a 2,288-to-428 vote.[3] As labor conflict began catching up with Bisbee, the Queen offered miners, muckers, and car men $4.00 a day, and

Brewery Gulch, Bisbee, as it appeared at the time of the 1907 strike there. Courtesy of Bisbee Mining and Historical Museum.

raised the pay for every other labor category commensurately. When the Western Federation of Miners began to sign up Copper Queen workers, the Industrial Association declared that "you may be sure that we who are satisfied with conditions here are not going to be told by outsiders what course we must pursue to remain in Bisbee."[4]

Bisbee bore a superficial resemblance to Butte, Montana, in 1907, as Butte is described in David Emmons's recent *The Butte Irish*. In both Butte and Bisbee, management bragged about high wage rates. Labor peace was based upon an understanding between the older, settled mining workers of Bisbee, many of whom were Cornish, and Copper Queen management—a situation comparable to the Irish-controlled Butte Miners' Union's arrangements with Amalgamated-Anaconda. Open dissension among the rank and file was generally absent in both places, until (again, in both places) around 1907. When the Bisbee strike began, many of the strikers were young men and relatively recent arrivals, while many of the nonstrikers were middle-aged men with families. Again, it was much the same way in Butte.[5] But there the resemblance ends. Emmons's explanation of the sociology and politics of early-twentieth-century Butte is based upon characteristic Irishness, the Irish culture of the plurality of the Butte work force. Bisbee did resemble Butte in many ways, but the only comparable work-force segment in Bisbee, albeit a smaller portion of the total, was Cornish. The men from England's Cornwall coast were typically Methodist working-class immigrants, with a cultural affinity for underground hard-rock mining work. Many of them had a general distaste for Irish-dominated American labor unions.[6]

Labor peace based on high wages and cozy arrangements made between a long-resident, settled mining population and management were common to both Butte and Bisbee. Hostility directed against recently arrived mining workers was also common to both. But the ethnic factor—Irish in Butte, Cornish in Bisbee—was as different as it could be. Specific ethnicity does not explain the old-resident and new-arrival antagonism in Bisbee, and logically, specific ethnicity may not be the best explanation for Butte either. The anti-immigrant, anti-Mexican biases shared by Cornish, Irish, and other northwest European groups were more relevant.

The Western Federation of Miners tried to create a Bisbee Miners' Union by combining a population of newly arrived South Slavic workingmen with a relatively small pro-union Anglo and Irish workers' population. Most of the South Slavs were ethnic Serbians and Slovenes who had come from Serbia and Croatia. The potential recruits among the Anglo-Irish-Americans were men who at one time or another had had WFM cards at mines and mills in other western states. The mining West was booming in early 1907, and Bisbee, like many other mining areas (Butte included) was experiencing the usual influx of new employees that accompanies a mining boom.

The Western Federation did not simply ride the crest of the wave during boom times at the mines and mills, but neither had it a developed policy for expansion and contraction of organizing effort during periods of labor-force growth and decline. However, flush times in Bisbee did offer an exceptionally good opportunity for organizing. The WFM organized opportunistically. During a boom period, the copper companies could be induced to raise wages, the union federation could justifiably take the credit for the higher wages, and the workingmen would feel the strength of a new union local while they had more money in their pockets, which they might then be willing to spend on union dues. But flush times at Bisbee did *not* offer the WFM an opportunity for replacing an Old Guard of immigrant-exclusionist conservatives with an enthusiastic, radicalized group of unionists who favored ethnic inclusion. Most of the new recruits would be non-English-speaking South Slavs, if the South Slavs could be induced to join.

When the WFM organizers came to town, copper management in Bisbee began eliminating men whom it considered sympathetic to unionism. Many of these men were English or Irish. By mid-February 1907, eight hundred men had been laid off. There was no strike at that point: the companies were moving much too fast for the union federationists. Many laid-off men who otherwise would have been strike participants left Bisbee and the nearby Douglas smelter area in February just as the union big guns, including Joe Cannon, Percy Rawlings, and Mother Jones, were arriving.[7]

What the WFM organizers had left to work with was a relatively small English- and Irish-American population, a relatively large South Slavic population, and Mexican immigrant and mixed European immigrant populations of indeterminate size. There were, altogether, about 5,000 mining workers at Bisbee early in 1907. On April 8, a group of South Slavs who had joined the union went to the mine managers to demand union recognition. They were rebuffed, and the strike began on April 10.[8]

There was moderately strong strike support, even as many men were leaving town. Strike supporters were a majority of the unskilled and semi-skilled work force, but the mines did not close. The newly created Bisbee WFM local had about 1,700 members, albeit briefly; and there were probably about 2,000 strikers.[9] The companies had begun blacklisting union miners before the strike. Throughout the several-week-long active phase of the strike, many mining workers, both Anglo-Irish and South Slavic, were losing their jobs and entraining, generally in groups, for other localities, hoping to find work. At the same time, Western Federationists posted at the Southern Pacific depot in El Paso and the Benson, Arizona, railroad station, tried generally without success "to turn back men who are coming into the [Bisbee] district from all portions of the country."[10] Some of the South Slavs who left town had families; some Cornishmen who left town after being blacklisted were reportedly single.[11]

The South Slavs quickly became functioning union members: they were the majority attending union meetings during the strike.[12] A big meeting was held at Bisbee's Medigovich Hall and "80 percent of those present were Slavonians, Italians, and other foreigners."[13] As previously mentioned, it was the South Slavic unionists who demanded union recognition; and finally, it was the same group of men, in particular, whom the copper companies refused to rehire.[14]

The Industrial Workers of the World also came to Bisbee during the strike. They came in a supporting role, as Mother Jones had done, to help the WFM. Tom Hickey, a talented Socialist and IWW speaker, appeared and Vincent St. John was scheduled to arrive soon afterward. Carmen

Acosta came from the Clifton district to organize Mexican and other Hispanic workers. The national Socialist Party was sending Eugene V. Debs. Both Marion Moor of the WFM's Executive Board and D. E. Semple, a WFM man with some journalistic experience, came. Moor and Semple were WFM radicals, and Semple, who began editing a newspaper which promoted the Bisbee organizing and strike effort, mildly favored the IWW in 1907. The active phase of the strike ended before St. John and Debs were able to reach Bisbee.[15]

The Bisbee strike effort smacked of failure from start to finish. Copper-company management and the Bisbee Industrial Association were certainly too fast for the miners' union. Management and the Industrial Association coordinated an antistrike campaign. Groups of antistrike Bisbee machinists, some engineers, pumpmen, pipefitters, and blacksmiths, some of whom were nonunion, but many of whom carried either current or expired WFM cards, held meetings. Their union cards, some of which were months or even years behind in dues payment stamps, had been acquired at other camps and some of the men at the meetings were probably WFM Union-at-Large members.[16] The meetings were held by individual groups of craftsmen, in imitation of American Federation of Labor crafts union procedure, and all of the skilled and semiskilled groups voted against the strike, despite some definite prostrike sentiment among the machinists and engineers.[17] Many of these men had used the Western Federation of Miners as a source of sickness-and-death-benefit insurance and as a surrogate lodge hall, but they did not want it to represent them as a labor bargaining agent in Bisbee.

The Bisbee skilled and semiskilled men were a natural constituency for the WFM, but they were also a diminishing portion of the mining work force at the modern, efficient, expanding twentieth-century mines in Arizona. Although the immigrant South Slavs and Mexicans were not taking their jobs away, the skilled Anglos and Irish (and especially Cornish, in this instance) were unwilling to tie their collective destinies to the emerging version of twentieth-century WFM unionism. The immigrants threatened to drag the English-speaking men into labor confrontations not of their own choosing, and they could expect that immigrants would eventually outvote them at union meetings, too.

The most active phase of the strike ended in late April, although the strike wasn't formally declared over until the day before Christmas.[18] Despite the strike failure, the new Bisbee Miners' Union, Number 106, survived the strike.

A functional understanding of Bisbee mining labor depends upon an understanding of the importance of the two broad ethnic categories—

"Americans," and "foreigners" and Mexicans. Individual ethnic histories and special cultural and sociological information about particular ethnic groups explains little in 1907 Bisbee. Nor, as mentioned above, was the Cornish community comparable to that of the Butte Irish. The distinctions made between newly arriving mining workers and older, more settled mining workers do not explain the Bisbee labor trouble either. Bisbee was a mixed industrial city. Newer arrivals were men responding to work-force expansion in a relatively high-wage job market, and many of them were family men. In fact, the relationship between the WFM and the Bisbee South Slavs in 1907 was similar to the WFM's relationship to the Clifton-Morenci Italians, Mexicans, and other Hispanics in 1903, and also its relationship to the Bingham Canyon, Utah, and White Pine County, Nevada, Greeks, South Slavs, and Italians in 1912. Specific ethnicity, the unique behavior of particular ethnic communities, did little to shape these conflicts. A more complex ethnicity—the us-against-them mentality that pitted the interests of so-called Americans or English-speaking men against those of recent European immigrants and Mexicans—was a root cause of ethnic work-force trouble in the Southwest and lower intermountain region during the early twentieth century.

Ordinary working miners at western copper camps who opposed the Western Federation of Miners' organizing drives did not necessarily disagree with its standard wage, hour, and working-conditions demands. Controversy over wages, hours, and working conditions was to become common again after 1912, often because of IWW, rather than WFM demands. Meanwhile, there were angry machine miners, timbermen, and blacksmiths, most of whom were Anglo or Irish, who opposed organizing immigrants, and sought a means to express their anger. Angry ethnic exclusionism was seldom expressed in social-class terms or western-labor-movement terminology. Working miners who attacked western industrial organizing head-on would have been fouling their own nests. Instead, when local English-speaking union men opposed organizing of recent immigrants, their hostility was expressed in ethnic and racial terms.[19]

An example indicates the intensity of feeling against WFM unskilled-worker organizing during these years. It was probably inspired by D. E. Semple's moderately successful trip from Bisbee to nearby Douglas in late June 1907, to organize the Douglas smeltermen.[20] The editor of the Douglas *Examiner,* a prolabor newspaper, pilloried WFM leadership for even attempting to organize WFM locals at Bisbee and Douglas. The *Examiner*'s editor accused potential Anglo and Irish WFM union recruits of sinning by merely associating with Mexican mining workers, and claimed that the Mexicans were too craven to join unions.

It requires manhood to build up a Federation Union. What could an organizer expect in a community where a white man is afraid to talk English, for fear of offending his wife's relatives?

Where peonage flourishes in all its primeval purity. Where the jails consist of caves; prehistoric Aztec dwellings, whose domestic arrangements need no changing to accommodate the low browed, mouse eyed, vermin ridden pelados who are compelled to work ten hours, eat on the trail, and steal on the side to keep carcass and mentality in the same neighborhood. Where the Copper Queen is in her glory, paying out $2.25 a day and getting back $2.50, the victim being compelled to steal government timber to make up the deficit.[21]

Jerome

Jerome, Arizona, was next. In 1909, WFM organizers sent from national headquarters faced more of the same hostility directed against unskilled and ethnic organizing there. The Jerome Miners' Union at the big United Verde Copper Company camp in Yavapai County staggered through an internecine quarrel in which rival sets of union officers led by Walfrid Holm and John Opman tried to grab the JMU's official records and office keys from one another. The Jerome incident looked like a power struggle, and Vernon Jensen's account attributed it to the copper company's subversive infiltration of the union.[22] Joe Cannon went to Jerome to try to resolve the local's fraternal warfare. Cannon summed up one side's argument this way:

the union was getting too radical, [they said], and that it must be held in check, that it had no business to interfere with the cases where the foreman was compelling the men to pay him so much a month for their jobs, and it was a mistake to have brought Ben Goggins here to try to get the Spaniards and Italians into the Union, the company does not like it and it is a mistake to go against the wishes of the company in matters of this kind.[23]

Ben Goggin was a Spanish-speaking organizer sent from Denver headquarters by the WFM's national leadership. There were immigrant men of several nationalities working at Jerome, and Goggin was sent to make Jerome something bigger than an American local operating for the benefit of an ever-shrinking proportion of skilled mining workers.[24] The Jerome local had had a similar situation several months earlier. A Serbian organizer,

"Judich," had come to Jerome, and local membership "had grown more rapidly than it had in years, perhaps than at any time since the union had organized." It was because both Judich and Goggin had been so successful in gaining recent-immigrant adherence that the union's anti-immigrant faction had blocked the organizing drives. During each organizing campaign, the Jerome local grew to over three hundred members from perhaps half that size.[25]

The anti-immigrant WFM faction at Jerome wanted to dominate the local by stopping its recent-immigrant influx. If they failed to dominate the local, the anti-immigrant men had prepared a backup position. The immigrant exclusionists already had 152 names ready for use on a charter application to be sent to the American Federation of Labor.[26] The exclusionists were resorting to blackmail. They would either stop the immigrant influx, or they would join with the WFM's AFL rivals.

As at Bisbee in 1907, there were machinists, blacksmiths, and engineers who were, in several respects, the natural allies of the WFM men, as well as being their residential neighbors in the mining camp and smelter communities. Anti-immigrant English-speaking men, of course, were only a part of Jerome's work force; but, as at Bisbee, their numbers were being augmented unfairly by nonmembers who were voting in the Jerome local. Joe Cannon maintained that an actual voting majority of the traditional membership of the Jerome local *favored immigrant inclusion.* These members, he maintained, were being cheated out of administrative positions in the local because the United Verde Company was colluding with the exclusionist anti-immigrant men.[27]

One element in the Jerome Miners' Union's 1909 fight appears clearly out of place. The usual two factions were present; men who were being called radical, and who favored immigrant inclusion, and men deemed conservative, who favored exclusion. But John Opman, one of the leading exclusionists, was anything but conservative on other issues. During the heat of the IWW-versus-WFM controversy in 1907, Opman had been president of the Jerome Miners' Union, and during his presidency the JMU sent its "Resolution No. 2" to the WFM national convention. In it, the JMU unanimously demanded that the WFM yield to the pro-IWW position, and threatened to pull the entire local out of the WFM if its demands were rejected at the convention. The JMU and some other WFM locals demanded that WFM headquarters meet its financial commitments to the IWW, which were in arrears. In effect, the WFM was being asked to rejoin the IWW. Opman also threatened to make the JMU "a local of the IWW." He sent the IWW's third annual convention assurances of the JMU's "hearty cooperation" in 1907. Subsequently, he was implicated in a half-baked scheme to capture the WFM's Arizona locals for the IWW.[28] Opman, then, exclusionist and outspoken *opponent* of radicalism in 1909, had been pro-IWW, and thus a *supporter* of radicalism in 1907. Opman's anti-immigrant stance during the JMU power struggle could have been a thoroughly duplicitous tactic intended to destroy the moderately radical faction within the JMU; or else, quite possibly, it genuinely represented the opinion of IWW sympathizers within the Jerome Union in 1909. In the JMU, at least, some of the anti-immigrant men were probably IWW sympathizers.

Globe

Globe's factional struggle matched Bisbee's and Jerome's, and then some. The 1902 battle in Globe had ended with an anti-immigrant factional victory and union constitutional changes which codified the new Globe Miners' Union power configuration. But the wrenching power struggle within the Globe union continued. By 1906, the situation was reversed. Alfred John Bennett, one of the men who had convinced the WFM's 1903 national convention to back the Clifton-Morenci strikers, had become the president of the Globe Miners' Union, and the local was being described as "the most revolutionary [union local] in the Southwest."[29]

In 1907, Bennett, P. W. Galentine, and William Wills represented the Globe Miners' Union at the WFM's national convention. National convention delegates argued furiously, day after day, for and against the Industrial Workers of the World. In a series of crucial votes over a week's time, they adamantly rejected IWW's new leadership and finally they decided to sever the WFM's affiliation with the IWW. The Globe Miners' Union was the third largest local in the WFM in 1907, and it cast the biggest block of votes against the pro-IWW forces, represented at the miners' convention by Vincent St. John and Fred Heslewood. The Globe opposition to the IWW was especially important because the biggest of the convention delegations, the group from Butte's Local 1, was almost evenly split between pro- and anti-IWW men, and the second biggest group, from Goldfield, Nevada's, Number 200, was heavily pro-IWW.[30]

P. W. Galentine of Globe said that he had come to the 1907 convention uncommitted to either side. Advocates of both the Charles O. Sherman (pro-WFM and anti-IWW) and William Trautmann (pro-IWW) factions had solicited him, Galentine said, and he had only decided to oppose the Trautmann group after having had a private discussion with Mother Jones. William Wills blamed both sides for causing the controversy, and claimed that many of the local's members back home in Globe felt the same way.[31]

Alfred John Bennett, of course, was the presumptive leader of Globe radicalism in 1906 and 1907, and Wills and Galentine were his associates. These Globe radicals, who apparently favored ethnic inclusion, began by riding the fence on the IWW issue at the national convention, but finally backed the anti-IWW faction there. The content and specific meaning of WFM radicalism and conservatism varied with circumstances, and varied independently of the immigrant inclusion-exclusion issue.

Radicalism can better be described than defined. Western miners, muckers, timbermen, and other mine workers frequently used the word and understood its meaning. In earlier years, many ethnically English and Irish miners had been angry men, real enemies of their employers, and willing to consider violent means to achieve workers' ends. The rhetoric that many of them used was antimineowner, and sometimes, by extension, anticapitalist. They demanded changes in working conditions, and in the 1890s, their list of demands was fairly long.

But violence had often proved counterproductive and the capitalist system was surviving and flourishing. For English-speaking miners, the eight-hour day and the $3.00 or $4.00 daily wage had become more common, and so their list of demands was shortened a bit. By 1907, western miners' radicalism was a shifting set of major reformist goals which often, but not always, included ethnic-racial toleration. Radicals were generally activists. They wanted to effectuate as many reforms as possible, as soon as possible, and said so.

After the flaming western labor-management wars of 1892–1904, conservatives were generally defensive WFM unionists who had had their fill of union trouble. Conservatives remained organized to protect their own perceived workplace status gains. WFM conservatives wanted to either shorten the radicals' list of proposed reforms, or to eliminate the list altogether. The conservatives feared that the radicals' list would cause unending labor-management warfare—warfare that might cost them their own hard-won gains at the workplace.

The three Globe convention delegates went back home to fight the IWW and ethnic inclusion issues again. D. E. Semple, only recently arrived from Bisbee, and long-time radical activist Tom Hickey began a pro-IWW newspaper in Globe, the *Globe Miner*. The newspaper tried to solicit support for the IWW among immigrant workers. The Globe Miners' Union and its ally, the Globe Socialist Party local, both fought the *Miner,* accusing it of "trying to stir up a race prejudice among the union miners of Globe."[32] The Globe IWW men did not develop a miners' organization there, but they did create a small IWW Globe Public Service Local the following year.[33]

Neither the IWW nor the WFM had enrolled pluralities of South Slavic, Italian, Finnish, Mexican, and Spanish American working populations of Globe in 1907–8, but the Miners' Union included some of them. Globe's exclusionist 1902 contract was still in effect in 1908, and pro-immigrant men wanted to eliminate it. GMU members voted in a referendum on whether to continue "the Contract System." Either confusion or deliberate duplicity caused the non-English-speaking mining workers to vote to continue the contract system, although some of them regretted their votes immediately after casting them. Ed Crough of WFM national headquarters, which was still opposed to the 1902 contract, came to Globe and attempted, unsuccessfully, to encourage non-Anglo-Irish GMU members to petition for another referendum vote on the contract, as previously mentioned.[34] The radical candidates were in full control of Globe Number 60 after winning the September, 1908 union local elections. The refurbished radical leadership began buttressing its strength within the Globe Miners' Union by recruiting more immigrant new members. Albert Wills, who may have been related to Globe delegate William Wills, began organizing on the job, and hundreds of new recruits began joining. The copper companies were furious: recruiting inside the workplace was a violation of the conservative 1902 contract. Most of the new members were South Slavic and Italian.

As at Jerome, and, to a lesser degree at Bisbee, the rapid recruitment of non-Anglo, non-Irish men was part of the power struggle between WFM radicals, some of whom had IWW leanings, and WFM conservatives, who did not. The 1909 Jerome fracas demonstrates that either side might recruit a recent-immigrant plurality with which to throttle the other, although the radicals certainly did so more often. At Globe, as at Jerome, recent-immigrant organizing by radicals provoked a strong conservative response about a year later.

By 1907, there were actually *three* factional contingents within the Globe Miners' Union. District organizer and executive board member Marion Moor reported that "the Capitalists endeavor to place as members in No. 60 [the Globe Miners' Union] all their Labor Lieutenants and conservative wage slaves in order to defeat any radical measure advanced by the true union men."[35] The Globe power configuration actually *was* comprehensible, but the imbroglio needs sorting out.

First, there were the "true union men," who, in Marion Moor's words, sometimes promoted "radical measures." These included Galentine, Bennett, and Wills, whose faction controlled the GMU in the spring and summer of 1907. These men could also be described as moderates, since they were neither friends nor committed opponents of the IWW. Despite their radical credentials, they opposed the IWW at the 1907 WFM Convention.

Second, there were men who supported D. E. Semple and Tom Hickey. They, too, would have been described as radicals, but unlike the moderate-radical Bennett, Wills, and Galentine group, they had the IWW credentials to prove it.

Third, there were the men whom Marion Moor called "Labor Lieutenants and conservative wage slaves." As was true at Jerome, tipping the balance in a union election or important vote through a last-minute addition of newly initiated immigrant voters had an anti-immigrant counterpart. If conservatives could find some ethnically Anglo or Irish former union men whose dues were in arrears, or an occasional mine-area boilermaker or railroad man who could be induced to pay the miners' federation for an additional union card, or even men who knew how to pretend a WFM affiliation, then the conservatives could tip the balance in union elections and crucial votes for their side just as surely as the radicals and moderates could do so. And the conservatives intended to do it, in Globe, during 1908.

Cornishmen were the preeminent conservatives in Globe in 1908. Globe had begun as a "Cousin Jack" camp in the 1870s, but some of the Cornish at Globe in 1908 were recent arrivals from the mining area around Houghton, Michigan.[36] The Globe Cornish were not necessarily longer-resident, settled men, and the Cornish who were involved in Number 60's power struggle were Cornish *union* men. But the struggle was about inclusion and exclusion, and so it proceeded along ethnic lines.

The Cornish "almost unanimously" opposed Albert Wills's organizing efforts. So did a majority of other Anglo and Irish workers. The radicals (a minority of the Globe English-speaking men) and all of the unionized South Slavs and Italians supported Wills. Old Dominion (Phelps Dodge) and Miami Copper Company management locked out their own workers in January, 1909, in order to enforce their demand that Albert Wills cease recruiting employees on the job, in the mines. Management seemed obdurate, and the Globe Miners' Union members argued among themselves about an appropriate response. Finally, 296 conservatives outvoted 205 radicals, and the miners' union agreed to accede to company demands. Albert Wills was accorded a "vote of thanks" and relieved of his duties, and the 1908–9 immigrant organizing drive at Globe was over.[37]

While Arizona was preparing for statehood during the following year, the fight at Globe resumed. Again, the focus was on ethnic inclusion and exclusion. Four hundred Globe residents petitioned the Arizona Constitutional Convention, demanding that strictures against employing recent-

Labor Day in downtown Globe, 1911. Courtesy of Arizona Historical Society, Tucson (#61104).

immigrant mining workers be included in the future state's constitution. The anti-immigrant proviso was intended to force Globe's South Slavic, Italian, Spanish and Mexican workers out of the mines and mills. After learning of this, the Western Federation of Miners' Executive Board threatened to censure the Globe Miners' Union again, just as the GMU had been censured when it adopted the Globe contract in 1902. But Globe pro-inclusion men, once again in charge of the GMU local, informed national headquarters that Globe Number 60 did not approve of the citizens' petition, "and that the matter has never been discussed by its [Number 60's] members at any meeting."[38]

The WFM's Executive Board wanted to help nudge the new Arizona constitution in a prolabor direction, and it dispatched board member Joe Cannon to Arizona with $1,000 "to be put into a [prolabor] newspaper."[39] Standard Arizona history characterizes the 1910 Arizona Constitutional Convention as having been generally prolabor. The territorial legislature had already produced an Arizona Literacy Law in 1909 which was hostile to recent immigrants, and the Constitutional Convention was considering more anti-immigrant legislation in 1910. The conventional characterization, as expressed most clearly in Joseph Park's work, equates prolabor attitudes with anti-immigrant attitudes, and assumes that the legislative expressions of ethnic bias developed at the convention were derived from the prejudices of ordinary English-speaking workingmen and from the WFM itself.[40] Pressure for the 1910 legislation, the Kinney 80 percent plan, came from two major copper-mining areas. Bisbee and Douglas residents sent a petition for the adoption of the Kinney plan which was similar to the petition from Globe. But neither the Globe nor the Bisbee-Douglas petitions were drawn up by union locals. Also, few of the constitutional-convention delegates were mining workers, and only a small minority were even workers by any definition. Two of the fifty-two convention delegates listed themselves as miners, two more were machinists, and two were skilled railway employees (one of whom was a locomotive engineer). None of the others had any visible connection with mining-industry blue-collar employment. Most were cattlemen, farmers, bankers, lawyers, and merchants, including (in the latter category) the convention's powerful president, former signator of the 1902 Globe contract and future governor of Arizona, George W. P. Hunt of Globe. Only two of Arizona's thirteen counties had any sort of labor representation at all. Regardless of whether or not the men ostensibly representing labor promoted them, the voting on anti-immigrant constitutional issues was close, and the convention was plainly divided over whether or not to pass such provisions.[41]

Neither the eight-hour day, WFM support for the Socialist Party, nor the extension of recruiting to include mill and smelter workers, several of the principal issues which had helped to define WFM radical activism and conservatism during 1901–4, mattered much by 1910. Arizona unionists, by 1910, were beginning to describe supporters of immigrant inclusion within the rubric of radicalism, and supporters of exclusion as conservatives, with the pejorative emphasis placed just as frequently on one characterization as on the other. In the 1910 Arizona labor movement, the participation or nonparticipation of European and Mexican immigrants and Spanish Americans had become both the means to power and the goal toward which local union control would be directed.

The Western Federation of Miners was trying to accomplish a potentially impossible task. The exclusionists in the traditional WFM constituency and the much larger mass of potential new recruits were too far apart. Many people within each of the two camps were committed enemies of one another. Yet the WFM's chance for future success in the Southwest depended upon uniting the discrete factional elements without driving either the dissident conservatives into AFL craft unions or, perhaps, driving the dissident radicals toward the IWW. Even more trouble threatened. southwestern copper-company management was becoming more skillful at using the WFM's internal ethnic problems against it, and the nascent IWW would eventually learn how to do so, too.

Despite all of this, the WFM salvaged a bit of success from its 1907 southwestern copper organizing drives. From September 1906 through July 1907, new WFM locals opened at Clifton, Bisbee, Ray, Metcalf, Globe, and Douglas, Arizona, and also in West Jordan (near Bingham), Utah. Two others, at Star, Arizona, and at Ely-McGill, Nevada, began in 1908. Of these, Ray and the new Globe local failed to last out 1907, and only Ely-McGill, Douglas, and Bisbee lasted more than three years. The Ely-McGill, Douglas, and Bisbee locals survived, although they did not prosper, until the next spate of organizational activity began in 1912.

When the 1907 Panic struck the copper communities in October, wages were reduced and men were laid off, and some mines were closed down. There was practically no serious union organizing in late 1907 and early 1908.[42]

WFM headquarters learned to appreciate the virtues of immigrants as strikers during 1907–10. Italian and Finnish workers had responded to WFM-IWW immigrant organizers on the Mesabi iron range in Minnesota in 1906. The immigrants organized effectively and struck in 1907. IWW organizers were successful with recent-immigrant workers at McKee's Rocks, Pennsylvania, and a strike erupted there in 1909.[43] In the same year an old, reliable WFM local began to fight a lockout that turned into a strike against the Homestake Mining Company at Lead, South Dakota. The confederation "concentrated its greatest effort on the large contingent of foreign-born workers. Generally the native-born Americans would desert the union before the foreign-born," they discovered. Ultimately, only the recent-immigrant miners, who were Slavs, Finns, and Italians, were loyal to the union in the Homestake strike.[44] In 1910, a thoroughly organized group of eight hundred "Austrian" (probably South Slavic), Hungarian, Polish, and Russian immigrants struck at the Globe smelter in Pueblo, Colorado, for an improvement in wages.[45] In 1910 too, a group of Mexican gasworks laborers in Southern California who had been organized by the IWW struck. The Mexican workers wanted to eliminate a wage system which gave Italian, Greek, and American workers wages higher than theirs, and they won. The gas workers' settlement provided for higher wages, and also stipulated that only IWW members could be employed there in the future.[46] By 1910, neither the WFM nor the now-separate IWW had reason to doubt the strike potential of recent-immigrant industrial workers.

The WFM staggered away from its defeats and debilitating internecine warfare with the IWW into the arms of the United Mine Workers of America and the AFL. The active rapprochement process began in 1908 or 1909, and in 1911, the WFM affiliated with the UMWA, and through the affiliation, rejoined the American Federation of Labor.[47]

The WFM's return to the AFL is probably best understood in the light of Vernon Jensen's explanation of the WFM's motives. He wrote that the WFM's leaders primarily wanted to build a powerful, successful labor organization, capable of achieving the demands of its members. The eventual effect of the AFL reaffiliation may have pulled the WFM toward labor conservatism, but this was not necessarily its leaders' intent. Charles Moyer never made a positive public statement about the WFM's purpose in reaffiliating, and so he left the reaffiliation issue open to historical interpretation.[48]

The grand prize potentially available from reaffiliation was enhanced AFL support for WFM causes. Skilled tradesmen—carpenters, engineers, electricians, and others—frequently threatened WFM strike efforts. Most skilled-crafts union members were uninterested in the WFM's overtures to recent-immigrant unskilled workers. The reaffiliation opened up a conduit between the AFL craft groups and the WFM industrial unions: the WFM probably hoped to draw craft workers into its existing WFM locals at the mines, mills, and smelters. There is evidence that the WFM had at least a minimal amount of success in this endeavor. But it was potentially a two-way conduit. "Look out for craft unions of engineers, of firemen, of timbermen, of ropemen, of machine men, of muckers, etc. among the miners," warned the IWW's *Solidarity* magazine.[49] In essence, the IWW was warning that the WFM itself could begin to unravel, which was exactly what had started to happen in Bisbee. Crafts groups were potentially powerful enough to force drastic alteration or destruction upon the WFM. But the Federation's immediate hope and desperate need was for improved organizing effectiveness. WFM leaders dreamed of future organizing drives in which English-speaking southwestern locals would successfully recruit unskilled recent immigrants with the reliable, puissant assistance of friendly, fraternal AFL craft unions.

By the beginning of the 1907 depression, immigrant unskilled workers had become the majorities at many western mining camps.[50] In 1909 and 1910, the Industrial Workers of the World began planning a southwestern organizing drive to parallel the WFM's extended effort. The San Diego

IWW chapter had assisted in the successful 1910 Mexican gas workers' strike, but the gas workers' strike was the only significant IWW success in the Wobblies' attempts at attracting southwestern Mexicans and other Hispanics. There were probably two or more IWW locals at Phoenix, Arizona, as late as 1909–10. The Phoenix IWW contingent began publishing *La Union Industrial*, which was described as "the only Spanish paper in the United States teaching Revolutionary Industrial Unionism."[51] The 1910 San Diego gas workers' strike had been conducted by the Spanish-speaking Public Service Workers' Union. The San Diego Wobblies were trying to develop "a big revolutionary union of Mexicans throughout the Southwest."[52] The all-Mexican Public Service Workers' Union was the very antithesis of the industrial-union concept, because it functioned as a splinter group independent of Anglo and other immigrant gas workers. The IWW was encouraging ethnic segregation, rather than integration.

Perhaps the inspiration for the IWW's Mexican organizing drive came from its association with the Partido Liberal Mexicano at San Diego. According to the Wobblies' *Solidarity* magazine, "[Lázaro] Gutiérrez de Lara, who went through Mexico with John Kenneth Turner is in San Diego assisting organizing the Mexicans in the IWW with great success."[53] Gutiérrez de Lara was probably instrumental in organizing a Spanish-language local of Union Number 13 in San Diego.[54] He was a leading member of the PLM, imprisoned in Los Angeles along with Ricardo Flores Magón, Librado Rivera, Manuel Sarabia, and Antonio I. Villareal in 1907.[55] He had appeared before the U.S. House of Representatives Rules Committee to defend Mexican revolutionary activism in 1910.[56] Gutiérrez de Lara's influence apparently helped forge the IWW-PLM link in San Diego.

The IWW was seeking political reinforcement through association with revolutionary politics, but ethnic bifurcation was a predictable byproduct of the deliberate siphoning-off of Mexican workers into separate union locals. The Wobblies certainly hadn't invented ethnic bifurcation: Vincent St. John, who was still a leading WFM policy maker in 1907, had suggested that some WFM locals be "chartered by nationalities, as branches" during the 1907 WFM annual convention.[57] But ethnically segregated union branches had potentially grave consequences. Segregating unions by nationality could exacerbate ethnic divisiveness in working-class communities. Ethnic segregation could also promote the kind of intra-ethnic factional infighting which had almost destroyed the 1907 WFM-IWW Clifton-Morenci-Metcalf organizing campaign. The IWW's early southwestern organizing plans, tentative though they were, threatened to increase work-force disunity.

The San Diego IWW also asked the IWW's General Executive Board to begin organizing work in California, Arizona, New Mexico, and Texas.[58] But the campaign was stillborn. The Wobblies' western organizing circuits continued to carefully skirt the edges of the Southwest, extending to Los Angeles and San Diego, and to Salt Lake City, Butte, and Denver; but not into Arizona, New Mexico, or West Texas.[59]

Fewer than 20 percent of the workingmen in southwestern copper areas were members of organized labor unions in 1912.[60] At national headquarters, the Western Federation of Miners still wanted to put Anglo and Irish Americans and non-English-speaking men, skilled and unskilled workers, together in southwestern union locals. The newly independent IWW was still relatively insignificant in the Southwest, and the San Diego IWW locals were apparently unconcerned with the ultimate problem of integrating opposed groups into industrial unions. In 1912, the WFM again announced:

> We recognize that the greatest problem confronting the Federation today is that of bringing the unorganized workers of the metalliferous mines, mills, and smelters under the banners of the Federation.
>
> Throughout a large part of the jurisdiction of the Federation there has been practically no advance for the membership because they recognized that thousands of men could be secured to take their places. We must bring up the rear guard to protect the vanguard, that should be our next great struggle, and along with it we should seek to close up the ranks in partially organized fields.[61]

Fifty WFM organizers were recruiting in 1912, more than in previous years.[62] Twenty-eight of the WFM men were employed in the West, especially in Utah and Colorado; and for the first time, fewer than half of them had Anglo-American or Irish American surnames.[63] The WFM was beginning to develop a genuine potential for organizing the ethnic unskilled.

BINGHAM CANYON: ALWAYS A UNION, SELDOM A STRIKE, 1904–1909

*We do not wonder that anybody would rather go anywhere
than stay in Bingham, which is the most repulsive mining
camp that we know of in the United States. We do not dep-
recate its unfortunate inhabitants, but we refer to its physical conditions, which are uncomfortable, forbidding, and
unsanitary. Bingham has been most fittingly described as
"a sewer four miles long."* [1]

One of the biggest copper mines in the United States was being carved out
of Utah Copper Mountain at Bingham Canyon, Utah, in the early years of
this century. The men who worked there lived in the town of Bingham and
several nearby communities, all of which were crowded into a long, narrow
mountain canyon about twenty-five miles southwest of Salt Lake City.
Bingham was never attractive, and it had begun to look old before its time.
One of its earlier critics described it as "a camp of weather beaten tumble
down shacks . . . . with a street cut up by ore wagons . . . [and] one has to
stand up or walk in mud four to six inches deep." [2] The camp dated back to
1863, but it was first incorporated a year after the Utah Copper Company
arrived in 1903. [3] It remained substantially without sidewalks or paved
streets until the First World War. The creek which wound through the camp
became "a garbage dump, sewer and junk yard par excellence." [4] The community's water was of substandard quality. [5] Disastrous accidents were frequent there. Within one five-month period, a Copper Belt Line ore train
crashed on the mountainside and the train locomotive bounced down into
the town; a large boulder rolled down the mountain and practically leveled
a miner's house; and a big fire destroyed several buildings in town. Serious
mine accidents in Bingham averaged about two every three weeks during
early 1912. [6]

Bingham, Utah, in the early 1900s. Courtesy of Utah State Historical Society.

Much of the industrial aspect of Bingham Canyon and nearby areas was the work of a brilliant mining engineer named Daniel Cowan Jackling. Jackling planned to recover low-grade Bingham Canyon ore profitably by using large steam shovels to strip the surface and to mine the ore, rather than constructing mine shafts. His plan called for the use of concentrating and smelting facilities so massive as to achieve profits through economies of scale. Jackling and his ideas were hired by men connected with the Guggenheim family in New York, and thus, indirectly, with the Standard Oil Company and the Rockefeller family. Charles R. MacNeill and Spencer Penrose, who were directors and officers in various Guggenheim enterprises, placed Jackling in charge of the Utah copper operation in 1904. Jackling later helped direct the investment syndicate's copper mining and processing facilities in Ely and McGill, Nevada, in Ray, Arizona, and in Hurley and Santa Rita, New Mexico.[7]

In 1903, the Western Federation of Miners identified Charles R. Mac-Neill as an especially dangerous antagonist. He had a reputation for firing mining workers who joined the union, for using strikebreakers instead of negotiating in labor conflicts, and for refusing to speak to committees of striking workmen.[8] According to George G. Suggs, Jr.'s study of the Colorado mining war, both MacNeill and Daniel C. Jackling rose within the Guggenheim copper organization because they had proved their toughness and efficiency against WFM miners in Colorado during 1903.[9]

The WFM had maintained a small local at Bingham since 1901, two years before the arrival of the Guggenheim syndicate mining operation.[10] Like the union local in Butte, Montana, the Bingham Miners' Union was on the ground early. It was one of the oldest Western Federation copper locals. But unlike the Butte Miners' Union, the Bingham local had no links to Utah Copper management, neither ethnic, sentimental, nor contractual. Local 67's membership included a settled work-force contingent of indeterminate size.

Bingham Number 67 did its own organizing, which included organizing among the generally non-English-speaking workingmen who had recently arrived in the mining area, and it was similar to Butte Number 1 in this respect, too. Neither the Clifton nor the Bisbee copper areas had operant WFM locals already in place when big corporate low-grade industrial operations were begun in those districts.

Wherever there was no union local in place and whenever the Western Federation had to send an organizer fresh from national headquarters to develop a local, there was a special problem: Denver headquarters was forced to provide some sort of dynamic. Creating a union local often required intense wage, hour, or working-conditions issues which could engender work-force activism. A local would then have something more to offer nonunionized employees than they could readily obtain for themselves. The union could also offer sickness, accident, and death benefits, but at some western camps, ethnic mutual-aid and benefit societies served this function just as well as a local could. When an organizer worked in an unorganized camp, he had to convince his potential recruits that their complaints and needs were actually class grievances, and that the union offered a genuine remedy for class grievances. Then he had to convince them to pay membership fees.

With an already-existing Western Federation of Miners local, things were different. A functioning local did not require a dynamic situation for organizing. National organizers would make occasional forays into unorganized mining areas, but the WFM could not afford to keep them there regularly. The Bingham Miners' Union was easily able to proselytize potential recruits whenever it chose to do so. The BMU had a year-round office in Bingham Canyon. It was not patched together during a one-time-only organizing drive: it had grown organically. Immigrant workers were gradually added to an extant Anglo-Irish and Swedish immigrant group. The Bingham Miners' Union began inducting Finnish immigrants by 1904, Italians in 1904–5, South Slavs in 1904, and Greeks and Cretans, somewhat sporadically, in 1906.

The BMU was very small and may have operated without a regular office until 1904. In November of that year, the BMU's union hall opened. Members brought in chairs, hung a big sign outside, and even purchased a "union horse," probably intended for local delivery work.[11] They also began to keep written records of their financial transactions and formal minutes of their meetings.

In the beginning, the union officers' surnames were invariably of English, Irish, or Swedish origin. But there were already immigrant Italians and Finns working in the metal mines and mills at and near Bingham. Finns first arrived in northern Utah during the 1880s and Italians in the 1890s, working in the Carbon County coal-mining areas which were southeast of Salt Lake City. There were also labor activists among the Italians and Finns. In a 1901 coal strike against the Pleasant Valley Coal Company, the miners' negotiating committee apparently included five English, two Irish, "and one Italian and one Finn, selected to represent their nationalities." The Finns, in particular, supported the strike wholeheartedly.[12]

The first groups of Greeks and Cretans came to work in Utah mines in 1903.[13] They were brought by a labor agent named Leonidas Skliris, and they came to break strikes: first on the railroads and then in Utah Fuel Company coal camps in Carbon County.[14] From Carbon County they went on to the Bingham area where a labor organizer spoke to them in early 1905. He said that it would be

> a hard matter to start a union there [at the Murray, Utah, smelter] on account of the number of Greeks working at the smelters, the Greeks outnumbering the other men four to one. The Greeks were being furnished the smelters by an agent in Salt Lake City, who was receiving a monthly fee from the Greeks to keep them in employment. I talked with some of the Greeks in regard to joining the union. One of them told me that the Greek captain would not let him join the union. I think that the Greek captain is the Greek agent at Salt Lake City.[15]

Skliris had a formidable reputation. He was suspected of having planned the fires which destroyed a Greek competitor's boardinghouses for workers, even though his competitor's scale of operations was so small that it had not been a serious threat to Skliris's business.[16]

Leonidas Skliris began sending Serbians, Croatians, Slovenes, Albanians, and Syrio-Lebanese to northern Utah as early as 1903. Thousands of Serbians, in particular, headed for the Carbon County coal mines beginning in 1904. Many coal miners moved from Carbon County to the copper area farther north in the early 1900s.[17]

Bingham Local 67 always accepted immigrant initiates during the years when BMU minute book records were kept.[18] Italian immigrants had begun joining early.[19] During late 1904, there were more Italian and South Slavic immigrants inducted than all other initiates combined.[20]

There were already Scandinavians and Finns in the Bingham Miners' Union. Some spoke English, and some did not. Scandinavians were being nominated and occasionally elected to union office in 1904–5.[21]

For several months during 1905, no South Slavs or Italians joined the local. Then in late September and early October, both Slavs and Italians began to join again. Similar lapses in ethnic initiations occurred several more times between 1905 and 1909 at Bingham, and included, after 1906, surges and lapses in the initiation of Greek immigrant workers.[22] The reasons for the erratic pattern of immigrant interest and disinterest are not clear.

There was another, more comprehensible pattern to ethnic-group participation in Bingham Canyon unionism. It was often observed in those days that unusually many workingmen, especially non-English-speaking men, joined WFM locals everywhere in the West during the organizing campaigns which preceded strikes. But strikes did not explain the sudden surges and lapses in ethnic adherence to the Bingham Miners' Union. Bingham also had a steady, minimal influx of new members. There were three to ten new initiates at each typical union meeting. One or more Anglo-Irish-Americans and one or more Scandinavians or Finns usually joined the union at each meeting.

The BMU did not continually proselytize among the Italian, South Slav, Greek-Cretan, or Japanese populations in Bingham. Instead, it organized somewhat sporadically. When the Bingham Miners' Union decided to build itself a new union hall in mid-1905, it empowered a committee of two Americans, two "Austrians" (probably South Slavs), and two Finns to solicit funds. When eastern and southern Europeans began pouring in again in late 1905, the union planned language translation of its meetings for the benefit of "the different nationalities."[23]

Coincidental, informal communication about Local 67 must have brought many of the southern and eastern Europeans to the union. Frequently two or more men with identical surnames would be initiated into the union on the same night, suggesting that brothers, cousins, or perhaps former fellow-villagers were joining the union together. The union's reputation, which was spread by word of mouth, probably rose or fell with changing conditions at the workplace and in the immigrant communities, which probably accounted for the waxing and waning of immigrant interest in unionism.

Ethnic unionization was not gradual, happy, or comfortable at Bingham. For one thing, there was no accretion of immigrant influence in the BMU local. Recent immigrants of all ethnicities except Japanese joined the union, but they also quit it. Of course, Anglo and Irish workers quit too: miners and smelter workers were generally a peripatetic lot. But the BMU seemed to gain momentary immigrant adherence only to lose it again, and South Slavs, Greeks, or Italians were not generally elected to union office in Bingham.[24]

Perhaps the very fact that the Bingham Miners' Union recruited recent immigrants at all is surprising, in view of contemporaneous ethnic antagonisms. Anti-immigrant sentiment pervaded the lower intermountain West and Southwest during 1906–8. The Christmas, Arizona, and McGill, Nevada, incidents previously discussed were indicative of widespread xenophobia. The *White Pine News* at McGill and the *Daily Mining Expositor* at Ely both hoped editorially in late July 1907 that community pressure would force local Greeks, Italians, and South Slavs to quit their smelter jobs, leave White Pine County, and never return. Further north, in Great Falls, Montana, unionized local barbers and restaurant workers and small businessmen tried repeatedly to force Greek residents out of the community.[25]

In and around Bingham there were violent incidents involving Greek and Cretan workers. According to a recent study on the influence of padrones involved in Bingham Canyon labor, one early 1908 incident amounted to industrial sabotage. Two Cretan trackmen destroyed three railroad train cars and some rails. Shortly thereafter, five Greek smelter workers beat and threatened to kill an American railroad section foreman because of a job-connected incident.[26] Throughout the late spring and summer of that year, there were murders and attempted murders involving accused assailants who were Greek.[27]

Other sets of ethnic antagonisms pitted Greek against Greek, Greek against Cretan, and Serbian against Croatian and Slovene. Much of the Greek and Cretan fighting at Bingham Canyon was internecine warfare, and Serbs, Croatians and Slovenes often shot at one another during the summer of 1908. Newspapers reported "threats of assassination" being hurled back and forth, "Austrians [South Slavs] living in deadly fear of being shot and killed," and some Slavs moving to Salt Lake City to avoid the violence.[28]

Could the Bingham Miners' Union have accommodated Serbs, Croats, Slovenes, Greeks, and Cretans, as well as Italians, Finns, Scandinavians, Irish, and Americans simultaneously during 1906–8? Perhaps the union could have done so, but it did not. Most of the Slavic initiates during 1908 had Serbian surnames: Croatians and Slovenes may have avoided Local 67 during that year. There were, however, local Slavic mutual-benefit societies. Any meaningful analysis of ethnic recruitment by central western and southwestern labor unions during 1906–8 must weigh the difficulties posed by both external xenophobia and internal ethnic antagonisms. The violence and the outpouring of vitriolic hatred surely inhibited effective working-class organizing at Bingham, and adversely affected the WFM local's chances for growth.

Bingham's Number 67 was unlike the Arizona locals in its approach to the immigrant-recruiting question. The Globe, Clifton-Morenci, Bisbee, and Jerome locals' earliest beginnings were linked to traumatic ethnic antagonism and violence; Bingham's were not. Ethnic factors may appear to account for the difference between Bingham and the Arizona mining districts; that is, their differing histories may seem to be explainable in terms of ethnic cultural differences and differing Anglo and Irish responses to Mexicans and to European immigrants. But specific ethnic cultural differences are insufficient explanation for differing historical outcomes. Greeks were only one of the several distinct ethnic groups in Bingham's early-twentieth-century labor history, just as Clifton-Morenci's story includes not only Mexicans but Spanish Americans and Italians; and the histories of Jerome, Globe, and Bisbee include South Slavs. (There were also significant numbers of Spaniards at Clifton-Morenci and Jerome.) Each mining district had a unique mix of ethnicities. But there was a distinct similarity of response to unionism, ethnic problems, and mining-corporation ethnic policies across the entire Southwest and lower intermountain West.

The BMU weathered the pre-1904 years without becoming polarized over the issues of eight-hour days, blacklisting, union shop, or contracts, and there was no factional trouble at Bingham over ethnic recruitment, as there had been in Globe and Jerome. The real voice of Bingham Number 67 was E. G. Locke, who was an officer of the local and a convention delegate almost continually during 1901–12. Locke's remarks and voting at the 1907 WFM convention were anti-IWW, which would mark him as less-than-wholeheartedly radical, and which suggests that Number 67 itself was not radical.

The BMU struggled to augment its membership, as both the local and groups of nonunion non-Anglo-Irish mining workers fought for improved wages and working conditions during 1904–10. At the West Jordan smelter near Bingham in 1904, men working twelve hours a day for $1.50 wrote up a list of demands, brought them to the company's offices, and then became frightened and ran away. Both in 1904 and 1905, WFM organizers, at least one of whom was sent from Denver headquarters, reported that the men working under similar conditions at the Murray smelter were afraid of or indifferent to unionism.[29] In early 1905, three men were "appointed to canvas the camps with a list of Benefit[s]." At midyear, two of the union's hardest working and most dedicated officers, F. J. Mallet and E. G. Locke, argued for a general campaign to increase union membership, apparently without result. But immediately thereafter, Local 67 began planning to post notices around the mining area "printed in different languages," announcing to delinquent members that "unless they pay up to a certain time they will be expelled."[30]

In June, 1906, the Bingham Miners' Union began listing demands to be presented to the Utah Copper Company, and it made preliminary preparations for a possible strike. The wage demands were explained to the Italian and Finnish union members by two bilingual unionists. For the first time, some Greeks began to join the union local, and they did so just in time for the upcoming struggle. BMU leaders were trying to maximize the local's strength in case of a strike. They also tried, for the third consecutive year, to organize the work force at the nearby Murray smelter. Organizers were asked to determine "why the smeltermen, they do not join the union." This time, eighty-five men were successfully organized into Mill and Smeltermen's Union Number 201.[31]

But there was no 1906 strike. On June 16, the BMU voted "that our Sec[retary] be instructed to ask . . . for advice in regard to whether the WFM will stay by us . . . in case of strike." On June 30, in a "special vote on shall we present our demands to mining Co.," the strike was voted down, 123 to 106. There was, however, incidental success. Wages went up, 25¢ a day for some men and 50¢ for others, in December. The strike threat and the feeling that accompanied it had probably pushed Utah Copper into increasing men's wages.[32]

But even when Local 67 could not organize a strike, it remained combative. Utah's eight-hour law was being violated by mining companies, and repeatedly, union members reported the violations. Sometimes they took the violation information to the county attorney and demanded an investigation. In late 1908, the BMU began printing and posting copies of the eight-hour law around the mining camp.[33] The Bingham Miners' Union also wanted a metal mine inspection law, and tried to push legislators into forcing the mining companies to enhance mine safety.[34] The dearth of safety precautions itself almost caused a strike. A massive cave-in closed the Utah Copper Company's Highland Boy shaft and men were trapped somewhere down under the rockfall. The company seemed to treat the cave-in in a cavalier manner, and the trapped men were not being rescued. In a heated discussion, "a great many Brothers declared themselves in favor of all the men working upon the mine ceasing production of ore until such time as the imprisoned men were rescued[.] [Other men] whose mental and moral courage failed them opposed such action for fear Scabs would take their jobs." Then the union appointed a secret committee to watch the rescue operation.[35]

Both in the 1905 Highland Boy rockfall disaster, when men who were ready to quit opposed men "whose . . . courage failed them," and during the June 1906 strike vote, major decisions were closely contested. Those who wanted to fight the copper companies and those who did not may have been radicals (or, more precisely, *activists*), and conservatives. The BMU was deeply divided, and the crucial issue was activism—in strikes, eight-hour violations, safety, and during the Highland Boy emergency. The Bingham local had become so badly factionalized that acting WFM national president Charles E. Mahoney and national organizer Frank Schmeltzer traveled together to Bingham in August 1906 to attend meetings of Local 67 and to try to straighten out the "turmoil which had arisen in that local."[36] But bad as things were in the BMU, neither side chose to play the immigrant-inclusion card. Immigrant mining workers were already being accepted as inductees, and the Bingham activists did not try to gain power through engineering an inundation of new recruits, as contemporaneous activists did in Arizona. Consequently, in Bingham, there was no need for a conservative counterstroke to eliminate immigrant recruitment.

The failure to strike certainly cost the BMU prestige among Italian immigrants during the summer of 1906. In mid-August, when Charles De Molli, a well-known Italian organizer whose speeches often drew big crowds, visited Bingham Canyon, his public appearance was canceled because hardly any Italians were interested in hearing him. But by October, the BMU was recovering. The Bingham local ordered a special printing of the union constitution in Italian, because the Italians had begun returning to the fold.[37]

In early 1907, the Bingham Miners' Union began another wage-amelioration effort. Again, men began joining in unusually large numbers. At each of several meetings in February and March, twenty-five or more new men, most with non-English, non-Irish surnames, were initiated, and a dozen or more new men joined at almost every meeting through the spring and summer. But from mid-spring on, none of the 1907 initiates was Greek or Cretan.[38]

This time, events began to push the Miners' Union. In early May, some men at the Murray smelter walked off their jobs because of a specific wage complaint. They returned almost immediately; their wages had been raised. Then, six hundred English-speaking United States Smelting and Refining Company employees walked off their jobs at the Midvale smelter near Bingham, demanding higher pay.[39] In June, there was a brief walkout and near-strike at the Galena and Telegraph Mines, a small operation near Bingham, where union men soliciting recruits "were ordered off company ground."[40]

The BMU itself moved slowly, cautiously, almost timorously. On April 20, the local discussed "The question of bringing in the non-union men." In July, the local went after "a list of names . . . of a number [of] men who have worked in camp a long time and have refused to join the union." In August, a group of unionists planned to go to the bunkhouse area near town to "round up all non-union men." The union created a set of wage-scale demands, which were equivalent to contemporaneous wage levels at Butte. The recent-immigrant, unskilled members of the BMU were initially neglected by the local's leadership during early July planning sessions, but then the job titles most often held by recent immigrants were added to the wage-demands list belatedly. On the same night, the wage-scale demands were "read and explained to the different nationalities."[41]

But there was no 1907 strike. Local 67 was ready: the negotiations with the Utah Copper Company had come to a dead end. However, the national Panic of 1907 came in the autumn, copper prices fell, and the company cut production and began reducing its work force and cutting wages. Local 67's organizing campaign was over.

The work situation at Bingham Canyon and at the similar set of copper communities in White Pine County, Nevada, was very unusual in 1907–8. The work regimen of Bingham's modern pit mine practically forced the Miners' Union to unionize non-Anglo-Irish workers, because there were so few other potential recruits available. The BMU definitely needed Finnish, Greek, South Slavic, and Italian recruits.

At the time of the 1907 wage drive, Utah Copper Company records listed many pitmen, dumpmen, and trackmen, all paid at the rate of $2.25 for a ten-hour day.[42] These were typical occupations for unskilled, generally immigrant workers at a big pit mine. The men were surface workers in an ore stripping operation and not underground workers, and so they were

Bunkhouses for single workingmen at Copperfield, Bingham Canyon, 1927. Courtesy of Utah State Historical Society.

not protected by eight-hour workday legislation. Of course, some shaft mining still continued in Bingham, but the proportion of skilled shaft miners was steadily diminishing as the big pit at Utah Copper Mountain got bigger.

Clifton-Morenci, by comparison, still had shaft mines. The copper-company time books there listed large numbers of miners, laborers, and timbermen, rather than pitmen and dumpmen. Many of the Clifton-Morenci shaft mining jobs, even those categorized as labor, required a considerable degree of caution and experience and some degree of skill because of the limited amount of space, the use of explosives in confined areas, the proximity of mine timbering, machinery, cables and trackage, and the special lighting conditions. Many of Bingham's workers were less skilled and more readily interchangeable.

But, because a big pit mine employed steam-shovel operators, crane-men, and machinists, many Anglo and Irish skilled men were still needed at Bingham Canyon. But skilled men tended to join American Federation of Labor crafts unions and railroad unions.[43] There were proportionately more railroad employees in pit mines than in shaft mines, too. The number of recent-immigrant unskilled men also increased, of course. *But the numbers of skilled men who would not be joining the WFM continued to increase as well.* The result was that the relatively few Anglo and Irish WFM members were increasingly outnumbered, not only by recent immigrants, but by occasionally hostile AFL and Railroad Brotherhood men. Because only a relatively few remaining English-speaking men were available as potential union recruits, the Bingham Miners' Union was especially driven toward accommodation with recent-immigrant workers, regardless of local members' pro- or anti-immigrant sentiments, and regardless of whether the immigrant initiates were Greek, South Slavic, or Italian.[44]

Working conditions at "the most repulsive mining camp . . . in the United States" got worse during the Panic. In January, 1908, oilmen's pay fell from $2.50 to $2.25 for ten hours' work and an occupation called trackman-walker-switch tender fell to $1.75 per day.[45] Many Greeks may have been designated as outside common labor, a job title that does not appear on the Utah Copper Company's "Mines" list; and this job title too paid $1.75 and $2.00 daily.[46] The $1.75 daily wage for ten hours of work (an hourly rate of 17.5¢) was probably the lowest wage rate offered to any major category of labor anywhere in central western and southwestern copper mines after 1903, not even excepting the big mines near the Mexican border.[47] (There were, however, even lower rates paid for *smelter* work in Murray, Utah, and still lower rates paid at the American Smelting and Refining Company's smelter in El Paso.)[48] In addition to the low pay at both Bingham and the Murray smelter, "the Greek working men had to dig up every month for their jobs": they had to kick back money to the padrone, Leonidas Skliris.[49]

Labor contractors, or padrones, had attracted the BMU's attention in 1907, when the local assigned an Italian "business agent" the job of investigating the kickbacks collected by an Italian padrone.[50] In April, 1908, Local 67 created a general plan "in regards to Greek Labor" with the support of Bingham IWW Local Number 93. The *Bingham Press-Bulletin* ran a series of editorials against "peonage and other outrages perpetrated on the miners of Bingham," and the Miners' Union planned to present "a bill to do away with the buying of jobs" to the Utah State Legislature in 1909, on behalf of both Greek and Italian workers.[51] The Greeks themselves protested vocally against the monetary exactions of the labor contractors, "these tramps who suck our sweat."[52] In June, George Demetrakopoulos, Leonidas Skliris's assistant and interpreter, was murdered at a Carbon County, Utah, coal camp which employed many Greek miners.[53]

Greeks began joining the BMU during 1908. The Miners' Union assigned an organizer, W. F. Burleson, to the Greek work force. The BMU decided to spend money on library facilities "to teach the Greeks the English

Language." The local intended to obtain additional funds from new Greek and Cretan initiates, and then, in concert with both IWW Local 93 and the new WFM Mill and Smeltermen's Local, Number 201, to use half of the new monies for library expenses.[54]

Although Greeks had begun joining the BMU, there were still relatively few of them compared to the number of Italian and South Slavic recruits. The pervasive power of Leonidas Skliris's operation suggests a reason for Greek reluctance, but Skliris's tight controls could just as well have driven Greek and Cretan workers in precisely the opposite direction. Greeks could have chosen to embrace unionism as a source of both organizational support and sickness and death insurance. Some Greek workers did try to buy insurance at Bingham and were swindled in 1908. Several Americans sold Greeks phony accident insurance and pretended that WFM membership was included, free, with the insurance purchase. The men who were thus duped apparently blamed both the swindlers and the WFM for their losses, and consequently, were even less likely to want to join the BMU.[55]

In July 1908, the Utah Copper Company lowered some unskilled wage rates. In mid-August, three hundred Greeks abruptly walked off their jobs, and the company, just as abruptly, restored wages to their previous levels.[56] The BMU was definitely interested in these events. On the last day of August, the local discussed "the Greek Question" and the "education" of the Greeks. Local 67 and Local 201 arranged a dance together, late in the year, "for the benefit of the [Library] Reading Room."[57]

Again in September 1909, three hundred Greek workers, quite possibly the same group of men who had forced a restoration of wages a year earlier, walked off their jobs at Bingham Canyon. Again the issue was wages, and this time, hours as well.[58]

An estimated twenty-five or thirty Italians working with the Greeks struck with them, and soon afterward, twenty-six Japanese working nearby struck too. Most of the Greeks were muckers, and about four hundred miners who depended on mucking also stopped working. The Utah Copper Company's operations temporarily ground to a halt, except for some Anglo and Irish skilled men, who continued working. After five days, management's Daniel C. Jackling announced a substantial 25¢ pay hike. Jackling said that the proffered settlement was not a concession, because it had already been planned, and that the whole incident had resulted from a "misunderstanding."[59]

There were two Greek leaders, described variously as William and Joe Callangakas, or else as Jacob and John Golocokis. A WFM national Executive Board member and "Judich," the Serbian immigrant organizing specialist who had worked successfully at Jerome some months earlier, both came to help at Bingham. The WFM sought Anglo and Irish support for the Greek strikers. Most of the English-speaking men avoided overt connection with the strike, but when it was over, they timidly assured the WFM leaders visiting Bingham, and the Greeks as well, "that they were always with the strikers . . . [and] that they are union men first, last and all the time (except when they are required to be)."[60]

The Greek strikers had become a catalyst for labor protest in 1909. WFM national leadership was ready to support Greek-led labor action. Then the Greek strikers, for the first time, although not the last, remedied another specific grievance by themselves. Leonidas Skliris intended to furnish strikebreakers for the Utah Copper Company, when the Greeks intervened with a "reception that this reptile . . . will never forget as long as he lives."

> Notwithstanding the presence of twenty-five armed deputies, the striking Greeks commanded him to leave the town at once and made the superintendent of the company understand that they will never have anything to do with such a scoundrel scab herder and a grafter, and they proceeded to carry out their command by taking him by the arm and leading him down the road with jeers.[61]

The Greeks were different from other Bingham Canyon ethnic groups in their general lack of cohesive group social structure and in the size of their sporadic walkouts on the job.[62] But there were obvious reasons for the difference. First, as a Murray, Utah, interviewee complained in 1905, "the Greek captain would not let him join the union." For a time before 1912, Leonidas Skliris kept Greeks away from the Bingham Miners' Union. Similarly, Skliris effectively discouraged the development of Greek sickness and benefit societies until the advent of the big 1912 strike. The swindling operation described above would have discouraged Greek adherence to the Miners' Union, too. Since conventional avenues of organization and protest against poor pay and unpleasant working conditions were closed to them, the Greeks, of course, protested sporadically anyway. "Self-organized" protest was by no means new nor is it especially significant. "Spontaneous" labor activism generated by several different ethnic groups was reported by many earlier historians.[63] But following the story of the Bingham Miners' Union itself offers the best opportunity for understanding the ethnically complex workers' efforts at conditions ameliorization and unionization in pre-1912 Bingham Canyon.

The Bingham Miners' Union maintained lines of communication with all of the immigrant and nonimmigrant groups working in and around the mines and metal processing facilities (even including the Japanese on occasion), with the churches, small businesses, and railroads, and with the American Federation of Labor unions both in Bingham and Salt Lake City. Both the Bingham Canyon IWW local (Local 93) and the WFM Mill and Smeltermen's local (Local 201) functioned as fledgling dependencies of the BMU.

BMU leadership's acceptance and encouragement of ethnic labor was genuine, although on many occasions, less than enthusiastic. The BMU accepted Finns, Italians, Greeks, and South Slavs, but if it had consistently and carefully canvassed for ethnic recruits, it would have become a predominantly ethnic local, with ethnic elected officers. The BMU's Anglo- and Irish-American and occasional Scandinavian leaders never pushed ethnic recruitment that far. They were probably unwilling to award themselves minority status in the BMU. But throughout 1905–8, the miners' union was also heavily engaged elsewhere. The union constantly mediated in quarrels between local business and skilled labor elements, on one side, and the IWW Local, Number 93, on the other. The Bingham Miners' Union had created the Bingham IWW local, and although Local 93 had a radical agenda, it depended upon the BMU. The Bingham IWW local had English, Irish, and Scandinavian officers, and probably a membership to match.[64] Most of the recent immigrants who became union members were organized, not by the IWW, but by the Bingham Miners' Union or by its later creation, the Mill and Smeltermen's Union.

◄ 6 ►

IMMIGRANTS AND ENGLISH-SPEAKING MEN STRIKE TOGETHER: BINGHAM CANYON, UTAH, AND WHITE PINE COUNTY, NEVADA, 1910–1912

Trouble rumbled on in Bingham Canyon. Incident followed incident in a persistent pattern: almost eight years of walkouts, near-strikes, threats, and demands, with occasional small concessions by management and labor. The two sides were like sparring heavyweights, warily circling one another in the ring, throwing occasional jabs, probing for the opening that might lead to a knockout.

The Bingham Canyon labor movement was solidly based. The on-the-ground, functioning unions there had a penchant for industrial organizing. Bingham's immigrant ethnic workingmen had developed some group cohesion through mutual societies, and even Greeks may have planned things together as informal members of coffeehouse associational groups.[1] Most workers, however, were not union members. On the other side, the Utah Copper Company could neither disarm nor dispatch its Bingham Canyon opponents. The company's importation of warring factions from Europe and ethnic outsiders from East Asia had created hostility, but not enough to eliminate joint labor action. The imported ethnic groups were neither reliable strikebreakers nor trustworthy allies in management's struggles against English, Irish, and American unionists. If a strike came to Bingham Canyon, management could not be sure of mobilizing enough help for itself, even when strikebreakers, gunmen, private guards, state police, or the federal army were employed on its behalf. Forces like these had been used in the West before, but Utah Copper could no longer be certain of their effectiveness.

The experiences of Bingham South Slavs, Italians, and even Finns and Japanese were becoming increasingly similar to those of the Greeks, especially after 1908. When the big Bingham strike of 1912 began, South Slavic strikers behaved much as the Greek strikers did.

In 1910, the Bingham Miners' Union men once again planned to strike. This time, WFM national headquarters deliberately discouraged them. President Charles Moyer interceded to prevent the strike, probably because he feared failure and did not want to risk the prestige of the WFM on a big debacle in the West.[2] For the third time in four years, Local 67 had tried to coordinate a strike without success.

But WFM national headquarters was interested in Bingham Canyon, and the Bingham Miners' Union began to turn to it for help. The national Executive Board discussed the 8,000 workers at Garfield, Murray, and Bingham, where "Seventy-five percent of the men employed are foreign speaking and are mostly Greeks and Austrians, making it difficult to organize."[3] In 1911, the Bingham local's officers requested that WFM headquarters pay the cost of "keeping an Italian organizer in the field." In January, 1912, "A communication was read from Bingham Miners' Union No. 67 asking that national headquarters place a Greek, Austrian, and English-speaking organizer in the Bingham district."[4] Organizing at Bingham, which the IWW's *Solidarity* newspaper described in 1910 as "the cheapest camp in the country," was continuous and repetitive.[5] The problems and arguments of earlier years echoed on from 1910 into early 1912. During the years of dissatisfaction, half-prepared strikes and minor protest, Bingham constantly simmered, but it never seemed to boil.

One 1911 incident indicated that something bigger was coming. Leonidas G. Skliris, the padrone, had returned and was as active as ever in Northern Utah. Skliris collected money from Greeks and Cretans long after he had placed them at jobs. His activities made cohesive ethnic organization among the Bingham area Greeks practically impossible. "Many times been trying to complain for the Greek padrone L. G. Skliris but we afraid that never get job at Utah Copper," Greek complainants wrote.[6] The principal complaint was that jobs cost the men $20 each.[7] Bingham Greeks were also charged special fees, and monthly payments were required for vague services supposedly rendered by the Skliris firm. Skliris and his brother operated a store too, and Greeks were probably forced to patronize it. Skliris's agents even handled accident-injury claims (and may have processed them inequitably) for Greek and Cretan workers.[8] At least one of the copper company's special police was Skliris's cousin.[9] Leonidas Skliris's pervasive power in the Bingham Greek community was used to help management against labor, just as it had been used in 1905. In early 1912, the Greeks tried to organize a "fraternal order" that was apparently intended to be a surrogate labor union. The Skliris men destroyed it.[10]

National Western Federation of Miners' activism also hinted at excitement to come. In mid-April, 1912, President Charles Moyer, J. C. Lowney and Yanco (A. J.) Terzich visited Bingham. From Bingham, they proceeded on to Ely and McGill in White Pine County, Nevada, about 250 miles southwest along the railroads, at the invitation of E. A. Redwanz, the financial secretary of the McGill Smeltermen's Union. This tour suggests that WFM headquarters had planned to play a role in the labor conflict that was about to begin in both Nevada and Utah.[11]

Once again, in May 1912, several hundred Greeks walked off their jobs. The Murray smelter was still paying some unskilled workers $1.75 per day. The men in Murray wanted a 25¢ pay raise, and "They allege that the company has increased the amount of work demanded to the extent of almost double their labor."[12] The wholesale price of copper had risen rapidly since late 1911, and the Utah Copper Company was expecting a huge additional profit in 1912. Utah Copper was enjoying a gradual production increase, an almost steady decrease in costs, and an increase in net profits. The company's primary goal was cost cutting: "During the month of September the average cost of producing a pound of copper was reduced to 7.18 cents, which makes it certain that the company will before long be making copper at between 6 and 7 cents a pound." Cutting labor expense was considered a most effective means of improving upon 7.18¢ copper.[13] Because of Utah Copper's commitment to cost cutting, the Murray smeltermen would have a difficult fight.

The leaders of the strike were Greek charge wheelers, who earned $1.90 to $1.95 daily. There probably were no more than sixty of these men at the Murray plant, and they met and began planning to fight for increased wages early in April. The charge wheelers obtained the adherence of the mass of lower-paid smeltermen, including Greeks, South Slavs, and even unskilled Anglo-Irish-Americans. The Greek smelterers were not WFM members when they struck.[14]

Company spokesmen blamed the WFM rather than the Greeks themselves for the strike, and in fact many of the strikers themselves were later rehired.[15] But neither the BMU nor the Mill and Smeltermen's Union had initiated the strike. "Organizers Leake, Alfirevich, and Oberto [from national headquarters], on learning of conditions at Murray rushed to the camp and immediately began organizing the men into the Western Federation of Miners" after the strike had begun. Union recognition was not an issue in the Murray strike. It would become an issue later.[16]

Strikebreaking began immediately under the auspices of the Skliris organization. The violence that occurred during the strike was associated with the strikebreaking effort. By early June, the Murray strike had failed.[17]

The Western Federation of Miners helped plan the strikes that followed.[18] WFM headquarters sent word to Bingham Canyon that the Butte Guggenheim-owned mines had just increased miners' wages by 50¢ a day, and smelter workers' wages by 25¢ a day.[19] The WFM's precise role in the planning which followed during the summer of 1912 is unclear. Vernon Jensen wrote:

> In the summer of 1912, the local at Bingham met to devise plans for establishing a wage scale. A local committee was appointed. Several other meetings were held. John Lowney, executive board member, arrived from Denver and participated in the planning. Campaigns were carried on among other A.F. of L. unions, numerically small: the machinists, carpenters, molders, boilermakers, blacksmiths, the Associated Union of Steam Shovelmen, and locomotive engineers and firemen.[20]

But the events that Jensen describes seem to have been inspired by actions initiated by the unskilled workers themselves. The WFM's Executive Board was notified in late July by E. G. Locke, the Bingham local's secretary, that "there was an agitation on for an increase in wages and that a mass meeting was called for Saturday evening, 3 August 1912." Locke also asked for assistance from WFM headquarters.[21] According to a later account by Charles Moyer, the unskilled workingmen themselves "were going to demand an increase in wages and an improvement in conditions. We had done what we could to organize the men of the metal mines, and when these men began to show that they wanted to do something for themselves, we went to their assistance."[22] In August, the WFM tried to begin negotiations with company management on the workers' behalf. The Utah Copper Company, utilizing the same methods that had served it well in 1907, 1908, and 1909, announced a general 25¢ wage increase in mid-August without holding any direct discussions with the union or the workingmen.[23]

On September 11, the WFM took a strike vote at Bingham, and approximately 1,800 out of 2,000 men voted in favor of striking. About four hundred unskilled, mostly immigrant underground men began the strike six days later.[24]

The immigrant unskilled workers were both the main participants and

Serbian baptismal dinner at Highland Boy, Bingham Canyon, early 1900s. The ear-liest South Slavic communities in Bingham Canyon and White Pine County included very few women. From Peoples of Utah Collection, courtesy of Utah State Histori-cal Society.

part of the leadership of the strike. Reporters attributed the strike to "for-eigners," especially Greeks and Serbians.[25] Even the WFM, which had helped originate the labor action, announced that "To the Greeks, however, must be given the credit for showing the greatest spirit of solidarity and dis-cipline."[26] Anglo-Irish-American unskilled and semiskilled workers played a mixed role early in the strike. They had been pushed into striking, and some were opposed to it.[27] But a committee of strikers' representatives, formed about two weeks later, consisted of "two Americans, two Greeks, one Austrian, and one Italian."[28] Soon, "Americans, Cretans, Greeks, and Italians" fought side by side in a major gun battle against strikebreakers and sheriff's deputies.[29] Although the Americans were participants, they did not lead the other ethnic groups. Unskilled men were also joining the Bingham Miners' Union. Seven hundred new members joined several days after the strike began.[30]

Some of the strikers owned homes in Bingham Canyon. A large contin-gent of Serbian strikers owned shack homes at Highland Boy, adjacent to the town of Bingham, and a few Greek strikers owned homes in various locations, although most of them probably lived in boardinghouses.[31] Many of the shack homes were worth $75 or less, indicating, as at Clifton-Morenci in 1903, that the striking homeowners were not necessarily a settled, propertied, stable portion of the community.[32] The assessed value of a typical Bingham unskilled worker's house was less than 15 percent of his average annual income in 1912.[33] But the Serbians and Greeks thought of themselves as homeowners, as some of them were to prove during the strike.

For many of the Greek strikers the activities of Leonidas G. Skliris were the primary strike issue. When Skliris was mentioned in a speech before a mixed crowd of Serbians, Bulgarians, Greeks, Italians, and Americans the crowd responded with a roar.[34] Some Greeks and Cretans "avowed that they would return to work without any increase in wages providing Leonidas G. Skliris, employment agent for the Utah Copper Company . . . [was] dismissed." The Greeks repeated the same statement to the Governor of Utah, when he came to investigate the strike.[35] Manager Daniel Jackling promptly replied with a stiff defense of Skliris and Utah Copper's use of Skliris's services, but Jackling forced Skliris to resign three days later.[36] The immigrant unskilled workers had won two victories, a twenty-five cent wage boost and at least temporary freedom from Leonidas Skliris when the strike was only a few days old.[37]

The copper area in White Pine County, Nevada, most of which was Guggenheim-owned, was also struck. The Nevada Consolidated Copper Company operated a copper mine at Ely and a smelter at McGill, and other mine-connected communities, including East Ely, Ruth, Kimberly, Lane, Copper Flat, and Riepetown were nearby.[38] Nevada Consolidated was newer and smaller than Bingham: Guggenheim management had just purchased it in 1910.[39] "Nevada Con" employed a total of about 5,400 men in 1912.[40] Unionization had come to Ely in 1902, as a result of an incident in which an Ely mine superintendent shot and killed three miners who were protesting a wage cut. The small and newly organized WFM group at Ely had subsequently won its old wage scale back.[41] Like Bingham, Ely-McGill WFM unionism had not originated in specifically ethnic turmoil, as some Arizona WFM unions had.

Ely and McGill were generally more pleasant than Bingham. Some wage rates were higher at Ely in 1912: miners and timbermen earned $3.50, which was also above the Clifton-Morenci scale. The largest group of low-wage men earned $1.75, and some common laborers were paid $2.00.[42] There was a Greek-operated store at McGill, which was apparently tied to

Leonidas Skliris's businesses, but the McGill store operation was comparatively unobjectionable.[43] But at the beginning of September, twenty "Austrian" smelter workers requested a 50¢ daily raise. They hoped to lead a general unskilled workers' strike on the wage issue; but the other smelter-men failed to respond, and the twenty men were fired.[44]

Most McGill South Slavs were Croatians, and there was a large, active Croatian lodge in McGill. Croatians, of course, were perceived as racially distinct from Serbians, and were generally Roman Catholics. Serbians generally attended Eastern Orthodox services and associated with Greeks. The predominance of Croatians rather than Serbs in the South Slavic Nevada copper communities may help explain why Leonidas Skliris's grip was weaker in Nevada.[45] In early 1912, approximately two thousand organization men in the "Greek Community" at McGill voted for a community board of directors there, indicating a level of combined organization far more substantial than anything at Bingham.[46]

The wage demand by the twenty Slavic workers was symptomatic of labor trouble, but it did not cause the strike. The WFM did. Within hours after a strike was voted in Bingham Canyon, WFM President Charles Moyer, with his close associate, general organizer and sometime executive board member Guy Miller, was on the westbound train headed for McGill.[47]

In McGill, Moyer proclaimed that he had come to Bingham and Ely-McGill after visiting Butte, and that everything which had already been accomplished in Butte could be duplicated in Utah and Nevada. He said that the Western Federation had "closed a three-years' agreement with the Amalgamated" in Butte, which included a pay raise, and that the WFM would press for a pay raise and some form of "union recognition" for Bingham and Ely-McGill too.[48]

Moyer spoke on the record, and he intended his newspaper interview to help kick off the White Pine County organizing drive. But his interpretation of the events in Butte was deliberately disingenuous. The Butte Miners' Union contract was old news, and it was only a renewal of the existing long-term contract there. Butte's Local 1 had not only been officially recognized for years, its relationship with Butte management was more than cordial. Union and management were embarrassingly intimate. Wages in Butte, ranging up to $4.00 a day in mid-1912, were traditionally higher than most wages elsewhere; a fact which was fairly well known in some quarters and which was unlikely to change. Also, Moyer did not mention that the Butte local was in the throes of internal warfare in 1912, partly emanating from its refusal to support the cause of dismissed Finnish mining workers.

The Butte Miners' Union was generally unfriendly to recent-immigrant miners, and Butte could not possibly have provided a model for Bingham and Ely-McGill workingmen to emulate.[49]

Charles Moyer's later stand on the issue of recognition can best be understood in the light of these initial statements. Butte's recognition option was substantially unavailable to the Utah and Nevada strikers, who believed that management was their enemy, and whose relatively weak WFM union locals were helping ethnic workingmen. Moyer may have believed that written contractual relations could be won in Utah and Nevada, but his announcement about bringing Butte conditions to Bingham and Ely-McGill was intended to deceive. WFM negotiators subsequently deemphasized the recognition demand, treating it as an expendable bargaining chip. But for its own reasons, the Utah Copper Company chose to fasten upon the recognition issue as a cudgel, a cudgel with which it could beat the union bloody.

Events moved rapidly in White Pine County. On the night of Sunday, September 22, the Central Labor League in Ely, with Charles Moyer in attendance, voted to fight for increased wages for both themselves and the Bingham strikers. The next night at McGill, the Miners' and Smeltermen's local inducted eighty new members and voted unanimously to support the Bingham wage and union-recognition demands. Hundreds of southern and eastern Europeans in McGill also joined the WFM strike. At Riepetown near Ely on the following night, the Lane Miners' Union pledged itself to support Bingham, also unanimously. Even Americans at the Riepetown meeting, about one-fourth of the total in attendance, voted strongly in support of the strike demands. Already at least two organizers were in the Nevada Consolidated ethnic communities, recruiting Greeks, Italians, and South Slavs.[50]

The White Pine County Greeks and South Slavs had begun joining the union soon after arriving in Nevada. Unionized English-speaking men and nonunion Greeks, South Slavs, and Italians soon found common ground in two great labor issues there. First, there was an Ely-McGill padrone problem, although Bingham Canyon's padrone problem was worse. The immigrants coming into White Pine County were sometimes described as "contract labor," and their continuing monthly payments to a padrone were sometimes described as a sort of peonage. Real contract labor operations had been illegal since 1868, but padrone activity was often pretty close to it, although accusations about contract labor were virtually unprovable. But WFM men, both at Bingham and Ely-McGill, insisted that padrones were essentially contract labor agents, and that they could produce groups of strikebreakers at a moment's notice, using illegal and unfair methods of operation.[51] Immigrants, of course, disliked padrones too, and many were more than willing to cooperate with a union effort directed against contract labor.

Eight-hour legislation was the other great issue at Ely and McGill. Nevada's eight-hour legislation, as applied to smelter workers, was a relative latecomer. The eight-hour issue had been more or less settled in Utah in the 1890s, and Arizona settled it, albeit with lasting animosity, in the 1903 Clifton-Morenci strike. The events at Clifton-Morenci effectively convinced some of the men who attended the 1903 WFM national convention that Mexican and Italian immigrants could organize for major labor action on the eight-hour issue. The Nevada law passed in 1907, and in 1909 some McGill smelter workers struck for eight hours in a situation identical to the one which had brought out two to three thousand men at Clifton-Morenci six years earlier. McGill's Anglo and Irish unionists and South Slavic, Greek, and Italian nonunion workers struck in January, 1909. The January eight-hour strike was a failure, but in July, 1909, WFM Lane Miners' Union Number 251 struck the Veteran Mine in Ely. As the July strike began, the Lane union included both recent immigrants and English-speaking men, but most of the three hundred strikers were Greek and Serbian union members. The July 1909 strike forced a small pay raise.[52]

By 1912, at least 13 percent of the Greek smelter workers at McGill were WFM members, and the Lane Miners' Union included all nationalities, again probably excepting Japanese.[53] Nevada's 1912 strikers were more united than were Utah's, and several factors explain the difference. The Nevada Greeks, who were a particularly important element in the 1912 strike effort, had achieved a measure of ethnic unity—the two-thousand-member Greek Society—which had eluded the Utah Greeks. The Nevada men had already had experience fighting against management *together;* the Utah men had not. On the other hand, support from the surrounding residential community was probably *not* a factor in 1912 striker cohesiveness. White Pine County xenophobia had been exceptionally intense, and the White Pine residential communities were strictly segregated along lines of ascribed ethnicity.[54] But the ugly xenophobia of 1907–8 (described above) had lessened by 1911. As Russell Elliott observed, the "economic barrier" was breached before the communities' residential barrier was.[55]

Ely and McGill lingered on the edge of the precipice for several days. The McGill newspaper which interviewed Nevada Consolidated employees after they voted to support the Bingham Canyon strike reported that there was an ambivalent attitude among them.

> While a good many union men and others not members of the union are credited with saying that they are opposed to a strike at the same time supporting a demand for increased pay, there is probably no doubt that if a strike is brought about a majority of the employees will go out rather than take sides with the controversy.[56]

Strike votes were taken on the night of Tuesday, October 1. The McGill Mill and Smeltermen's local authorized the WFM's Charles Moyer to begin the strike at his discretion. The Ely strike began the following day. McGill struck about two weeks later. Moyer used the strike meetings to restate his demand for "recognition of the union," which he said, "means nothing more than that the company enter into an agreement with the union for a specific period."[57]

Following the standard script, Nevada Consolidated raised wages just before the strike began. Nevada Con also signed an agreement with Ely machinists and offered the steam-shovel operators an agreement which would have amounted to recognition, and which included a pay raise big enough to make the steam-shovel men "the best [paid men] . . . for the same class of labor in the United States." Twenty and twenty-five-cent daily raises were offered to the unskilled men.[58]

The wage increases and the measure of recognition given these sometime allies of the Western Federation probably diluted strike sentiment. WFM leaders had come to White Pine County seeking support for the Bingham Canyon strike, and they had won it quickly and easily. But there was no general consensus among Ely-McGill workers on striking against Nevada Consolidated on local issues.

A big antistrike meeting was held in McGill on October 3. A. L. Wilde, the general business representative of the Associated Union of Steam Shovel Men, Charles F. Nicholson, third vice-president of the International Machinists Union, an unnamed "Greek speaker," and Guy Miller, Charles Moyer's second-in-command, attended the meeting and asked permission to speak, but were refused. Instead, the audience heard speeches by local men.[59]

One speaker after another rose to announce his satisfaction with local wages and conditions and his opposition to the strike. Most claimed to be union men, and many of them probably did belong to labor unions. But they were certainly not a representative group of McGill workers. Included were three carpenter shop employees, one of whom was a head carpenter, a steam-shovel engineer, a smelter foreman and an assistant smelter superintendent, a machinist, a master mechanic, two railroad locomotive engineers and a railroad locomotive fireman, a spokesman for the McGill business community, and several other white-collar and security employees, all with northwest European surnames. The men at the meeting voted themselves a self-constituted antistrike organization for the duration of the Ely-McGill labor conflict.[60] The organized antistrike group provided effective opposition to the strike. Many carpenters, railroad operatives, and steam-shovel men were to return to work before the strike ended.

A dramatic labor-management battle was being waged at Ely-McGill and Bingham. More than 8,000 men left their jobs and virtually the entire complex of mining and smelting industries from Bingham Canyon to the Great Salt Lake closed down; several thousand men more left their jobs in White Pine County.[61] During the first few days, both in Utah and Nevada, the trades unions—steam-shovel operators, blacksmiths, carpenters, machinists, engineers, boilermakers, and others—generally supported the strike.[62] The Utah Copper Company and Nevada Consolidated refused to negotiate from the outset.[63] Both sides collected resources and prepared for war.

The Utah Copper Company hired and deputized three hundred armed guards even before the strike had started.[64] The company also planned to secure the services of the Utah National Guard, if it could convince the governor to send it.[65] Utah Copper wanted armed forces because it intended to employ strikebreakers, which both sides understood from the very beginning of the strike. The only delay in using strikebreakers would be caused by the difficulty in locating and assembling them while the American copper market was booming and the labor market was tight.[66] Daniel C. Jackling, Utah Copper's manager, said that "as soon as he is guaranteed protection for the men, he will place men at work in the property." There were rumors as early as September 20 that strikebreakers were beginning to arrive in Bingham, and that the company was arranging hotel accommodations for them. Three hundred Cretan strikebreakers arrived in Utah on September 21, and by September 23 "nearly a thousand strikebreakers [had] been assembled at such places as Scofield, Castle Gate and other [coal-mining] camps besides those already in Bingham." The several hundred Japanese mining workers at Bingham remained off the job but refused to commit themselves to the strike effort, and Greek and Italian section hands on the Denver and Rio Grande Railroad also refused to leave their jobs during the strike's first week.[67]

In response, perhaps a thousand armed workingmen seized a part of the big pit on Utah Copper Mountain and dug emplacements. They reportedly had large quantities of dynamite on hand. "The strikers feared that an attempt would be made to [bring] strikebreakers in from the outside and they are declared to have admitted that their men were posted on the road to prevent their entry into camp. They are said to have declared that they would shoot the crews of the trains carrying the men and would take such measures as seemed necessary to stop the men from entering the camp."[68]

Strikebreaking was expected at Nevada Consolidated, too. "Nearly all the foreigners at the copper pit are armed with revolvers and rifles. Some stray shots were fired this morning."[69] But the White Pine County sheriff selected some of his deputies from the strikers' ranks, and at first there were no strikebreakers. Nevada Consolidated began closing and boarding up its facilities almost immediately after the strike was declared. Smeltermen at McGill continued working "only while no attempt was made to break the strike at the mines." But when Nevada Consolidated began preparing to reopen the mines, "a mob of 50 striking Greeks and Austrians armed with revolvers and clubs drove 200 laboring men coming on shift away from the gates of the [smelter] works."[70]

The strikers were armed and angry. They threatened strikebreakers, company officials, and sheriff's deputies. The armed McGill strikers were mostly Cretans and the strikebreakers were probably Greeks.[71]

On October 17, near the gates of the smelter, two strikers, Nick Papagiannakis and George Prinaris, were shot dead by sheriff's deputies, and a third, Mike Economulos, was wounded. Shooting had begun as a crowd of shouting strikers faced a crowd of strikebreakers who had gathered within the smelter area.[72] Greeks and Cretans continued to dominate the smelter area, and sometimes ordered Americans away from the smelter. Thirty company "gunmen" were imported from Salt Lake City to face the Greeks and Cretans. The White Pine County sheriff at first refused to deputize them, but later he apparently did so surreptitiously. Nevada's Governor Tasker L. Oddie quickly declared martial law, perhaps as a means of quashing the arrest warrants which had been issued against the men who murdered Papagiannakis and Prinaris. On October 26, armed guards and state police occupied the smelter and the McGill smelter strike was called off a few days later.[73] The Ely workers gave up their strike on October 28. The company's wage increase, which had preceded the strike, was the workers' only ultimate measure of victory.[74]

Despite the mid-October incidents, there was less violence at Nevada Consolidated than there was in Utah. Nevada Consolidated had not generally evicted the strikers from company-owned property, and had limited its use of strikebreakers. At both McGill and Ely, it was reported that "The companies are not forcing the men out of the company-owned houses, but on the contrary, men with families who have signified their wish to remain in the district have been notified that they can remain in the company houses rent free for the present at least, and that water and lights will be furnished also."[75] At Bingham, by contrast, the Utah Copper Company wanted to give the striking workers' housing to incoming strikebreakers, and so the company decided to force the strikers out of their homes.

The Utah Copper Company owned approximately 5,500 acres of land in and around Bingham Canyon.[76] (Some of the smaller companies operating at Bingham also owned extensive acreage.) Many of the workingmen, as previously explained, were homeowners. They owned shack homes situated upon copper-company land.[77] Utah Copper valued the land for its industrial potential: most of the 1912 shack area is now being mined. Utah Copper's land was also a *closed camp,* over which the company was able to maintain thorough surveillance.[78]

On October 10, the Utah Copper Company began using its closed camp to its best advantage. Open warfare between the Bingham Greek workers and deputy sheriffs began because "The Greeks were ousted from their shacks on the east mountainside temporarily yesterday and were informed that they would have to vacate or go to work this morning. While they were out of the houses deputy sheriffs made a search for weapons. . . . The deputy sheriffs intend to climb the mountain again today and it is considered certain that resistance will be made." The same policy was used against the Serbians.[79]

> It was claimed that George Bean, a foreman at the Highland Boy mine, was preventing Austrian strikers from going to their homes. It was represented that Mike Zikovitch had told the foreman that he wanted to go home to his wife and family, but that Mr. Bean had driven him back. Other Austrians also reported similar experiences with the foreman at the Highland Boy mine. Mr. Bean was quoted as saying that all of the Austrian strikers would be driven from the company's ground.[80]

Strikebreaking and eviction continued throughout October. Frequently, men from one side or the other were caught and brutally beaten.[81] On October 1, 150 Japanese were back on the payroll.[82] Strikebreakers reopened large-scale operations at the big pit on October 9, when minor fighting was reported. Then the company began rehiring and reemploying hundreds of its own skilled men, probably to sap the resistance of the Bingham-area skilled tradesmen who were still on strike.[83] Hundreds of new men were hired—"steamshovel men, machinists, miners and skilled copper men," "recruited, it is said, from the Pacific coast and various other parts."[84] Another group of strikebreakers, most of whom were Americans, came to do the unskilled work.[85] By October 16, company guards had entrances and exits at the big pit surrounded and controlled. Several hundred men fought a gun battle for control of the pit on October 25.[86] By the end of the month, the company was using Greek strikebreakers against Greek strikers. According to WFM observers, "One of the methods adopted by the Utah Copper is to throw a bunch of Greeks into jail, charge them with murder or some similar crime, then send agents among the Greeks, telling them the union would do nothing for those in jail and promising to release their friends if they returned to work. This method was successful in some instances."[87]

The company initiative which probably finished off the 1912 Bingham strike was an offer of increased wages. First, Jackling announced that "An increase in wages to our employees at the Garfield plant has been authorized and announced, effective November 1. We have also increased the scale of wages of our locomotive engineers, locomotive firemen and trainmen working in connection with the steam shovel operations at the mines." He also spoke vaguely of increases for other "classes" of employees, and of pursuing a new general policy of revising wages upward "provided the relatively high price of copper then and now prevailing should be sustained." Jackling said that the wage increases were intended to reward Utah Copper's loyal employees, and not the strikers. "The increase now made applies only to such plants, departments, and employees as were not directly affected by the recent strike and is intended for the benefit of such employees only as have remained or been willing to remain in the company's service throughout the period of disturbance."[88] "We shall use our own discretion in the matter of reemploying strikers," said Jackling. "This can be called discrimination, selective action, good judgment, or whatever one pleases."[89] More strikebreakers arrived in early November, more Greeks were arrested, and the WFM began to speak of terminating the strike, "just as soon as the Utah Copper Company posts notices around the camp notifying the miners that they have been granted the same concessions as were granted to the men at Ely."[90] On November 29th, Jackling announced wage increases for men whose wages had not been raised during the previous months, "and like the increase applied on September 1 to our underground employees, [it] is made voluntarily and entirely aside and apart from the effect or consideration of recent labor disturbances."[91]

The great Bingham Canyon strike was practically over. Before the end of the year, production returned to near normal although replacement workers were still being imported as late as the following February.[92] The WFM ruefully admitted that management had defeated labor at Bingham Canyon, although it claimed that the company had been hurt in the process.[93] But some important things had changed.

Unskilled mining workers, particularly Greeks, had been striking for higher wages and liberation from padrone control, and they had achieved at least temporary victories on both of these issues.[94] Management had also been punished, albeit briefly, and the immigrant workers had ineffaceably demonstrated their potential for achieving power. The impetus behind the 1912 strike had come from the immigrants at Murray, at Bingham, and to a lesser degree, at Ely-McGill as well.

The Western Federation of Miners was also an important participant in the Utah and Nevada strikes, more thoroughly involved than it had been in any of the previous major strikes in the lower intermountain and southwestern copper industry. The WFM had proselytized for industrial unionism at Bingham, helped to plan and direct the strikes, and had generally helped direct and inform the Bingham-area miners. Information about the 1912 Butte contract and its sliding scale based upon the wholesale price of copper provided inspiration.[95] On September 24, for instance, the Bingham strikers were reported "jubilant" because of "the advance yesterday in copper past the 18 cent point, as the contract with the Butte miners calls for an increase to $3.50 per day upon such figure being passed in the copper market."[96] The Bingham miners also had obtained information about comparative costs of living and working conditions at Bingham, Butte, and some of the other western mining camps.[97]

The WFM carefully publicized the Bingham strike, and tried to coordinate the two major strikes in Bingham and Ely-McGill. The Western Federationists asked all workers "to stay away from Utah" during the strike, correctly surmising that wandering miners could be temporarily hired by railroads or the Carbon County, Utah, coal camps until they were needed for strikebreaking in the copper areas.[98] The organizing effort at the mills near the Bingham pit was successful: many of the men at the Magna and Arthur mills and the Garfield smelter struck in support of the Bingham mining workers, and workers at the big Tooele, Utah, smelter agreed not to handle Bingham ore.[99] The WFM also paid out some strike benefits: single men at Bingham were paid $3.00 a week, and married men were paid $6.00.[100]

WFM President Charles Moyer tried to develop strike possibilities at the Guggenheims' Chino Mines Division in Hurley and Santa Rita, New Mexico, and at their Ray Consolidated Copper Company in and near Ray, Arizona. "We have the situation as well in hand at Ray and Santa Rita as at Bingham and Ely but do not want to extend the strike to those places,"

Moyer boasted. Possibly, Moyer may have wanted to create strikes at Guggenheim mining properties across the Southwest, but he would not have been able to do so. Hurley-Santa Rita and Ray remained quiet, except for the Santa Rita steam-shovel men's strike, noted below. Moyer's expressed reluctance was merely cover for his failure at those mining areas.[101]

The skilled-trades men at Bingham and Ely-McGill had been very important for the strike's chances of success. WFM national leaders really tried to win strike support from all of the important skilled-crafts groups, with partial success.

The Bingham strike tested a new kind of Western Federation of Miners strike demand for written contractual relations with management. The decision to actively seek contracts with employers has been described as indicative of growing WFM conservatism. John Laslett, restating the IWW position on WFM contracts, wrote that "contracts prevented one group of workers from going to the assistance of another when the need arose" but precisely the reverse occurred at Bingham.[102] The WFM behaved like a conventional AFL labor union in search of a written agreement; but the miners behaved conventionally in order to attract the fraternal assistance of other AFL groups, and fraternal AFL unions provided some degree of help to the Miner's Union because it was a conventional, contract-seeking union.[103] But the WFM's goal was to organize a genuine industrial union local among unskilled, non-Anglo-Irish workers. That was by no means a conventional or conservative idea in 1912.

National officers and organizers of the Western Federation had traveled to Bingham in the summer of 1912 and had spoken directly to local Bingham trades unionists. The WFM men had also traveled East to speak to the national officers of skilled-trades groups. Most national trades-union leaders assured the WFM officers of their support, but the leaders of the skilled-men's locals were less reassuring.

The trades-union locals tentatively agreed to cooperate with the WFM before the strike, but they became progressively less willing to cooperate after the strike had begun in September.[104] The *Deseret Evening News* claimed that only coercion from national labor union officials in the East had pushed the reluctant Bingham skilled tradesmen off the job.

> It leaked out yesterday from reliable sources that when the black-smiths employed at Bingham voted on the question of the strike, there were but two votes cast in favor of such a movement, while there were 97 against it. The grand council, however, affiliated with the Western Federation of Miners, ordered the local lodge to strike.

There is a visible feeling of bitterness among the mechanics and artisans thrown out of work because of the strike. An official of one of the affiliated unions said today:

"This thing has been forced on us. None of us wanted to strike and we had no grievance. Take the engineers and firemen, for instance, they were and are entirely satisfied: the shovelmen have no kick coming and I am sure that the boilermakers, blacksmiths, and machinists are content. What we want to do is to get back to work, yet we can't do it, because the foreigners outnumber us."[105]

Two of Bingham's skilled-craft groups demonstrated the poles of strike response. The steam-shovel operators at Bingham supported the strike with exceptional fervor, while the railway crewmen were quite unwilling to support it at all.

The Associated Union of Steam Shovel Men was a new union; it got an AFL charter in mid-1912.[106] It was already striking. The steam-shovel men, together with some railroad union allies, were conducting the first strike against the Guggenheim management at the newly opened Chino Copper Company in Hurley and Santa Rita, New Mexico. The steam-shovel men planned to strike there for a wage increase in May, but by late June, they had been replaced by strikebreakers at the ore shovels.[107] When the Bingham shovel men struck, they demanded not only safety measures, paid holidays, "union shop" arrangements, and other local Bingham demands, but they also demanded reinstatement for the shovel men at Santa Rita.[108]

The steam-shovel men were slightly better-paid than most other skilled mining employees were, even before the strike. However, they were especially loyal to the Bingham strike, probably because they wanted to establish their credentials within the labor movement.[109] At Ely, copper-company officials tried to negotiate separately with the steam-shovel men. The shovelers were offered a big pay raise and a two-year written agreement, but they rejected the offer.[110] After the rejection, the company replaced some of the steam-shovel men with strikebreakers.[111]

The railway operating employees were quite different. A Chino Mines (Hurley and Santa Rita) locomotive firemen's and engineers' strike had failed along with that of the steam-shovel men there, but the Bingham and Ely-McGill railroad unions did not try to link the New Mexico strike with the Utah-Nevada strikes.[112]

The Bingham mine's locomotive engineers were privileged. The Utah Copper Company had *raised* the engineers' wages during the 1907 Panic. The locomotive engineers had taken no active part in the 1909 labor trouble, and again their wages, along with those of the firemen and brakemen, were raised in October, 1909. Again in April, 1912, the three railroad crafts groups were the only categories of employees whose pay was increased. Next, Daniel Jackling listed them among the employees entitled to raises in October, 1912.[113] Not surprisingly, the railway operatives were the first to quit the strike and return to work at Bingham.[114]

The Bingham Canyon local of the Brotherhood of Locomotive Firemen and Enginemen had been unresponsive from the outset. Charles Moyer had asked for their support, and originally the engineers and firemen had agreed to give it. Then they changed their minds. Some of the Ely-McGill engineers and firemen were more cooperative.[115] The WFM leaders appealed to the national leaders of the railway operating unions and to their local lodges in other parts of the United States, and some of the other lodges responded with a joint condemnatory letter directed at the Bingham locals, urging their cooperation with the strike.[116] Moyer also spoke directly to the Firemen and Enginemen's president, William S. Carter. Carter, a lifelong labor-union conservative, responded by writing a letter to the Bingham Canyon local. The letter said that if the local "had no contract with the Utah Copper they might do as they saw fit in the premises, but that in case they came out it would not be considered a brotherhood strike."[117] Apparently, some of the Bingham railroad men did refuse to work during the strike's first several weeks, but most of them were back on their locomotives by mid-October.[118]

A portion, but only a portion, of the American work force joined the recent-immigrant workers in active picketing and fighting. Others refused to help. Some Bingham Canyon steam-shovel men were eager to divorce themselves from A. L. Wilde, the national shoveler organization's local representative. Wilde, they said, had "taken too active a part in the controversy to suit many of them." Some of the Ely-McGill steam-shovel men felt the same way. The McGill carpenters, too, went back to work early. Despite official support of the strike by the AFL national trades unions, many Americans avoided the strikes, and some of them expressed subdued dissatisfaction with them.[119] The hoped-for collaboration between the Western Federation of Miners and its AFL fellow unionists had almost happened nationally. Only the railway union's William Carter had blocked national organized-labor support for the Bingham and Ely-McGill strikes. But even if the railroads had not transported copper ore and strikebreakers, the strike response was still far short of total unity. National collaboration between Moyer and the presidents of the carpenters, steam-shovel men, and machinists was arranged, but *local* collaboration between the higher-paid,

specially privileged, skilled Anglo-Irish-American workers and the relatively underprivileged unskilled immigrant workers did not necessarily fol-
low from the national-level agreements.

Some Bingham and Ely-McGill workingmen had begun leaving the
strike areas in September.[120] By late November, *Miners' Magazine* reported
that "The majority of the Bingham strikers have left for other fields where
conditions are at least a little more tolerable, about 1000 of the miners yet
remaining."[121] Many of the Greeks left to fight for Greece in the Balkan
Wars during December.[122] Some unskilled workers of various ethnicities
who had remained had joined the WFM locals, of course, early in the strike.
A few unskilled men even joined at the end of it.[123] But the strike effort did
not weld an enduring alliance between the immigrant unskilled workingmen and the WFM.

The WFM claimed to have won a great general victory for "thousands"
who were "enjoying an increase in wages and improved conditions" all
over the mining West—implying that the wage increases had been forcibly
extracted from the companies by strikes and the threat of strikes.[124] The
companies adamantly denied that they had been coerced into increasing
wages. They insisted that their wage policy was a free-will offering which
had been negotiated neither with union officials nor with union members.
The companies declared that on the contrary, they intended to punish, not
reward, unionists. They would accomplish this, they said, by firing some
unionists, and especially by denying the union recognition.

It is unlikely that the WFM expected to get meaningful recognition
from the Bingham strike, although such recognition was desirable. *Miners'
Magazine* had been very specific about the causes of the springtime strike
at Murray, near Bingham. Wages were the only significant issue at Murray. Wages were the primary cause of the Bingham strike too, although
Leonidas Skliris's operations subsequently became a second major issue.[125]
The WFM claimed that it was seeking a contractual wage agreement similar to the one at Butte, and probably made that claim in order to attract
skilled-trades unionists. But once the strikes had begun, the Western Federation completely dropped the recognition idea.[126]

However, the Utah Copper Company mentioned recognition extraordinarily often. On October 4, Spencer Penrose, a company vice-president,
said that "The Utah Copper Company will never recognize the union at
Bingham, even if the mine is closed forever."[127] That phrase about closing
the mine was repeated by corporation officers in Boston several days later.
On October 7, the *Salt Lake Tribune* announced that "The Bingham strikers
are willing to return to work without recognition of their union."[128] On the

same day, a steam-shovel-men's committee and a committee of six Bingham mine strikers, none of whom was either a union officer or negotiator, went to see Daniel C. Jackling. He refused to speak with them. "The committee reported that Jackling said they were no longer employees because they had left the works, and gave them to understand that if they desired to do business with the company they would have to return to work at the company's terms, the company accepting such applicants for jobs as it desired."[129] Shortly afterward, "When Mr. Jackling was asked if any miners had called to see him to discuss the strike, he replied that none had, and that it would be impossible for a miner to come into contact with him." As mentioned above, wage increases were made, according to the company, voluntarily.[130]

Another part of the legend which Utah Copper management wished to create about the strike helps explain the company's unnecessarily vociferous rejection of union recognition. According to Jackling's interpretation of the strike, the WFM had coerced the skilled American men into striking, and it had duped the unskilled immigrant men. "We have of course only sympathy for those who were forced out on strike against their wills because they feared for their personal safety and only sympathy for those who were deceived and misled in the Ely district by Moyer and his crowd, as these same men deceived and misled our workers at Bingham."[131] In an absurd coupling of the two notions of "union recognition" and the "misleading" of immigrant workers, the Nevada Consolidated general manager said that the strike was "a struggle for recognition and carried on exclusively by foreigners."[132]

The use of the recognition issue, the notion that unskilled immigrant strikers were duped, and the carefully articulated arrangements regarding wage raises and negotiations were all elements in a general management strategy which served to keep the union confederation, the skilled men, and the unskilled men apart. Many of the Anglo-Irish-American workers at Bingham and Ely-McGill already had achieved union recognition by virtue of their membership in skilled-trades unions. Nevada Consolidated's management actually signed written agreements with individual members and groups of unionized boilermakers, machinists, steam-shovel men, and other skilled tradesmen at Ely-McGill; but it did so surreptitiously, both during and after the strike there.[133] There were formal negotiations, and a Western Federation of Miners' representative even participated in some of them.[134] The agreements were not publicized, and the unskilled workers were neither represented nor made a party to them.[135] The WFM was probably salvaging what it could from a bad situation, but it was also helping to perpetuate the notion that the way of WFM unionism was to create a series of surreptitious understandings between skilled men and company management which excluded the unskilled men. The WFM was opportunistically grasping for institutional advantage. The Moyer-led leadership group would not risk alienating Anglo-Irish-Americans in return for the hope of future support from recent immigrants.

Another strike theme, especially at Bingham itself, was that of the copper companies' struggle for the allegiances of immigrant strikers, Anglo-Irish-Americans, and even Western Federation unionists. Both the corporations and the unions knew that a unified industrial labor movement could conceivably defeat management at Bingham. But the Anglo-Irish-Americans were already better paid, better organized, and were working under relatively better conditions than were the immigrants. The copper corporations were delivering a message. They were demonstrating that they were ready to scale down the privileges of the highest-status workingmen if forced to raise the standards for the men at the bottom. If the companies had to raise someone's pay, it would be at someone else's expense. They would not cease their effort to cut production costs by holding down the total wage bill.[136]

The Bingham-area strike indirectly furthered industrial unionism in the central western region by creating industrial-union consciousness. Thousands of Utah and Nevada copper-industry workers had battled management, and they had come reasonably close to victory. The WFM's reaffiliation with the AFL also had come close to providing the requisite degree of crafts-union support. In a final analysis of the strike's effectiveness, Charles Moyer blamed defeat primarily upon the unionized opposition: "it will go down into history to the ever lasting shame of the Railroad workers, who so efficiently assisted the Copper Trust of Bingham Canyon, Utah, to defeat the workers."[137]

The 1912 Utah and Nevada strikes were among the most ambitious unionization drives made anywhere in the United States before the First World War. But President Charles Moyer's reach far exceeded his grasp. The Utah and Nevada campaign was an effort at tying a walkout and strike by about ten thousand unskilled workers, most of whom were nonunion southern and eastern European immigrants, to labor action which included smaller, individually organized and potentially hostile groups of semi-skilled and skilled Anglo-Irish-American men in several localities, and then tying all of this, in turn, to related efforts made in various outposts of the Guggenheim copper empire across the western United States. Moyer gambled upon the strength of his newly reestablished ties with the national leadership of the skilled trades. He overestimated the power of that national leadership to control events in the relatively remote western communities.

Greeks, South Slavs, and Italians had demonstrated that they could effectively strike against a major American copper corporation in 1912. The 1903 Mexican, Italian, and Hispanic strikers of Clifton-Morenci had developed organizational cohesion from within their own ethnic mutual societies. There were no comparably organized elements in the Bingham Canyon Greek and South Slavic communities.[138] In Bingham Canyon, the Miners' Union's organizing work partially substituted for the lack of mutual-society participation. Although the Clifton district Spanish Americans, Mexicans, and Italians were comparatively more cohesive than were the Utah and Nevada strikers, the Arizona men had a greater *opportunity* to function cohesively. Most of the 1903 strikers had come, on their own, into Arizona from a vast southwestern hinterland, while the Greeks, South Slavs, and Italians were more thoroughly controlled by labor agents associated with the railroads which had brought them to Bingham and Ely-McGill. The Greeks' and South Slavs' demand for equitable wages was not quite the same thing as the Clifton-Morenci strikers' fight against Mexican and Italian wage scales, but the mistrust of local Anglo- and Irish-American coworkers, based upon earlier experiences on the job and in the community was similar in both instances.[139] The events of 1912 demonstrated that western immigrants and English-speaking men could strike together, and that several distinct immigrant nationalities could become the main element in a potentially large, powerful, organized labor movement in the western copper industry.

Planning and carrying through a fight for improved wages, hours, and working conditions against a major U.S. corporation was intrinsically difficult. Ethnic groups needed the internally generated leadership and internal cohesion of ethnically based societies such as mutualistas, sickness-and-death-benefit societies, and the improvised ethnic clubs and unions which sometimes developed during the planning stages of strike efforts. But ethnic groups also needed U.S. labor unions. Without recourse to the Bingham Miners' Union, the Greeks, Italians, and South Slavs could temporarily walk off their jobs, physically intimidate and threaten depredation against copper-company management and property, and, most commonly, quit their jobs and seek work elsewhere. What the Bingham Canyon workingmen had been unable to do without union assistance was to conduct a major strike. The Bingham Miners' Union, through its national, state, and local connections, could find money and legal help, could threaten disruption of the copper company's transportation and power sources, and most importantly, could at least threaten to affect the general financial well-being of the copper corporations. Bingham Canyon and White Pine County immigrant workers moved toward both ethnic cohesion and unionization during the great strikes of 1912.

◄ 7 ►

JUSTICIA AND *IGUALDAD* AGAIN
AT EL PASO AND RAY, 1913–1914

Neither the WFM nor the IWW was able to organize effectively in the Central West and Southwest during 1913–14. But there were ethnic initiatives. Mexicans and Spaniards fought copper-corporation management, both in El Paso, Texas, and at Ray, Arizona, during those years.

The Western Federation of Miners was slumping, and the slump looked potentially fatal. The Bingham Canyon and Ely-McGill strikes of 1912 were, temporarily, the end of the line for the WFM in the southwestern and lower intermountain states. Even though the miners' confederation retained its ties to AFL skilled labor and kept some of its ethnic organizers, WFM leadership had no organizing plans for the western heartland. The Industrial Workers of the World had been practically ignoring the western states and territories since 1911, and continued to do so.[1]

Organized labor seemed to be in trouble everywhere. The national economy went downhill in late 1913, and the price of copper fell from 16¢ to 13¢ a pound.[2] Many men were out of work. But despite hard times, there was plenty of strike activity, most of it far from the western copper areas.

There were unorganized garment workers' strikes in New York and Chicago during 1910–13, partly assisted by organized labor.[3] The Lawrence textile mills were struck in 1912, and the Paterson mills were struck in 1913. The IWW helped direct and organize the Lawrence strike through its Local 20, which had been in Lawrence since 1910.[4] The Paterson strike was generally similar to the one at Lawrence, although unlike Lawrence, Paterson was a clear IWW defeat.

The United Mine Workers of America participated in major upheavals which were contemporaneous with Lawrence and Paterson: in the West Virginia coalfields in 1912 and 1913, and in Colorado in 1913–14. These were similar in size to the clothing-mill strikes. Each involved thousands of workers. The coal strikes had at least a tinge of what was contemporaneously interpreted as radicalism, especially the Colorado strike, whose major participants were armed, angry recent immigrants. Both strikes were decidedly violent, and the violence in Colorado earned it national notoriety.[5]

In 1909, in the Black Hills of South Dakota, the Homestake Mining Company began locking out WFM union miners. The Western Federation spent much of its national treasury fighting Homestake, and then lost the fight. After the WFM's much less expensive but equally unsuccessful battle at Bingham Canyon and Ely-McGill, its next big effort was the strike against the Calumet and Hecla Copper Mining Company on the Michigan copper range in 1913, which ended in defeat, too. Then one of the WFM's most important component parts was destroyed in 1914, when the Butte Miners' Union (Local 1) split into radical, moderate, and conservative factions and then ruined itself in internecine warfare.[6]

Some general labor histories have implied that much of the early twentieth century was a *period* in the history of American labor.[7] They describe consistent growth patterns throughout the prewar decade. A close examination of the health of the AFL, IWW, and WFM during 1912–14 suggests a different interpretation.

All three—the AFL, IWW, and WFM—ceased to gain in membership during 1912–14, and all three were riven with internal dissension. In 1909, the American Federation of Labor began an expansive phase during which its membership rose each year, from about 1,428,000 to about 2,020,000 by early 1914. Then it declined to 1,946,000 in early 1915. Similarly, the AFL issued fewer union local charters in 1914 than it had at any time since 1909. The AFL national conventions of 1912 and 1914 were both relatively acrimonious. A large minority, which included the United Mine Workers and the Western Federation of Miners, frequently voted against the AFL majority at the 1912 and 1914 conventions on issues relevant to the encouragement of industrial unionism. The coal and metal miners, the Brewery Workers, and several temporary allies supported Max Hayes's campaign against Samuel Gompers in 1912.[8]

The IWW was described by Melvyn Dubofsky as languishing in 1911 and reviving itself at Lawrence in 1912. Nineteen twelve "seemed like the dawn of a newer, freer era," wrote Dubofsky, but by the summer of 1913, "the IWW seemed on the verge of disintegration." In 1913, of course, the IWW was still striking in Paterson, but "open dissension broke out among Wobblies on the West Coast," and the national convention was "rent by conflict." The IWW didn't begin to recover until 1915.[9]

The Western Federation of Miners experienced a drastic decline in paid-up membership in 1914. During that year, it issued seven new charters, but twenty-six locals' charters were surrendered. Nineteen fourteen was a year of national recession, and so it was obviously a bad year for labor organizing, but it was a particularly bad year for union groups with potential organizing interest in the Southwest and lower intermountain states.[10]

Layoffs, short hours, and a general scarcity of jobs became widespread across the western copper areas south of Montana in late 1913 and early 1914. Most of the western copper areas from Utah and Nevada south to the Mexican border fell silent and slept until early 1915.

Fernando Velarde had been working for the IWW in Arizona since its genesis at Phoenix in 1906. He was described as a tireless worker. Velarde had organized with Frank Little, briefly, at Clifton-Morenci-Metcalf in 1907, with both men dedicating themselves to the WFM and the IWW, and they had almost succeeded in jump-starting unionism there. Velarde had organized a separate Mexican Branch of Phoenix IWW Local 272 in 1908. Then came, in 1909, La Union Industrial, "the only Spanish paper in the United States teaching Revolutionary Industrial Unionism." La Union soon ceased publication, but Velarde moved to Southern California, where the IWW was helping the Mexican Revolution via its connection with the Partido Liberal Mexicano in Baja California.[11]

In 1910, the San Diego IWW movement was calling for "a big revolutionary union of Mexicans throughout the Southwest." But the revolutionary movement never moved east from Southern California; and in 1913, Fernando Velarde, operating out of Los Angeles, requested support for another IWW Spanish-language newspaper which might inspire a southwestern organizing campaign. Velarde said that he couldn't obtain enough money and that IWW leaders were uninterested. Then he got his newspaper. It was La Huelga General (The General Strike). Huelga General lasted for only about a year, until September 1914. A third newspaper, El Rebelde, began about six months after Huelga General folded, and continued for about two and a half years. Both Huelga General and Rebelde were Los Angeles-based, and were infrequently distributed east of California.[12]

Was Fernando Velarde correct when he questioned national IWW commitment to southwestern Mexican unionism? Wobbly policy was not a

unified whole on ethnic issues. While some European-immigrant IWW recruits were easily absorbed into mainstream IWW activity, some remained
decidedly separate.

Sometimes, Wobblies' opposition to skilled-crafts unionism was con-
flated with their struggle against Anglo-American and Irish American
crafts-union members. After the 1909 McKee's Rocks, Pennsylvania, strike
against the Pressed Steel Car Company, for instance, the IWW's new *Solidarity* newspaper claimed that the results were a "brilliant" victory for the
fifteen European nationalities who had fought against the American-born
population.[13] In Lawrence in 1912, Joseph Ettor's recruitment work among
the Italians included making "vicious attacks on the natives," who, he said,
would only tolerate an Italian "so long as he wants to live next door to a dog
and work for $4.20 a week."[14]

But the IWW also had an ethnic-separation policy which ran counter to
its own acceptance of ethnic diversity. The IWW used so-called "language
federations" and ethnic "branch" locals on a national basis. Language federations were ethnically segregated locals in areas with distinct Anglo-
Irish-American and immigrant European, Asian, or Mexican populations.
The Public Service Workers' Union in San Diego was all Mexican, and was
an offshoot of an Anglo union, Local 13, there.[15] In 1912, a *Solidarity* con-
tributor argued that ethnically segregated locals were a divisive factor
within the IWW all across the country, and he called for their elimination.[16]
But the language federations continued to function as separate entities, at
least through the First World War years.

The several Spanish-language newspapers were ephemeral: they sometimes reached Phoenix, but were practically unknown in southwestern mining camps. No South Slavic IWW newspapers appeared in the western mining areas until after the World War either. Nor were there any IWW Greek
newspapers, despite the large Greek and South Slavic populations in many
western mining areas. Eastern Wobblies created most of the IWW's foreign-
language press; but even when the western-based *Industrial Worker* began
publishing a foreign-language page, it was devoid of Spanish, South Slavic,
or Greek coverage.[17] A Phoenix IWW member wrote to the *Industrial
Worker,* "I wish you would publish a page in Spanish." The *Industrial
Worker*'s staff did not heed his request.[18] Fernando Velarde and his associates at the Mexican branch of the Phoenix IWW were an independent little
band of IWW devotees, receiving no direct support from the IWW's western offices at Spokane. Manuel Rey, the only Hispanic IWW national organizer before the First World War, did not travel in the West. There were
Italian-surnamed members on the IWW Executive Board, but no Greek,

South Slavic, or Spanish members were included and there were seldom IWW Greek or South Slavic western organizers.[19]

The IWW sent speakers west from Denver and Salt Lake City to California, Washington, and Oregon throughout these years. There were active IWW locals in Salt Lake City and Phoenix, and the free-speech fight at Salt Lake in 1910 drew many Wobbly itinerants and several notable speakers to the edges of the desert-and-mountain mining country. A group of men associated with the failed Tonopah, Nevada, IWW Local 325 returned there and reestablished the IWW in Tonopah, briefly, in 1914. There was a tiny IWW local at the National, Nevada, gold mine in Humboldt County in 1910 and perhaps briefly thereafter. But in general, IWW organizers and speakers either ignored or carefully avoided most of the Central West and Southwest through 1915, treating the region between the Rockies and the Sierra like most nineteenth-century wagon-train emigrants. Wobbly organizers set off from the eastern edges of the plains, hastened past Western Utah, Nevada, New Mexico, West Texas, and Arizona, and went directly to the West Coast to speak and organize.[20]

The Western Federation of Miners was struggling to extricate itself from its troubles in the Calumet and Hecla strike in Michigan, its tangled connections to the Homestake picketing in South Dakota, and its far worse troubles in Butte. It had little organizing energy left.[21] Former Colorado men, including Vincent St. John and John M. O'Neill, the long-time editor of *Miners' Magazine,* had been the largest, most vocal, and most capable contingent of the Western Federation. Before the Colorado mining war of 1903–4, Coloradans were about a quarter of the Western Federation's total membership. The fighting, lockouts, strikes, arrests, and deportations in Colorado decimated the locals there. For a few years after 1905, the Montana locals, led by Butte Number 1, were the largest single component (about 20 percent) of the WFM. Beginning in 1905, Montana miners and former Montana men often dominated WFM national administration and continued to do so until Butte Number 1's troubles began in 1911. But Butte Number 1, in turn, was practically destroyed during 1912–14. The Arizona copper mines were the only union success story in the mining West during 1913–14, and WFM men from Globe and Miami, Arizona, were beginning to fill the vacuum left by the collapse at Butte. However, the absence of a large, solid base of regional support was still painfully evident as the WFM struggled on through 1913–14.[22]

As Arizona moved into the spotlight, so did the special character of her work force. Mexican Americans and Mexican immigrants, and, in smaller numbers, South Slavic, Spanish, and Italian immigrants were, together, the majority of Arizona's unskilled and semiskilled mining workers, and generally, they were not unionized. Unionizing them was stated WFM policy, as it had been since the Clifton-Morenci strike in 1903. But in practice, WFM leaders were less than eager to welcome Mexican workers into the union. The 1912 WFM convention heard a report by an ex-member who claimed that unionized Slavic miners in Bisbee were not paying their dues, and that underpaid "Mexican miners are slowly but surely driving out the organized men in this state [Arizona]." The convention members raised no objections to these statements.[23] President Moyer said that the issue of organizing Mexican workers was being brought "forcibly to our attention" by Mexicans themselves, who were joining a small, new WFM local at Mogollon, New Mexico. Although Moyer supported the notion of educating and organizing Mexican workers, he was reluctant.[24] In 1914, a WFM committee reported on Mexican immigration and Mexican workers in a similar vein:

> The unorganized worker is everywhere a menace to the organized. We must inspire the workers with the principles of unionism and unite them in a common effort to improve conditions or all will sink in the quicksand of misery and poverty. Great sections of the mining industry are wholly unorganized, many sections partially unorganized. The Mexican peons are invading the southwest. The easiest and most logical way to educate him is in the mining districts of Mexico. Local organizations are already formed in many of them; some have requested admission to the Federation.[25]

The Western Federationists would educate and organize among the new southwestern work force because necessity demanded it. They offered the Mexican mining workers a cheerless welcome to the WFM.

The Alianza Hispano Americana was building in the Southwest and included lodges at Clifton, Morenci, Metcalf, Jerome, Hurley and Santa Rita, New Mexico (the site of a newly expanded mine and mill complex), at El Paso, Texas, Winkelman, Arizona, and Mogollon, New Mexico. Earlier lodges at Bisbee and Globe, Arizona, had come and gone since the Alianza's early days. But the Alianza was primarily a sickness-and-death-benefit society. It provided insurance: the opportunity for socializing came as an incidental benefit, and the Alianza's general purposes were unrelated to on-the-job problems. Although at least a few mining workers belonged to Alianza lodges, the Alianza had little connection with any mining workers' job actions through the First World War era.[26]

The Liga Protectora Latina was a different story. The Liga was political and was interested in job opportunities. It was a fairly typical Progressive

Era defense organization, and its members were interested in work-related issues. But the Liga had only begun to grow in February 1915.[27]

Neither labor unions nor fraternal benefit associations, then, were organizing the Southwest's copper industry work force in 1913 and 1914. Yet there was one big southwestern strike: in El Paso, Texas, at the American Smelting and Refining Company smelter, in 1913.

There had been an earlier strike at El Paso's ASARCO smelter plant. Nearly one hundred and fifty Mexican smelter workers had walked out in 1907, demanding a wage increase from the $1.20 daily that they were earning, to $1.50. ASARCO had eventually offered them $1.40, but it had also replaced some of the strikers. About half of the striking workers had refused the proffered pay increase and had left El Paso, heading for Colorado.[28]

The El Paso–Ciudad Juarez area "attracted nearly every major revolutionary movement in the north [of Mexico]," according to Richard Medina Estrada's important study of El Paso area revolutionary political activity.[29] El Paso also attracted organizers from the Phoenix Mexican Branch IWW local. In early 1912, Fernando Palomarez, a prominent organizer, R. A. Dorame, who helped publish *La Union Industrial* at Phoenix, and a third man, S. Lomas, were arrested and held in the El Paso County jail, apparently because they had engaged in labor organizational activity. IWW men may have "talked union" at the ASARCO smelter on other occasions, too.[30]

That the revolutionaries and radical unionists had been nearby, before the strike, is certain. But when the ASARCO workers struck, they were neither unionized nor politicized. They were practically alone.

The county sheriff and his deputies, and eventually, the Texas Rangers helped ASARCO management. Urineo Avila, one of the strikers, was arrested for handing out prostrike leaflets and charged with disturbing the peace. A few black strikebreakers were put to work during the second week of the strike, and they were protected by nondeputized company guards. During the third week of the strike, a Texas Ranger shot and wounded one of the Mexican pickets who was trying to prevent strikebreakers from entering the works. During the same week, there was a strike-related killing, with ambiguous causes. ASARCO intensified labor-management hostilities by initiating legal action to eject some of the strikers from their homes on company-owned land. But during most of the strike, the strikers who picketed the ASARCO plant were disciplined and orderly.[31]

The occasion for striking may have been propitious. In 1913–14, racial-ethnic accommodation in El Paso was increasing. El Paso AFL unions already included some Spanish-surnamed men. The secretary of the Sheet

Metal Workers' local was named Villegas, and the El Paso Cigarmakers' local was mainly Mexican in 1913. Seventy-five Mexican clerks who wanted to take Sundays off in order to shorten what was apparently a seven-day work week had organized a clerk's International Union local.

Five ASARCO Anglo union carpenters went out on strike with the smelter workers. When the ASARCO strike was a little over a week old, some of these AFL unionists hosted a presentation at a regular meeting of the El Paso Central Labor Union at which a committee of ASARCO smelter strikers explained their strike to the assembled AFL skilled tradesmen. The strikers asked the Central Labor Union for an endorsement of their strike. They had been earning a miserable $1.40 for a twelve-hour workday, and they were demanding a 20 percent wage increase. They added a demand for an eight-hour day, and they had complaints about the company doctor, the company store, and their treatment at the hands of foremen. The strike had begun with only 100 men, but by mid-April, there were at least 1,000 men out.[32]

The Central Labor Union endorsed the ASARCO smelter strike. Fifteen dollars was donated "to aid them at once while all unions . . . [were] requested to help them financially."[33] More funds and supplies came later.[34] But the Central Labor Union's support was less than wholehearted, probably because it was far from unanimous. Two hundred and fifty other ASARCO Anglo or Irish workers, some of whom must have been union men, continued to report to work at ASARCO throughout the strike.[35] The AFL central labor body, which included ASARCO metal fabricators and electricians among its membership, could conceivably have tied up production at the big smelter and forced concessions from management. Some of the AFL men in El Paso must have been active opponents of the ASARCO strike, and the CLU was apparently unable or unwilling to force them into line.

The Central Labor Union's newspaper was seldom reticent about expressing hostility to "peon labor," but its potentially offensive verbiage slackened during the first two months of the strike.[36] By late June, the strike appeared doomed, and the local voice of the AFL resumed making comments implicitly critical of unskilled ASARCO labor. The U.S. Secretary of Labor, William Wilson, had just appointed Joseph S. Myers, the former head of the Joint Labor Board of Trade in Austin, as the new U.S. Inspector of Contract Labor for El Paso. The Central Labor Union expressed the hope that Myers would check what it considered a massive influx of contract laborers into El Paso. Many of these men, claimed the newspaper, were deserting their "families and charges" in El Paso, and the charity burden upon El Paso residents, they said, was becoming impossible to bear.[37]

National Western Federation of Miners' headquarters sent organizer C. H. Tanner to El Paso. The IWW, of course, was already in town. The first southwestern contest between the WFM and IWW for the allegiance of Mexican and other Hispanic workers had begun. Neither side had an operating union local in the community. The IWW, using Mexican organizers from Phoenix, had a head start, but the WFM again had the help of its AFL allies. Several months into the strike, the El Paso Central Labor Union urged the strikers to avoid connecting themselves to the IWW, and to join the WFM, and thus the AFL itself, instead.[38]

The idea of bringing C. H. Tanner may have originated in El Paso, rather than at the WFM's Denver headquarters. The El Paso CLU had already become aware of IWW activity in town, and it was decidedly hostile to the Wobblies.[39] The CLU may have felt an urgent need for help from WFM headquarters because the ASARCO strike was enhancing IWW prospects in El Paso.

Whether the inspiration for obtaining Tanner's services originated in El Paso or Denver, the WFM organizer sincerely tried to help the smelter workers. He reported back to Denver that he had told the strikers

> of this great trust, of its numerous smelters, its many mines. I told them that it was useless; they couldn't win. I told them they should have to be organized everywhere—at Santa Rita, at Hurley, at Hayden, at Ray—before they called the strike; that they were not a part of our union; that they could not expect support. I tried them. Their answer was: We will starve. We will never go back. We have the smelter closed.[40]

The WFM claimed to have signed up 413 men, and at El Paso a local was chartered.[41] El Paso Mill and Smelter Workers Local Number 78 survived the strike, albeit shakily, reporting forty members in 1914.[42] Fernando Palomarez, recruiting for the IWW, claimed that "the winning of this strike will be the means of organizing large unions of Mexicans all over Texas and the South," and signed up 200 men.[43] But there was no IWW local in El Paso when the strike ended.

The strike had begun to fail by late spring. The company had assiduously searched for strikebreakers, and had managed to assemble a work force of black Southerners, Mexican soldier detainees who had been driven across the international border, other Mexican workers who had been displaced from jobs on the railroad south of Ciudad Juarez, and white Texans.[44]

The Western Federation of Miners performed a final service for the El Paso strikers. C. H. Tanner said that he had found jobs elsewhere for the strikers, including some which actually paid higher wages with shorter hours. He did this through his connections with employment sources, especially railway agents, throughout the Southwest.[45]

Was the ASARCO workers' strike a significant part of the labor history of the Southwest? Mario T. García, in his history of the El Paso Mexican community, says that it was not. "Most Mexicans in El Paso and the Southwest," he wrote, "avoided labor agitation. Adjustment not resistance characterized their stay in the United States."[46] Certainly, there was no followup in El Paso itself. Many of the strikers were gone from ASARCO and its vicinity before the summer of 1913 was over. But Mexicans had been active participants in a series of small southwestern labor incidents, and in the big Clifton-Morenci-Metcalf strike of 1903. More Mexican working-class community activism developed in the Southwest soon after this strike, and still more developed in 1915. The El Paso strike had consequences. Some of the working people who took trains out of El Paso in mid-1913 may have detrained at the Arizona mining camps at which labor conflict next erupted. Perhaps this was the way in which labor consciousness spread.

Arizona's First World War-era labor activism began with a series of incidents at Ray. There had been distant preliminaries. Globe WFM Local Number 60 had been organizing at Ray, a few miles away from Globe, through early 1914. The Globe local was Anglo-Irish, and Ray was mostly Mexican and Spanish. The Globe men and the organizers from neighboring Miami seem to have planned to concentrate union clout in Arizona, beginning at Globe, Miami, and Ray. They then planned to use Arizona union power as a weapon to influence national WFM policy. The Globe and Miami campaign began with Globe Miners' Union "making a strenuous effort to organize the Globe and Ray districts," and requesting national financial aid to pay for its Ray organizer.[47]

Ray had originally been unionized in 1900, when its mines and work force were small. The WFM's Ray Local 102 disintegrated before 1907, when the modern Ray Consolidated Copper Mining Company began low-grade ore-stripping operations there.[48] Ray Consolidated attracted men from Hermosillo, Sonora, who began building a Mexican community near the Ray mine. The Mexican and Spanish American community was "Sonora," with a population of about 5,000 in 1914–15. "Barcelona," a Spanish immigrant miners' community which grew up next to Sonora, had over 1,000 people in 1914–15, and Ray itself, the company-controlled

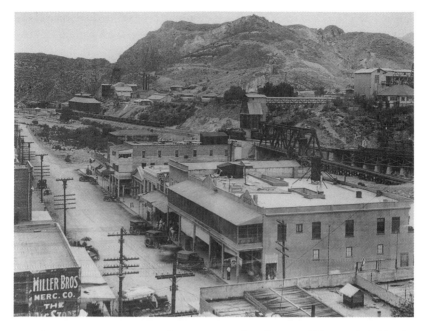

Ray, Arizona, 1919. Courtesy of Department of Archives and Manuscripts, Hayden Library, Arizona State University, Tempe.

townsite for Anglo and Irish workers also had about 1,000 people. The three communities were often collectively referred to as Ray.[49]

Ray, Barcelona, and Sonora were ethnically segregated, and the work forces around the mines and mills of both the Ray and Globe mining districts had had a history of mutual antipathy dating back to at least the 1890s. The Ray Consolidated Copper Company had been orchestrating an unremitting campaign of deliberate racist repression against the Ray-area Mexican and Spanish communities since 1910, when full-scale operations had begun there.[50]

Most of Ray was company-owned land, and the company dominated not only its own little fiefdom, but threatened residential dwellers and small businessmen on privately owned land abutting its property as well. Ray was heavily policed. Company officials were constantly ferreting out "troublemakers," including any businessmen or private citizens who were even marginally unfriendly to Guggenheim corporate interests, either silencing them or ejecting them from Ray by means of threats, beatings, and jail sentences. The Ray authorities, including a town "overseer," the justice of the peace, and the sheriff's department, assisted in the threats, beatings, and

139

jailings. The Ray justice of the peace, "Judge" French, bragged about his skill in defying lawyers, depriving defendants of attorneys, illegally trying felony cases, and securing convictions whenever he chose to do so. The "overseer," J. W. Dunlap, supervised and censored Ray social gatherings and entertainment. Dunlap refused to allow a circus to perform in Sonora, he said, because "times were hard [and] work [was] slack."[51]

Ray Consolidated used the proverbial carrot, rather than the stick, for some of its Anglo employees. When union recruiters came to speak to Hispanic workers, they were caught, threatened, and thrown out of the Ray area. Mexican WFM recruiters E. J. Moreno and Julio Mancillas were, respectively, jailed and beaten before being ejected from Ray.[52] But Ray Consolidated also knowingly employed Anglo union men: approximately one hundred WFM and skilled trades unionists, who, according to the Ray Consolidated superintendent, were "absolutely indispensable." Their union affiliation was overlooked: some among them were, in effect, company pets.[53] The copper company's management didn't hate unionists as such. Ray Consolidated management hated *Mexican and Spanish* unionists and the Anglo-Irish unionists who associated with them.

But not all Ray English-speaking men were pets. Many of the Anglo-Irish had something to hide. According to one estimate, at least half of the English-speaking men were refugees from previous western labor-management wars, some of them on mining-company blacklists and many of them working under assumed names. Ten-day men, migrant miners who were only incidental Ray residents, were also a significant fragment of the Anglo-Irish Ray population. Neither the partially blacklisted refugees nor the ten-day men were pets, and neither group had any particular reason to be anti-Hispanic.[54]

The major cause of Mexican and Spanish work-force hostility at Ray was not simply low pay or long hours. Most Hispanic workers were, after all, relatively new hires, who would not have taken mining work at stipulated wages only to reject the wages immediately thereafter. The real issue, again, was justicia and igualdad. E. J. Moreno "taunted the Mexicans for working for less than the whites, and agitated them to organize."[55] Organizing, for absolutely anything connected to the amelioration of workplace-related conditions, was absolutely forbidden to all Hispanic workers. The Mexicans' and Spaniards' sense of unfairness and inequality was most directly felt through their unequal wage status and their inability to join labor unions. Mutualistas, if they functioned at all at Ray, were no part of the problem. In fact, it is probable that Hispanic workers could have joined Ray-area mutualistas, if there were any to join, as long as the mutualistas remained essentially insignificant and irrelevant to workplace-related social concerns at Ray. Ray area Mexican and Spanish workers wanted wage equality, and perhaps just as much, they wanted the right to join labor unions.

Ray Consolidated's 1910–15 totalitarian control of Ray illustrates the virtual impossibility of workers' self-organization, or locally derived workers' autonomy in some places. The Ray-area workingmen initiated individual protests themselves, but they needed help. They solicited the assistance of outside unionists who might influence events in Ray from beyond the county line. The WFM was established in the Globe area, and Globe was only about one long day's walk away from Ray.

WFM men, probably based at Globe, began talking union at Ray in 1912, while Bingham Canyon and Ely-McGill were on strike. Although no explicit statement connects WFM organizers' activities in Ray with the Utah and Nevada strikes, it is most probable that the Ray and Hurley-Santa Rita proselytizing was part of Charles H. Moyer's dream of tying up production at Guggenheim mines all over the West as an extension of the Utah-Nevada strike effort. Utah and Nevada lapsed into sullen despondency after the 1912 strike. But at Ray, the Western Federation got more than it bargained for. Ray, Sonora, and Barcelona became a hornet's nest of social activism which would not subside until after the First World War.

Another series of events began at Ray with the theft of a horse during the summer of 1914. The August, 1914 trouble began as just another set of racial incidents. Pedro Smith, a half-Mexican, half-Anglo sometime miner and woodcutter, stole a horse in Ray, and was seen escaping into the mountains nearby. Smith was chased by Anglos, who were, in turn, ambushed and shot by Pedro Smith and two or more companions. In a sequence of related violence that lasted for over a week, a Mexican boss of an all-Mexican mine work crew was stabbed to death while he slept, several more men were shot, a town riot broke out, and some men were arrested. The number of deaths is uncertain, but it may have been as high as sixteen, all in some way related to the original horse theft. Four of the dead were Americans by local estimate, and twelve were Mexicans. Fighting in Ray and nearby Sonora, the segregated Mexican community adjacent to Ray, probably accounted for half the fatalities.[56] Mexican-Anglo antipathy ran deep, and the possibility for what Arizona newspapers commonly called "race war" was always close to the surface.[57]

Workplace issues in Ray were seen through the lens of Anglo-Mexican hostility, and workplace issues certainly triggered some of the August violence. One official of a small Ray-area copper mine remembered years later that the horse thief, Pedro Smith, had been one of many men laid off at the Ray mine when the price of copper dropped during the 1914 downturn. Smith was infuriated because he and his wife had not been paid for work already done. He was "known to have been in sympathy with the agitators among the Mexican miners thrown out of work by the shutting down of parts of the Ray mine." Shortly after the shutdown, a mine foreman was killed from ambush and mine equipment was dynamited. During the August violence, an *Arizona Republican* reporter whose sympathies were obviously not with the Mexicans guessed that many local Mexican men might join Pedro Smith and his brother in a "Mexican conspiracy" of mining workers. The alleged murderer of the crew boss during that August week was Librado Encinas, a miner whom the murdered man had fired from his job at the Ray Consolidated Copper Company in a dispute over work rules two weeks earlier. Two of the other Anglos killed in one of the affrays were Ray Consolidated timekeepers.[58]

This time, the Mexicans at Ray looked toward both Los Angeles and Denver for outside help and direction. They contacted Lázaro Gutiérrez de Lara in Los Angeles, and told him that the Ray Mexican community was being persecuted. Gutiérrez de Lara responded in the name of the Los Angeles "Mexican colony" by telegraphing Governor George W. P. Hunt of Arizona with a request for intervention. Hunt replied defensively, but promised to look into conditions at Ray. Gutiérrez de Lara was an old hand at southwestern organizing, and he had friends in both the national WFM and the Southern California IWW.[59] But it was Gutiérrez de Lara himself, rather than his former WFM associates, who originally drew Governor Hunt into the labor-management and ethnic community brushfire raging in Gila and Pinal counties. Globe, near Ray, was George W. P. Hunt's long-time home and his continuing power base. It was also the home of some of his most important Arizona friends and business associates. Governor Hunt and some of his Ray connections were about to help facilitate some real workplace changes in Ray, Globe, and even in Clifton-Morenci.

◄8►

LOS TRABAJADORES AND THE MIAMI MINERS' UNION COMBINE AT RAY, 1915

Copper labor-organizing activity began anew in Arizona in 1915. Arizona's 1915 strikes triggered a succession of labor-management wars across the entire western mining region between Butte and the Mexican border that continued through 1918 and permanently changed western working-class ethnic relations.

At the beginning of 1915, the price of copper was up, but Arizona wages were down. Wages had been cut 10 percent during the 1914 slump, and they were unchanged in early January 1915, when everything began to unravel in the new town of Miami, near Globe. On January 11, twenty-five boilermakers employed at the Inspiration Consolidated Copper Mining Company's Miami concentrator walked off their jobs in protest over the hiring of a nonunion employee. Within a few hours, angry carpenters, electricians, coppersmiths, trainmen, and others joined the walkout. No strike had yet been declared. On the following day, there was a single great issue: the concentrator men demanded the reinstatement of their old wage scale. Two days later, the WFM Miami Miners' Union voted overwhelmingly to strike for their old $3.75 daily wage. They joined the skilled concentrator workers in a big, combined strike.[1]

The 1915 Miami strike was quiet and well organized. Town merchants generally supported the strikers. The mines were shut down, and no strike-breaking was reported. Fifteen hundred men, Miami WFM members, mostly Anglo-Irish skilled tradesmen from the Miami concentrator, but also the Comité por Trabajadores en General [General Workers' Committee] all struck.[2]

Miami's *Silver Belt* newspaper reflected an awareness of the national copper-market conditions which would affect the strike's outcome. New York wholesale copper prices and copper output information were frequently reported. Management offered a sliding wage scale to be tied to the New York wholesale copper price, and the strikers, with considerable hesitation, accepted the new wage system on January 22.[3] After about two weeks, the Miami strike was over.

An Arizona Alien Labor Law was making its way through the federal court system in early 1915. The Alien Labor bill had been passed by the state legislature with considerable support from the Anglo-Irish populations of Globe and Miami. It required that copper-mining companies employ at least 80 percent American labor. The law was ruled unconstitutional in January, but its supporters anticipated either an appeal to a higher court, or a redrafting of the law to conform to federal strictures.[4]

Precisely which English-speaking men supported the Alien Labor Law is unclear. The law was seldom discussed openly in the Globe-Miami press by 1915. Governor Hunt favored the law: his Attorney-General, Wiley Jones, was preparing briefs arguing for its constitutionality in 1915. The Alien Labor Law was half of a two-pronged attack on management by labor. The big copper-mining companies would be forced to either dispense with their noncitizen employees, or else they would be facing Arizona union activism bolstered by the noncitizen employees' support. Some covert support for this essentially exclusionist legislation may have come from Arizona unionists for whom inclusion was only a fallback position. However, the Arizona Alien Law's proponents and the advocates of newly revived Arizona union activism may have been two distinct groups. Anti-immigrant men probably promoted the Alien Labor Law, and pro-immigrant unionists may have opposed it.

Governor George W. P. Hunt had investigated the August 1914 Ray murders and the general situation at Ray. He had concluded that Ray's Hispanic mining workers were justifiably angry because, as he had written in his diary, "the condition is bad there, Feudalism [*sic*]."[5] Globe-Miami unionists had been feeding the flames of worker hostility intermittently for at least three years, and by June, 1915, conditions at Ray had reached the boiling point.

Ray, Sonora, and Barcelona were angry communities—angry about the great Mexican-versus-Anglo social problem in its many forms. The Mexi-

Workers at the concentrator at Ray, approximately 1915. Courtesy of Arizona Historical Society, Tucson.

can Revolution, thundering away 150 miles to the south, had demonstrated an anti-gringo spirit at Cananea and at other towns near the international border.[6] In Ray, Barcelona, and Sonora, there were also the myriad slights and actual insults on commercial streets, at bars, and on the job. But most of all, there was the Mexican-versus-Anglo social problem as created, enforced, and perpetuated by the Ray Consolidated Copper Company. Ray Consolidated's influence was everywhere in the communities as well as on the job, and Ray Con's anti-Mexicanism had more than an ethnic-racial meaning. It was the anti-Mexicanism of the Anglo rich, middle class, and social elite visited upon the Mexican lower middle class and poor, and was consequently doubly potent.

In late June 1915, about a hundred Mexican men from the Ray communities had an organized, preplanned meeting. According to one report, they "were not out for more wages, but that [*sic*] they understood that the United States and Mexico were going to war and that they wanted to help Mexico fight the United States."[7] According to one observer, the meeting included "Mexican revolutionary agitators." Before they went home that night, the men at the meeting changed their minds. Instead of planning revolutionary action, they decided to strike against the Ray Consolidated Copper Company.[8]

The strike at Ray began on June 27. There were, eventually, issues of wages, conditions, and the right to organize, but the strike's origins suggest its true inspiration and meaning. The distant cause of the June meeting was the Ray murders and a series of small incidents. But the June meeting was also held to discuss the biggest, most basic issue in most Arizona mining areas: that of justice and Mexican-versus-Anglo equality. The activists in Ray chose a direct socioeconomic response over a vague political one. Their strike was initially not about wages, but about social change.

Some Ray strikers managed to communicate with Governor Hunt. They told him that

> they did not want to have anything at all to do with the WFM and that they wanted all the Americans run out of camp: that they didn't care what they had to work for, provided the Americans had to work for the same rate. Another report that gained credence among the Americans, inspired, no doubt, by the company, to the effect that the strike committee representing the strikers had notified the company that either they wanted the same wages as the Americans or else they wanted the Americans reduced to their scale . . . . the Americans, and when I say Americans I mean the Slavs, the Cornish and all those that were working, swallowed the bait, hook, line and all and the bitterness of the Americans against the strikers would have to be seen to be properly appreciated.[9]

The specific needs of the 1915 Arizona Mexican and Spanish strikers were very different from those of the strikers at Bingham Canyon in 1912. The Bingham Greeks, especially, struck against a labor agent. They, and to a lesser extent, the South Slavs and Italians as well, needed the organized countervailing power provided by the Miners' Union and its AFL affiliates in order to fight Leonidas Skliris and other padrones. The Bingham Greeks were generally men without families, very far from home, and lacking effective organization for any kind of social action. Also, some of them needed the sickness and death benefits which the Bingham Miners' Union could provide for them.[10]

Some of the Ray strikers had families with them and many of them were much closer to home. Labor agents did not cause major difficulties for them, and their Comité por Trabajadores led the strike effectively enough to have been dubbed "the Mexican union" by a portion of the Anglo press. Unlike the Bingham Greeks, the Ray Mexicans and other Hispanics had become effectively organized in time for the 1915 labor action.

Despite the real differences in the specific circumstances of the 1912 Utah-Nevada strikers and those at Ray in 1915, both struck against the same set of general conditions. All over the Central West and Southwest, foreign labor had been deliberately placed at a disadvantage by its mining-company employers, both at work and in the segregated residential communities nearby, and this massive, racially-ethnically defined disadvantage was the same equality, justice, and fairness issue for both Utah-Nevada and for Arizona workers.

Almost all of the Ray-area Mexican and Spanish workers walked off the job together, and Ray Consolidated closed some of its facilities shortly thereafter. The Anglo-Irish were about one-fourth of the total Ray work force. Most of them continued working, although about ten Anglo-Irish joined the strike. The English-speaking men's strike opponents held a mass meeting in opposition to the strike. Their meeting was similar to the October 3, 1912 meeting held by the McGill Anglo-Irish strike opposition. Many of those attending were non-Western Federation white-collar and skilled men, and perhaps others whose putative eligibility for participation was determined by their ethnicity, rather than their working-class status. The meeting participants voted almost unanimously to demand that the Western Federation of Miners disassociate itself from the Mexican and Spanish workers' strike.[11]

The Comité por Trabajadores was striking for the Miami miners' wage scale. The monetary difference was considerable. Miami muckers earned $3.75 daily, while Ray muckers were being paid $2.25. Miami machine miners earned $4.15; the same job paid $3.00 at Ray. The dispute was quickly enlarged to include other wage and hour issues, but also, the "right to speak freely on all subjects at meetings held at their own pleasure." Ray Consolidated offered substantially increased wages, but the Hispanic miners held out for the Miami scale.[12]

At Globe and Miami, Americanized English and Irish workers were an estimated 25 to 40 percent of the combined mine and mill work force in 1915. There were also some long-resident Cornish, Italians, Serbians, Spaniards, and Finns. A growing minority, but only a minority, of the Globe-Miami men were recently immigrated South Slavs and Mexicans.[13] The Ray strikers must have known that they had little chance of getting major wage increases quickly, but their demands had a broader meaning. What they were demanding was a sense of complete equality, as expressed through wage rates, with the Anglo-Irish workers in Globe and Miami.

They didn't get complete equality, of course. But when the strike ended, the Ray strikers had won 60¢ flat rate daily wage increases and several other concessions from Ray Consolidated. The strikers called it a victory.[14] Equality had not yet come, but they believed that the pendulum had begun to swing in their direction and ultimately they were right. As one correspondent explained it, "The Mexican and Spanish worker has now had a taste of power."[15]

The Comité functioned exactly like a union local. It organized picketing, posted notices, negotiated with management, and enforced strike discipline for an estimated 1,000–1,500 men.[16] Just as in 1903, Arizona Mexican and European immigrant workers managed to completely effect a combined strike without recourse to conventional unionization. Even though they were small and isolated, and even though gains and losses in western mining work tended to be impermanent, the Ray strikers had traveled far.

But achieving equality and justice was a process, and there was a long road yet ahead. To increase the impact of their strike and maximize their gains, the Comité por Trabajadores sought ancillary support. C. L. Salcido and Jose Miranda of Ray spoke to Governor Hunt in Miami, and he was willing to help.[17] They were also assisted by the WFM.

The search for help began early, when Ray Consolidated began to move against the strikers. Strikers were arrested, communication with areas outside Ray was partially cut off, and a contingent of armed guards began patrolling Sonora and Barcelona. Several strikers, including Refugio Neyera, M. de J. Minoz (or Muñoz), and A. N. Tribolet, were beaten, threatened with jail sentences, and then forcibly ejected from the strike area. All three men soon found their way to Miami.[18]

Miami's WFM Local 70 had invited the Governor to Miami. Hunt promptly announced that he was considering a declaration of martial law for Ray, in order to disarm the Ray Consolidated guard patrols. Miami men, both Anglo-Irish and Mexican and Hispanic, began raising money for the Ray strikers. Ray Consolidated, which had imported Utah Copper Company's Daniel Jackling to help coordinate strategy, delayed the striking employees' last paycheck, and encouraged local merchants to garnishee their wages. Local 70 hired a Phoenix attorney, F. C. Struckmeyer, to defend the strikers in court and help represent them in negotiations with the company.[19]

For a moment, during the last few days of the strike, there was a Western Federation of Miners' Ray union local, but consistent with its "no recognition" stand at Bingham, the Guggenheim-controlled Ray Consolidated demanded that the local be disbanded as a precondition for any strike settlement. The Ray strikers could derive no benefit from union recognition. Also, toward the end of the strike, they had begun receiving support from the Liga Protectora Latina, which had only recently been organized in Arizona. The WFM local's charter was returned to Denver headquarters.[20]

Immediately thereafter the Miami Miners' Union became the sponsor of Ray organized unionism. Two of MMU's leaders, George Powell, who was an ex-president of the local, and Henry S. McCluskey, its recently appointed regular organizer, along with Guy Miller, the Executive Board member who had been sent from national headquarters, worked in Ray during the strike. They encouraged many Ray strikers to join the locals in Miami and Globe. A few days after the Ray strike ended, the Miami local created a Ray branch, which soon converted itself into a revised version of the Ray Miners' Union. The resurrected RMU, with 634 new members, was still officially unrecognized by Ray Consolidated and its management.[21]

The Ray and Miami collaboration of mid-1915 was a very important new phenomenon in the Southwest. Yet all of its component parts were already there. Mexicans and other Hispanics, in combination with European immigrants, had managed the much larger Clifton-Morenci strike a dozen years earlier. Some Arizona Western Federation of Miners locals, when they had been under the control of pro-immigrant men, had recruited Mexican and other Hispanic mining workers as early as 1902. National WFM leadership, with national IWW help, had promoted a regional organizing campaign, intended to include immigrant and Mexican workers, in 1907. These earlier WFM southwestern organizing drives had a common feature. Pro-inclusion men created the pre-1912 union organizing drives in the Southwest, and used them as a means of supporting their political agenda. Mexicans, Spanish Americans, Italians, South Slavs, and Spaniards were recruited as a means of seizing control of individual locals. WFM radical ideology implicitly welcomed non-English-speaking participation in union locals, but Mexican and European immigrant workers had always been treated as a means to an end. The radicals' goal was the achievement of radical predominance, or sometimes the creation of a regionally unified work force. The immigrant and Hispanic men had never been simply welcomed, en masse, as equal, ordinary union members. But now, at Ray in 1915, that was about to change.

In Utah and Nevada, European immigrant workers were first accorded open access to WFM unionism several years before the big 1912 strikes. Although the Ely, McGill, and Bingham-area locals included European immigrants, most Nevada and Utah immigrants remained potentially organizable but unorganized. The 1912 strikes were the first combined local and national headquarters WFM organizing drive for massive immigrant recruitment in the lower intermountain West. The 1913 El Paso smelter strike also represented an important beginning. For the first time in the Southwest, WFM leadership had intervened to support a large Mexican workers' strike with no inclusionist or regional organizing issues at stake. When the Ray strike developed, all of the necessary antecedents for an even more ambitious WFM intervention had fallen into place.

Again, it is worth noting the absence of the Industrial Workers of the World in most of this. Some of the men who would later participate in IWW activism (in 1917) were already living in southwestern and central western mining communities, but there was generally no IWW for them to join. The Spokane, Washington, IWW organization and the many eastern outposts of IWW activity were certainly more consistently friendly to non-Anglo-Irish participation than were the western WFM leaders. But the eastern and West Coast men and women who organized for the Wobblies generally avoided Utah, Nevada, and the Southwest for their own complex reasons. When serious IWW recruitment began in the mining West in 1917, some of the IWW recruiters were former WFM men who had been there all along.

The existence of a set of conditions necessary for social change does not in itself explain the dynamics of social change. Sociological hypotheses cannot explain what happened to the English-speaking men and Mexicans and Spaniards in Ray. No egalitarian heroes, IWW or otherwise, appeared on the scene, nor did any of the major participants experience a change of heart, fit of conscience, or sudden conversion to kindness and racial-ethnic toleration.

The WFM's agents of change in 1915 were a group of "new" men, who were directing labor relations in a new town. Miami itself was just incorporating in 1915. The Globe, Miami, and Superior area was one of the fastest-growing copper regions in the United States. Many of the area's businesses and some of its copper-processing facilities were new. Miami's huge new International smelter had only been completed the month before the Ray strike began.[22]

George L. Powell was foremost among the new Miami leaders. Powell was typical of many Arizona WFM union officers in the early statehood years. He had not risen through the Arizona ranks, and in fact was not an Arizona miner at all, but a hired gun from farther north. He had attended a law school and a School of Mines. The first WFM office he held was probably that of delegate for Butte Mill and Smeltermen's Local Number 74 at the 1904 national convention. In 1912, as an activist, although perhaps not an officer in Bisbee Local 106, he had signed a joint letter of complaint about WFM national leadership which was published in the IWW's *Indus-*

trial Worker. George Powell was also an active member of Local Bisbee, one of the few functioning Socialist Party locals still left in Arizona after 1912. When Powell addressed a crowded SP meeting in mid-1913, even Arizona's Governor Hunt was in the audience. In 1914, George Powell sought election as WFM delegate to the AFL national convention, and lost. By 1915, he had already been, briefly, a vice-president of the Arizona State Federation of Labor and a president of Miami's Local 70. He had been living in Miami for less than two years.[23]

Henry S. McCluskey was an even more recent arrival in Miami. McCluskey was a precocious career unionist. While in his early twenties, he had become an international executive board member of a New York State glassworkers' union. He had come from New York to Arizona seeking a cure for life-threatening tuberculosis, arriving in Miami in February, 1915. By March, he had become Miami's new district organizer. McCluskey was twenty-seven years old in 1915.[24] Joe Bracken, another leader of the 1915 Miami Miners' Union, had been an outspoken Socialist and president of the Anaconda (near Butte) Mill and Smeltermen's Local 117 in 1903. He too had recently arrived in Miami.[25]

None of the Miami men who helped the Ray strikers in the spring of 1915 had ever been an active advocate of immigrant inclusion. None had played an active role in the WFM-IWW controversy of 1907–8. None, for that matter, spoke or understood Spanish. But theirs was a new, healthy union, closely associated with Globe Number 60. Since the virtual destruction of Butte's Local 1, the Globe and Miami locals combined constituted the strongest unionized area anywhere in Western Federation of Miners' jurisdiction.

The Globe Miners' Union was closely associated with Miami. The Globe local had been a passionate participant in nearly every kind of western miners' union trouble since its inception in 1896. Its members had been on both sides of the IWW issue and on both sides of the immigrant inclusion issue years earlier. Between 1907 and 1911, Globe's Local 60 had helped sponsor a Globe Socialist Party local, the nearby Pinto Creek WFM local, a Globe IWW local, and an Arizona State Union centered in Globe. The state union had had as many as three of its own organizers working in various parts of Arizona at any given moment. The Miners' Union Hall was the biggest building in Globe, and other Globe unions held their meetings there. In 1911, when the Arizona State Federation of Labor was begun, Globe Miners' Union men were among its first officers.[26] Number 60 was almost continually activist, but also almost continually factionally split. Its contractual relations with the Old Dominion Company were a hallmark of conservative and immigrant-exclusionist western unionism, but its immigrant-inclusionist and generally radical minority had come close to eliminating the contract in 1907, and had nearly forced immigrant inclusion in 1909.[27] By 1915, George W. P. Hunt, who had previously been one of Globe's leading businessmen and its mayor, and who still had strong ties to both organized labor and to some mining and real estate interests in Gila County, was the new state's governor.

The Globe Miner's Union was losing members in 1913, probably because of internal factional warfare. But while Globe was experiencing temporary loss of membership and money, the nearby Miami local had begun to prosper.[28]

The WFM's Miami men were obviously spoiling for the fight at Ray, but WFM national headquarters was a battered, bloodied operation by 1915, and not at all eager for more trouble in Arizona. Denver headquarters made no effort to enlist fraternal AFL support for the Ray strikers, as they had done for the Utah and Nevada strikers in 1912. However, Charles Moyer sent Guy Miller, and Miller was enthusiastic, not only about the chances for victory at Ray, but about prospects in other camps. Miller wrote to Moyer that "The men in many camps are certainly ready to organize, we should not stand back."[29] Charles Moyer gradually grew to fear the powerful new mass of WFM activity that was developing in Miami. He was also afraid that some of the men in Miami Number 70 were secret supporters of the IWW. Moyer complained that

> They [the Miami Miners' Union's leaders] seem to think that Miami is entitled to special attention, just why, I, of course, don't know. We also received a lengthy resolution [passed] by the Miami local addressed to the governor calling his attention to the situation at Ray and asking that he take immediate action to the end that constitutional rights may be had in that district, and a whole lot of other junk that we have heard so much of and which could naturally emanate from at least one of the committee which drafted the resolution, who was no other than Mr. J. L. Donnelly, the advance agent in that district of Haywood & Co. [the IWW].
>
> Now as to the Ray situation, I have my own opinion which I do not care to write, but if my conclusions as to the present status of things there are correct, then the sooner we send the Miami representatives home, put a charter in Ray and take charge of the situation ourselves the better we will be off. I have said in answer to the request for immediate action in Ray that I expected to be there in the course of a few days and advised holding the matter in abeyance until I arrived.[30]

At the end of October Moyer wrote that "Donnelly [John L. Donnelly, Acting Secretary of the Miami Local], as I anticipated, is mixing the dope in Miami, and Globe, and the helpless financial condition of the organization [the WFM] gives him a good strong hand."[31]

These exchanges marked a definite parting of the ways. Beginning in mid-summer 1915, the initiative for ethnic organizing passed from WFM national headquarters to Local 70's office in Miami. Thereafter, although national headquarters played a role in organizing activity, the Arizona WFM activists became the new leaders of western mining labor reformism.

The Miami men were building a powerful *regional* labor movement. The national WFM had an almost unbroken record of early-twentieth-century defeats. Its individual locals had obtained charters, and like the Ray and El Paso unions, had quickly surrendered them again. Arizona hard-rock miners were beginning to build a labor powerhouse, a strong and potentially durable western labor movement, independent of the vicissitudes of the Denver organization or its scattered locals.

The Miami men were opening the way to large-scale and long-lasting ethnic unionism. They even expected to see immigrant and Hispanic union local majorities, although they also hoped to supervise them. The Ray strike may not have been the most obvious first step, but Ray was a logical place to begin for several reasons. Mexican workers had proved themselves readily organizable; and Ray workers, in particular, were eager for organization. Mexican and other Hispanic workers were seldom tied to railroads and railroad-connected labor agents, as most of the workers in Bingham Canyon had been. Non-English-speaking men generally suffered inequitable treatment, but many of the Ray Mexicans and Spaniards embraced unionism itself as a partial remedy for it.

Previously, individual WFM locals had accepted ethnic inclusion, albeit for brief intervals. Conventional radicals had sought power in order to promote their agenda of extensive reform and revolutionary intent. The Miami men were not radicals; and their version of ethnic inclusion was regional, not local. The Miami Anglos' immediate objective was effective labor activism. They had come to understand that effective southwestern activism required Mexican and other Hispanic participation. With Hispanic participation, the Miami men could win victories in Arizona. Unlike their compatriots in most other WFM jurisdictions, the Miami men had begun to win.

◄ 9 ►

UNITY AND VICTORY
AT CLIFTON-MORENCI, 1915

Almost immediately after the Ray strike was settled, trouble began again at Clifton-Morenci. This time, more than ever before, external circumstances affected the pattern of labor unrest in Arizona.

Action began at Clifton-Morenci on September 1, 1915, with a general walkout of unskilled and semiskilled Spanish-surnamed workers. The strike effectively closed the mines and smelters for four months. It was settled with a written agreement on improved wages and working conditions which was approved by a U.S. government-appointed strike mediation team in early 1916.

Before the strike, there was organizing. El Club Cosmopolita, a new Mexican workers' group, was founded at Metcalf (near Morenci) in mid-July. Club Cosmopolita began with several hundred members. It was a probable labor-union surrogate, but was completely unaffiliated with either mutualista or WFM organizations.[1] The WFM's Guy Miller reported that "The Mexicans are alive and enthused throughout Arizona." He had "never seen such sentiment in favor of organization." Club Cosmopolita's membership became "immense" at the beginning and, Miller wrote, "the men have turned [into] organizers." Miller telegraphed union headquarters in mid-September, "Advise you wire L. Guiterrez DeLara 420 West Fourth Street, Los Angeles, organizers' terms and instruct him to come here."[2] Lázaro Gutiérrez de Lara arrived soon afterward.

Picketing at Clifton during the 1915–16 strike. Courtesy of Department of Archives and Manuscripts, Hayden Library, Arizona State University, Tempe.

There were about 5,000 unskilled and semiskilled mining workers at Clifton-Morenci-Metcalf in September 1914. Approximately 500 of them were Spanish and Italian immigrants. There were also at least 1,000 skilled English-speaking men at Clifton-Morenci. Mexican workers, of course, were the majority of all copper-company employees in the area. Most workers of all ethnicities struck, virtually in unison, on September 12.[3]

There was no strikebreaking in the 1915 Clifton-Morenci strike, partly because of the intervention of Arizona's Governor George W. P. Hunt. In a speech at Clifton on September 30, Hunt announced that "he would not tolerate any importation of hired thugs and gunmen in the capacity of strike-

Arizona's Governor George W. P. Hunt (center) visits Clifton-Morenci in 1915 to speak in support of the strikers. The man at left, identified on the photo as "Thomas Farrell, Mexican Orator," is probably Lázaro Gutiérrez de Lara. Courtesy of Arizona Historical Society (#55404).

breakers." Hunt also said that "when I come back to this community, and have to bring troops the principal officers of companies will be no different than the poorest Mexican they control."[4] An atmosphere of good cheer and work-force unity prevailed through most of the strike. Even the Anglo-Irish skilled men participated.

> On the evening of the 12th the craftsmen, realizing that for the first time in the history of the district, the Italians, Spaniards and Mexicans were united, called a meeting of the different crafts . . . and every craft unanimously voted to join the strike. For the first time the Americans were joining the foreigners in their struggle for organized labor.[5]

Even several Anglo-Irish foremen joined the WFM union locals and participated in the strike.[6] A carefully managed copper-company campaign to create ethnic animosities among the strikers failed, and the companies conceded wage and working-conditions improvements early in 1916.[7]

The informed U.S. reading public had only recently read about the Ludlow Massacre in the great Colorado Fuel and Iron Company strike of 1913–14. A detachment of Colorado state militia had wantonly attacked a strikers' tent settlement along the railroad tracks near CFI company property, deliberately setting the tents afire and killing over a dozen women and children. Vengeance was swift, and western Las Animas County became a battlefield. Miners, militia detachments, and company guards fought a small war in southern Colorado, until U.S. Army troops managed to separate them. When Arizona's Governor Hunt wrote about the Ray strike in his diary on June 30, 1915, the Ludlow Massacre was on his mind. "Some day there is going to be the cul. [Colorado] over again [sic] can it be averted," Hunt wrote.[8] Retrospective accounts of the Arizona strikes of 1915 credit Governor Hunt with having avoided "Ludlow Massacres."[9]

The Mexican Revolution was another tangible presence in 1915 Arizona. Action south of the border, and sometimes north of it, generated wild rumors and provided a forum for aroused anti-Mexican sentiment. In January, 1915, a "Plan of San Diego" surfaced in South Texas. It was a scheme for a general Tejano insurrection to retake the Southwest from the Anglos. A set of small raids into South Texas, originating in Mexico, began in association with the Plan.[10] The spring 1915 meeting at which the Ray strike was first organized may have begun as a Plan of San Diego meeting. Rumors were rife, especially in areas which were in close proximity to the international border. When the Clifton-Morenci strike began, a Tucson newspaper reported that

> Jesus Flores Magón, Mexican Socialist, is believed to be running a printing press somewhere in the southwest, turning out inflammatory literature for the purpose of preventing the recognition of Carranza at the Pan-American conference. No specimens of his handiwork have been seen in Tucson so far as known, but underground disturbances at Ray, Hayden and other camps are being investigated with the idea that he or his associates may be at the bottom of them.[11]

Some Anglo Arizonans awaited an imminent attack upon the Arizona State Prison at Florence, reportedly planned for mid-September, which was to be met with armed force. At the Clifton-Morenci strike area, the Arizona National Guard commander stationed nearly wrote to Governor Hunt on September 13, "I believe that owing to the local conditions and particularly to the relations with Mexico that Troops should be sent here immediately." A group of Morenci businessmen made the same request in mid-October.[12]

Privately held discussions in Ray and later in Clifton-Morenci repeatedly suggested that major violence could erupt momentarily. Since ultimately there was no significant violence in either strike, it seems possible that antilabor or anti-Mexican elements deliberately created mass hysteria, and that they were not actually anticipating large-scale labor-management warfare, or another Ludlow. Governor Hunt was definitely afraid of a Ludlow-like scenario. He feared that *management,* rather than Mexican workers, would initiate violence. The Ray strike offered a possible curtain-raiser. Several carloads of men had been brought into Ray, "where they were told they would be enlisted to fight the Mexican revolutionists." The Ray Consolidated Copper Company purchased large quantities of ammunition, and for a moment, another Ludlow seemed a possibility. The prolabor *Arizona Labor Journal* also reported that "the company has 25 or 30 men among the Mexicans who are attempting to persuade them to employ violent means to gain what they demand. It is figured that if they are successful in inciting violence the armed guards can kill off a few Mexicans and thus drive the others back to work with no further thought of organization."[13]

Not only Governor Hunt, but most other authorities, and the Miami local's George Powell as well, said that they were afraid of violence involving Mexicans, driven by Mexican demands for justicia and igualdad. Greenlee County deputy sheriff Fred Hill asked the governor to issue a proclamation to the Mexican population of Arizona which would state that "no matter what might happen between the U.S. and Mexico, every Mexican and his family would be given and guaranteed absolute protection."[14] The national guard commander recommended that his troops "be retained [near Morenci] . . . for a time" after the strike was over.[15]

George Powell addressed a State Federation of Labor meeting on October 6, with many Globe and Miami union men in attendance. Discussing trouble at Clifton-Morenci, Powell told the meeting that the WFM had offered vital assistance, because "only organization saved . . . [Clifton Morenci], that if it had not been organized, revolution would have resulted." Furthermore, Powell told the audience, he was afraid that soon "strikers will become uncontrollable." The general consensus at the meeting seemed to be that "there is increasing difficulty in controlling the Mexicans."[16] Powell was warning about "uncontrollable Mexicans" behind the Mexican workers' backs. Powell, the sheriff, the deputy sheriff, the governor, and the national guard commander were simultaneously warning English-speaking men about Mexicans and warning the Spanish-surnamed population about the Anglos and Irish. Claiming to be "in control" of the

Ray and Clifton-Morenci labor troubles, Powell and his allies in politics and law enforcement were actually holding a semiorganized contingent of anti-immigrant exclusionists at arms' length. During the Ray strike, a large group of Anglo-Irish petitioners, some of whom were members of labor unions, had demanded that Powell, Charles H. Tanner (who had also come to help organize in Arizona), and other WFM leaders "abandon their efforts to form an organization among the Mexicans." Powell and Tanner managed to derail the petition drive.[17]

The authorities and the Miami union men had a concerted plan for eliminating people whom they regarded as troublemakers. They averted their collective gaze when vocal strike opponents were forced out of Clifton, Morenci, and Metcalf. Helpful incarceration was also arranged there. Two Clifton antistrike Anglo unionists, Frank Tarbell and Harry McKenzie, were arrested for disturbing the peace, released on bond, and then reimprisoned. Some other English-speaking men fled the Clifton-Morenci area on their own initiative. A purported IWW plot there was crushed. Even the Morenci Catholic priest, who opposed the strike, was forced out of town. In Ray, a group of Mexicans tried to disrupt a Miami union meeting and were repulsed.[18]

One of the men forced out of Clifton-Morenci was J. Y. Ainsa, who the Arizona Copper Company employed to teach English to its Spanish-speaking workers. Ainsa tried to recruit men for the Alianza Hispano Americana, the oldest large mutual sickness-and-benefit society in Arizona. He made antistrike speeches, and apparently offered the Alianza as an alternative to WFM unionizing.[19] The other regionally organized mutualista, the Liga Protectora Latina, had been prostrike at Ray only a few months before the Clifton-Morenci strike began. The Liga may have even favored Governor Hunt in early 1915. But the Liga had been created to coordinate political opposition to the Claypool-Kinney Alien Labor Law, legislation which Hunt was surreptitiously promoting. In mid-1915, after Hunt signed an Alien Land Bill which was intended to bar landowning for Arizona aliens not intending to become citizens, the Liga turned against him.

The two large Mexican and Hispanic organizations in Arizona had become the opponents of both the governor and the WFM by 1915. The much larger unorganized Mexican and Hispanic mining-camp populations generally supported the strikes. Mexican and Hispanic labor activism in 1915 Arizona was not only unconnected to major mutualista organizing, it was diametrically opposed to the mutualistas.

The Ray and Clifton-Morenci strikes polarized and further factionalized both the English-speaking men and the Mexican and Hispanic communities in the mining areas.[20] Successful unionization had come to depend upon manipulation of the factional divisions within the two principal ethnic communities at the Arizona mines, mills, and smelters. Once again the Western Federation of Miners unionists were being presented with a tenuous opportunity to create a united working-class movement which could transcend ethnic divisiveness.

The Claypool-Kinney bill required that companies with more than five employees hire work forces that were at least 80 percent English-speaking.[21] It was obvious anti-immigrant legislation, and some of the same people who were assisting in Hispanic recruitment for labor unions were backing Claypool-Kinney. Its antecedents went back to 1896 and the Globe Miners' Union's exclusionist origins. The 1903 Eight Hour Law was, in part, anti-immigrant legislation. The 1909 Arizona Literacy Law and some of the phrasing in the proposed 1910 state constitution, together with the updated Kinney Bill of 1914, were all intended to check recent immigrants' employment in Arizona. The drive for some kind of 80 percent law, that is, for a law limiting an employer to a maximum 20 percent non-English-speaking work force, continued unabated through 1918. Accompanying it, by 1918, was the resurrected demand that some southwestern mining communities be made into "all American camps."[22]

Governor Hunt proclaimed the Arizona Alien Law on December 14, 1914. Several days later, Hunt was agreeing with a union-connected attorney that further public discussion of the law should be avoided. Hunt was willing to defend the law in private, but refused a request to write about it for a New York City newspaper. Hunt's Attorney-General was Wiley Jones, whose given name matched his political proclivities.[23] Throughout 1915, while Mexican workers cheered for Governor Hunt, Jones fought for 80 percent legislation. In January, he "defended the act as necessary to the state's police powers over dangerous gatherings." In September he claimed that national welfare and even national preservation—because Arizona copper, after all, was war materiel—required the passage and enforcement of the law. By including a population count of all of the Anglo-Irish, native-born Hispanics, Navajos, Pima, and Papago who lived in counties far away from the big mines, Jones was able to declare that the law was essentially unobjectionable, because there was a "relatively small number of aliens in the state."[24]

Hunt and his Arizona allies were apparently undeterred by warnings from U.S. Secretary of Labor William Wilson, Secretary of State William Jennings Bryan, and British and Italian diplomats about the mendaciousness of the law.[25] Arizona's Senator Henry Ashurst repeated the Hunt-

Recruiting Mexican mining workers into the Western Federation of Miners, 1916. This photo, taken at Morenci during the middle of the Clifton-Morenci strike, shows Henry S. McCluskey, the Miami Miners' Union's principal organizer (seated at table, left), and Luis Soto, Clifton-Morenci union officer and organizer (facing the typewriter on the table, right), surrounded by union supporters and potential recruits. Courtesy of Department of Archives and Manuscripts, Hayden Library, Arizona State University, Tempe.

Wiley Jones line in a preparedness speech to a Navy League luncheon on October 14, 1915. Dangerous aliens, said Ashurst, "are driving out the healthy patriotic American laborer."[26]

Immigrant exclusion, of course, was bigger and older than Arizona. Nevada had passed its major anti-alien legislation in 1914, requiring that mining corporations employ English-speaking underground miners.[27] In Colorado, the Ludlow Massacre aroused not only the socially conscious, but the xenophobic as well. Anti-immigrant racist verbiage reportedly increased because of Ludlow, and it "darkened the cloud of animosity that [Colorado] Slavic immigrants had lived under throughout the opening decades of this century."[28]

Speakers at Socialist Party meetings, while SP locals were still affiliated with WFM locals in some western mining districts, frequently voiced antiforeign sentiments. The Socialists urged organized labor to extend its hand to the unorganized and to abolish "all the onerous conditions of membership and artificial restrictions."[29] But, at the same time, some Socialists bemoaned the "low moral and intellectual standards of the foreigners from these sections of Europe," and they were unhappy about "Mexican peon labor."[30] Within the Western Federation itself, convention delegates no longer encouraged one another to "organize the Mexicans" as they had done in 1903. President Moyer, who had described Mexicans as "greasers" in 1903, announced at the 1911 national convention that organizing of Mexicans had just begun at Mogollon, New Mexico. However, almost a decade after the inclusion of Mexican workers in some Arizona locals, Moyer added that it was time to "educate and organize these people," because "it is reasonable to believe that they can be brought into the labor movement of the United States." A 1914 report to the WFM national convention, signed by a committee which included Yanco Terzich, a long-time ethnic organizer, and Guy Miller, was still calling unorganized workers a "menace."[31]

The Socialist Party did not help the WFM's organizing efforts among unskilled non-Anglo-Irish mining workers. The national Socialist Party received requests for Greek and Spanish publications, but had nothing to offer.[32] The Miami stalwarts who began proselytizing at Ray in 1914 probably spoke only English. On several occasions, Arizona WFM leaders were unable to locate Spanish-speaking men when they needed them. There was only one bilingual liaison between the 634-member, Spanish-speaking Ray Branch and the Miami Miners' Union in July, 1915; and in December, only one of the thirteen elected officers of the parent union, Miami Number 70, was Mexican. He was E. J. Moreno, who had recently arrived at Miami after being driven out of Ray. Moreno was elected the "Spanish conductor" of the Miami union. At the beginning of the Clifton-Morenci strike, the Miami leadership asked WFM national headquarters to send out Spanish-speaking organizers. Charles Moyer understandably replied that "If the men of Arizona are not in touch with available Spanish-speaking men, I hardly know where we will go to find them."[33] During the following year (1916) the Miami Miners' Union's George Powell and Henry McCluskey proposed that the WFM establish a Spanish-language newspaper.[34]

The long years of regional and national WFM anti-immigrant and anti-Hispanic behavior were easy enough to remember. Simple Anglo-Irish disinterest, insensitivity, and even hostility had been amply demonstrated. Most historians of working-class, Progressive Era America conclude that organized AFL labor was intolerant of ethnic-racial minority workers, and consequently unwilling and unable to organize them. Gwendolyn Mink calls "racial argument" the "dominant way in which labor expressed opposition to immigration." Racial nativism, according to Mink, was a "driving force behind union politics." Mink's account only takes cognizance of occasional instances of ethnic organizing by WFM unions, and she treats those as exceptions. She categorizes pre-1920 AFL labor union activity in general as exclusionist.[35] Similarly, Aileen S. Kraditor, in her book *The Radical Persuasion,* claimed that exclusionism was the predominant Socialist Party position on immigration and immigrant workers. Kraditor quoted Guy Miller, speaking at the Socialists' 1910 convention, as opposing "the forced mingling of people of different races," and she called Miller an exclusionist.[36]

Historians generally conflate and even confuse perceived WFM nativism with the racial nativism of the WFM's AFL associates; because after 1911, the WFM was, for the second time in its institutional career, an AFL union. Also, AFL racial nativism is easy to demonstrate because it can be contrasted with perceived contemporaneous IWW egalitarianism. In Philip S. Foner's working-class studies, the AFL and IWW appear to be complete opposites. The IWW "demanded that all workingmen be considered equal and united in a common cause," according to Foner. Practically alone, the IWW organized among Chinese, Japanese, and Mexican workers, Foner wrote.[37] Foner's interpretation of IWW racial-ethnic ideology is accepted by most current historians, but his interpretation does not apply to western states' and territories' working-class people before 1917. The IWW either did not participate, or, as in both the 1913 El Paso ASARCO strike and the Ray strike, it was only a minor player. The Wobblies were essentially irrelevant to most Utah and southwestern copper camp organizing from 1905 (when the IWW began) all the way to 1917. Fernando Velarde, Fernando Palomarez, and Frank Little had tried and failed to organize in the Southwest during 1905–17.[38] Most often, IWW national leadership either ignored or deliberately avoided organizing among Greeks, South Slavs, Spaniards, Mexicans, and Spanish Americans in western mining areas. In the Clifton-Morenci district, there was deliberate avoidance. In an exculpatory statement written several months after the strike at Clifton-Morenci had ended, an IWW spokesman explained editorially to Mexican workers that the Wobblies had avoided the strike for the miners' own good:

> Then it was that many mining workers of Morenci asked for the IWW, but the IWW, knowing that to go there in that moment would precipitate the most tremendous defeat for the miners, because two factions would have been formed; one accepting the IWW and the others not having clear judgement, would have followed the "Pie Cards" of the A.F. of L. who might have led them to return to work in order to break the strike, trying thus to bring the IWW into disrepute as they have done in other parts of

the country; now you see that the IWW are not disorganizers nor so fool-
ish or stupid as they were considered.[39]

In southwestern hard-rock miners' union organizing work, and especially
in racial-ethnic minority organizing before 1917, the WFM was practically
the only game in town.

Guy Miller was not an exclusionist as the term is used in this account,
and of course, generalizing about WFM exclusionist behavior is meaning-
less. The conventional interpretation of southwestern and Utah and Nevada
unionizing would dichotomize working-class organizing into a clash between the forces of a "good" IWW and an "evil" AFL. The WFM has been
adjudged guilty of nativism, especially after 1911, because it had become
an AFL union.

A group of men with previous experience as organizers of immigrants,
some of whom had been previously associated with inclusion, came to
Globe-Miami, Ray, and Clifton-Morenci in 1915 and early 1916. There
were, of course, Guy Miller, George Powell and Henry McCluskey; also
A. N. Tribolet and E. J. Moreno, who had begun working at Ray and had
then moved on to Clifton-Morenci. Ed Crough, who had worked against
Globe Number 60's conservative contract with the Old Dominion Company came to the Clifton area, too. Charles Tanner, who had worked hard
for the ASARCO strike in El Paso in 1913 became the secretary of Globe
Number 60 at midyear, and helped with organizing work at Ray. W. F.
Burleson, who had been organizing Greeks into the Bingham Miners'
Union several years earlier, and E. A. Redwanz, who had been the McGill
local's financial secretary and who was a prominent participant in the 1912
Ely-McGill strike, both came to Arizona. Burleson replaced George Powell
at Ray when Powell went on to Clifton-Morenci, and Redwanz worked at
both Miami and Ray. These men, except for Tribolet and Moreno, were
non-Hispanic and were experienced WFM unionists. Most were also experienced ethnic organizers. Most also, except for Tribolet, Moreno, and perhaps Tanner, were long-time westerners, but had only recently arrived in
Arizona.[40]

Lázaro Gutiérrez de Lara joined the Arizona action during the Ray murder episodes of 1914, and, as mentioned above, he returned to the Clifton
District during the strike there. Juan Rico came from South Texas to play a
subliminal organizing role in the Clifton-Morenci strike.[41] Both Rico and
Gutiérrez de Lara were drawn to Arizona by the opportunity for creating
coherent organizational unity among the Mexican and other Hispanic
workers, and both men were leery of the American Federation of Labor's

role in the strikes. Both the Mexican activists subsequently sided with the Miami men in their destructive quarrel with WFM national headquarters in Denver. Juan Rico had already brushed with AFL racial exclusion in San Antonio. As he later explained it, he had intended to join the AFL Typographer's Union in San Antonio in 1914, but he was told that "labor organizations could not and would not admit us to their ranks due to the fact that we were not white men." Both Gutiérrez de Lara and Rico worked with Anglo-Irish unionists in the name of working-class unity, although both preferred association with WFM, rather than general AFL unionism. Tomás Martínez and Fernando Velarde, based in Los Angeles, represented a further extension of Mexican and Mexican American leadership. As IWW members, they were unwilling to associate with Governor Hunt, the Greenlee County sheriff, or the AFL, and although they probably approved of the 1915 Arizona strikes, they were unable or unwilling to participate in them.[42]

The sides in the complex Clifton-Morenci strike were clear enough to the participants. By mid-strike, in November 1915, management's side included J. Y. Ainsa and some Mexican and Spanish American business and professional men, probably both the Liga Protectora Latina and the Alianza Hispano Americana, and some conservative Anglo-Irish unionists, including skilled crafts and railroad men. On the striking workers' side were at least two independent Mexican activists, both of whom had political connections to the Mexican Revolution itself, most of the Mexican, Spanish American, and Spanish community, most of the local organized Anglos and Irish, especially including the Anglo-Irish WFM men led by pro-inclusionists, the Arizona State branch of the American Federation of Labor, and the relevant Arizona authorities—sheriff, National Guard commander, and governor. The IWW and the few remaining Italian workers generally avoided both sides. The Clifton-Morenci strike was an organizing success because of the successful conjunction of WFM ethnic-inclusionist activists and Mexican activists.

There is no literature of racial-ethnic inclusion. U.S. social and working-class histories do not recognize a general *process* of inclusion. Instead, each historian who encounters the phenomenon explains it in his or her own particular, empirical terms. There are, for instance, several recent, thorough studies of black and white coal miners and muckers in eastern U.S. coalfield regions which, in effect, finesse the issue of inclusionary process. The earliest general essay on race issues in the coalfield work force was Herbert Gutman's "The Negro and the United Mine Workers of America." Gutman explained that racial and ethnic inclusion was promoted because it strengthened the United Mine Workers, and that basically decent and tolerant men converted the coalfield labor force to racial tolerance.[43] More recent studies are more detailed, but similar. David Alan Corbin wrote that the early-twentieth-century West Virginia coal companies practically decreed their workers' housing and living arrangements, and that the coal companies mandated both nonsegregated community life and nonsegregated working conditions. Italian immigrants, African Americans, and white Anglo-Americans were all treated equally, although often badly. The coal companies, Corbin wrote, broke down culturally determined behavior, and racial inclusion necessarily resulted.[44] More recently, Joe William Trotter, Jr., has described communities shaped by coal company "welfare capitalism," and blacks and whites shoved into close contact with one another at work. Returning to Gutman's emphasis on working-class "good guys," Trotter maintains that eventually "black and white miners developed mutual loyalties, and sometimes their commitment to each other was demonstrated in dramatic ways."[45] Ronald L. Lewis's explanation similarly attributes coal miners' inclusion to physical proximity. Lewis quotes an 1870s white Alabama miner who explained that "we who are compelled to work side by side with [African American miners] must drop our prejudice and bigotry."[46] Although all four accounts (including Gutman's) argue that racism was supplanted by multiracial working-class consciousness, there are differences. Corbin awarded the companies partial credit for breaking down racial barriers, although he avoided suggesting corporate altruism. Trotter offers the laurels to the miners themselves, rather than to the coal companies, and does suggest altruism. In his account, the miners heroically discarded their racist cultural baggage and became buddies. Lewis, like Corbin, avoids the altruism, but suggests that somehow, within a single generation, the men who had been forced to associate with one another began to accept "equality as a democratic ideal."[47]

Except for Corbin's, these coal-camp studies conclude that racial toleration began on the job. All four studies claim the coal companies forced their miners and muckers to see the light (so to speak), and either a little natural altruism or something like it did the rest of the job. This mode of explanation conceals more than it elucidates. The story of eastern coal-town altruism discovered during moments of shared adversity substitutes for an explanation of the process of inclusion. But there is also a scatteration of other, comparable studies which deny both the altruism and the democratic ideal.

The UMWA was an early AFL union, and some of its officers were closely associated with WFM leadership and in some cases, with WFM locals. But early UMWA interracial democracy in the eastern coalfields had no apparent effect upon AFL black-white relations in nearby Pittsburgh, where black "hoisting engineers" were accepted into an otherwise white building-trades union local as part of a repulsive ruse which cost them their jobs. Thereafter, building-trades racism continued unabated in Pittsburgh.[48] Anti-Asian UMWA racism also continued unabated. Alexander Saxton's book *Indispensable Enemy* describes western states' anti-Asian union sentiment in the same terms as Lewis uses to explain pro-African American sentiment in the eastern coalfields. Both AFL racism and UMWA anti-racism are described as being useful adjuncts for enhancing union growth. Saxton's account seems to negate the notion that the UMWA had adopted "equality as a democratic ideal" at the same moment that equality had been partially accomplished in the East.[49]

Western ethnic and racial relations changed, at least as much as relations in the East and South did in the early twentieth century. But historians describe increased *western* labor union toleration as pragmatic, limited, and anything but democratic. European immigrants were included in Denver-area WFM locals only because mining management's manipulation of ethnic-racial divisiveness forced the Western Federationists to accept immigrants, according to David Thomas Brundage.[50] Japanese and Chinese immigrant coal miners were accepted into southern Wyoming UMWA locals in 1907 mainly because, "If the newly established locals had denied them membership, they would have undermined their own effectiveness." Also, access to UMWA unionism in southern Wyoming was probably a unique local phenomenon, according to Yuji Ichioka, in his "Asian Immigrant Coal Miners and the United Mine Workers of America."[51] Ichioka argues that UMWA national leadership was not racially tolerant, at least insofar as Asians were concerned, and that acceptance of Asians in Wyoming cannot be associated with class consciousness. Instead, it was the result of nonideological pragmatism in a special situation.[52] The works of Saxton, Brundage, and Ichioka all deny the possibility that an inclusionist *process* was operating throughout the West during the early twentieth century. The weight of their evidence suggests that inclusion was an exceptional, rather than a common phenomenon, and that class consciousness was not a component of western AFL unionism.

But ethnically tolerant inclusion was the actual basis for the events in 1915 Arizona, and the results of the Arizona strikes rippled across the entire U.S. labor movement thereafter. The union organizers and Mexican activists from Utah, Nevada, Arizona, Texas, California, and Mexico began to speak in terms of an inclusionist ideal, although Anglo-Irish-Americans and Mexicans and other Hispanics expressed it in different terms. To the

Mexican and Hispanic American strikers, it was justicia, a readjusting of "Justice's unbalanced scales," after "30 years of oppression."[53] It also included as a newfound disinclination for deferential behavior. When Mexican and other Hispanic women and girls marched through the streets of Morenci in support of their strike, their extraordinarily assertive behavior drew, for the first time, genuine praise from the Anglo press. An *Arizona Labor Journal* editorial announced that the Ray strike had demonstrated to all unionists that "the Mexicans, whom we are always ready to condemn, were the ones who were demanding better pay and better conditions." "Everywhere the Mexican population is learning that it has been made a goat," and the editor implied that things were changing.[54] The Mexican and other Hispanic strikers' attitudes, according to a Tucson editorial, were not the result of recent labor organizing, but rather "a thing of long, slow growth. An agent of the Western Federation of Miners merely touched the match."[55] An Anglo strike observer wrote to the editor of a Clifton newspaper that "the people who were formerly talking in whispers and in guarded private conversations are now standing on their feet, looking the companies squarely in the eye and talking aloud."[56]

Strikers and strike supporters of the various ethnicities interacted throughout the Clifton-Morenci strike. A feeling of working-class unanimity pervaded the Clifton district. But Mexican and other Hispanic strikers also had a special, politically conditioned view of the strike which was uniquely their own. An important part of the Mexican and general Hispanic perspective, according to a federal mediation commission report in 1917, was "their political beliefs and the ideas of what they term their conception of the social struggle."[57]

The Clifton-Morenci strikers who were Anglo and Irish did not share these political beliefs. The English-speaking men expressed their own notions of ethnic inclusion in terms of racial egalitarianism. Anglo-Irish strike participants declared repeatedly that there was an unbroken history of racial discrimination in the Clifton district and that they intended to change it. They wanted the strike to create a new general racial equality. The U.S. Commissioners of Conciliation tried to arrange a strike settlement in which there was to be, explicitly, "elimination of race prejudices, and the development of the solidarity of brotherhood among the workmen." Also, there was to be a 5 to 20 percent wage increase specifically for "Mexicans and Spaniards."[58]

An important shift toward ethnic-racial inclusion had occurred; of that there was no doubt. But the question of altruism must be raised once again. Did bad men become good, or at least, better? Did the beneficent sunlight of egalitarianism suddenly penetrate the clouds and change all below with its warming rays? If not, why did racist unionism begin to diminish?

Part of the answer lies in the murky, but important set of demographic changes which had occurred at Clifton, Morenci, and Metcalf.

Before the adoption of the 1903 eight-hour law, most unskilled Clifton-Morenci mine, mill, and smelter workers' wages had ranged from $2.00 to $3.00 a day.[59] During mid-1915, most of the miners, muckers, and other mine laborers were still working at approximately the wage rates of early 1903. But the unskilled men in the concentrating, smelting, and refining departments were working only seven hours in mid-1915. Most 1903 men were being paid for ten hours' work each day, so the 1915 men were earning less than the 1903 workers had earned. Unskilled copper-processing jobs which had paid $3.00 in May 1903 paid $2.60 twelve years later, despite rising prices.[60] Both in 1903 and in 1915, only an infinitesimal proportion of the Spanish-surnamed workers earned over 40¢ an hour in the mines, although more Italians and Anglo-Irish had reached the 40¢ level by 1915.[61] In essence, wages for the 1915 Spanish-surnamed unskilled copper workers, who were the unskilled majority, were as low or lower than those of the 1903 Spanish-surnamed copper workers.

Payroll deductions decreased the unskilled men's take-home pay still further. The Clifton-Morenci copper companies deducted a hospital fee, a water fee, an "accident insurance" fee, a school tax, and in some instances, a "toilet key" fee from their employees' take-home pay.[62] Total deductions were higher for married men than for single men. Total deductions in 1903 were typically $3.75 a month for single men, and $4.25 for married men. By 1915, the deductions had risen to $4.30 and $5.50, respectively. The 1915 deductions had become the equivalent of more than two days' pay at typical unskilled wage rates, or about 7 percent of 1915 unskilled workers' monthly paychecks. Married men were surrendering half a day's pay more in 1915 than comparable workers had lost in 1903.[63] Some of the Clifton-Morenci men were very well aware that their take-home pay was decreasing.[64]

Also, as mentioned above, the workday varied in length, depending upon the companies' needs. During the first six months of 1915, an unskilled worker who worked on every available working day worked fewer total hours, at about the same hourly rate, than his counterpart had worked in 1903. The size of a 1915 workingman's take-home paycheck varied from department to department, even when pay rates were constant.[65] (There were, of course, fewer working days and shorter hours offered during periods of economic downturn.)

The 1915 employees were trying hard, probably much harder than their predecessors had, to save money. For one thing, they were less transient. The 1915 persistence rate was far above the 1903 rate, and well above rates reported for many contemporaneous unskilled American workers nationally.[66] Job absenteeism was also far less frequent than it had been in 1903.[67] Furthermore, the Spanish-surnamed portion of the 1915 unskilled labor force had a completely different pattern of company store use than the 1903 work force had had. Because they purchased less from the company store, the 1915 men were typically taking home 50 to 60 percent of their remaining pay, whereas the 1903 Spanish-surnamed workers had been keeping 35 to 40 percent of theirs.[68] The Spanish-surnamed portion of the 1915 Clifton-Morenci unskilled labor force was much more effectively retaining its total take-home pay compared to its 1903 counterpart. But the copper companies' wage policy was making it ever more difficult for the 1915 workers to save money.

Ethnic wage-and-job differentials, of course, still existed. In 1903, Italian and Spanish-surnamed miners, mine laborers, and mine timbermen received less pay than did Anglo-Irish who held the same jobs. Also, there were neither Italian, Mexican, nor Spanish American apprentices for skilled jobs in the processing plants in 1903. Only a handful of Spanish-surnamed and Italian employees held skilled or marginally supervisory jobs in 1903, and some of the men who had those jobs were labor recruiters.[69]

The 1915 job distribution was substantially unchanged. The Detroit Copper Mining Company no longer hired English-speaking men as laborers or miners. In fact, the only job title which included substantial numbers of all three major ethnic groups—Italians, Spanish-surnamed workers, and Anglo-Irish-Americans—was that of timberman, and timbermen were still being paid at varying wage rates based upon their ethnicity. Some Italians clearly had better jobs in 1915; Spanish-surnamed workers did not. There were still no Italian or Spanish-surnamed skilled-trades apprentices. In two instances, Spanish-surnamed men were being employed as machinists, along with Anglo-Irish, but the company listed them as Mexican machinists, and paid them less.[70] At the Arizona Copper Mining Company some job titles were being paid at a bewildering variety of wage rates. The wage rates apparently depended upon the whims of foremen, but the general discriminatory pattern still held. Anglo-Irish were generally paid more than Mexicans and other Hispanics.[71] Foremen were accused of being extortionate, and "the charge is also made that a short time before the strike was called the foremen were urged by the managers to make the men do in six days what they had been accomplishing in seven. The foremen were to receive seven days pay for six days work, but the men were to do more work for less money."[72]

About half of the known strike leaders were ethnically English or Irish, which reflects both the extent of Anglo-Irish participation in the strike and the fact of WFM (especially Globe-Miami) influence upon it.[73] Most English-speaking workers, of course, were skilled. But most of the Spanish-surnamed employees' leaders were also semiskilled and skilled men. The known leaders of both groups were miners (three), furnacemen (two, each earning $37^1/_2$¢ an hour), one carpenter, one timberman, and one mechanical department employee (who earned 54¢ an hour). No known strike leaders were laborers. At least one strike leader had a wife and children, and at least two did not.[74] Four of the strike leaders are known to have owned houses and lots worth in excess of $200 each, but there is no certainty that the other leaders owned real property at Clifton-Morenci.[75] The 1915 strike leaders included both moderately successful and exceptionally successful working men; but they were men who had not advanced to supervisory status, and who had not attained the very highest wage rates. They were, collectively, a more privileged group of men than the Clifton-Morenci-Metcalf leaders of 1903 or the Bingham leaders of 1912 had been.

The 1915 Clifton-Morenci work force was new. Most of the Mexican and Spanish workers were relatively recent immigrants, just as many of the 1903 strike participants had been. However, compared to earlier populations, the 1915 Spanish-surnamed men were more likely to have acquired property, saved their wages, and probably, to have had families. But the history of the wage and job offerings at the Arizona and Detroit companies in Clifton-Morenci was regressive. The Spanish, Mexican, and Spanish American work force was managing to acquire both property and savings, but it was doing so under increasingly adverse circumstances.

Although job discrimination was as bad as ever, there was one significant difference. By 1915, only timbermen could still make direct comparisons of their jobs and wages throughout the mines and conclude that the Detroit Company was basing their pay on perceived ethnicity. All other job categories had been made totally, ethnically segregated, so that jobs held by Mexicans and Spanish Americans were qualitatively different from those held by English-speaking men. For that reason, ironically enough, the chances for the success of a combined ethnic society-and-union drive to end racial discrimination had never been better. Clifton-Morenci Mexican, Spanish, and Spanish American workers, with a few exceptions, no longer had reason to demand *wage* equality with the Anglo-Irish at the Detroit Company mines, because they no longer had *job* equality with them. Instead, the Spanish-surnamed men were pushed toward demanding the Miami scale—that is, toward demanding wages comparable with those offered for their own jobs in better-paying western mining areas. The tendency was clear: at least at the Detroit Company, Mexicans and other Hispanics were less likely than ever to *replace* Anglo-Irish. Also, regardless of whether or not the Claypool-Kinney 80 percent law ever passed, the Anglo-Irish were less likely than ever to *replace* low-status Mexican and other Hispanic workers. On-the-job racial-ethnic inclusion had been rendered harmless, and thus desirable for both Hispanics and Anglo-Irish. What remained as prevalent as ever, virtually unchanged since the Globe Miners' Union had been founded two decades earlier, was management-induced, job-connected racial-ethnic unfairness. In addition, Clifton-Morenci wages were lower than ever, relative to rising living costs. The overwhelming sense of racial-ethnic discrimination engendered by these conditions was what the 1915 inclusionists intended to change.

Clifton-Morenci's 1915 wage-and-job configuration, while different from the equally discriminatory pattern of 1903, was even more blatantly racist. Copper-company management was gradually making it increasingly difficult for Hispanic workers to earn a living and to derive benefit from personal thrift and residential stability, even as it increasingly segregated them in lower-status jobs. The copper companies had finally contrived to create such a vast gap between Anglo-Irish and Hispanic workers that the two groups had ceased to be direct competitors for jobs and wages in any meaningful way. But, because of management's wage and job policy changes, both ethnic groups now had a real identity of interest. By 1915, Hispanic workers' most accessible means to wage and job improvement really was the Miami wage, and the fastest route to the Miami wage was, for this one brief moment, WFM unionism. The Anglo-Irish unionists saw things in much the same way, but sought a different goal from ethnic-inclusive unionism. The goal which the Arizona WFM men were aiming at was huge, obvious, but hitherto elusive: the chance for stable, growing, powerful mining-camp unionism, which the numerical and financial support of a large new group of recruits could give them.

Ethnic-racial inclusionists had become the WFM's majority at the big Globe-Miami locals in Arizona; and, at both Ray and Clifton-Morenci in 1915, they seized power. Using their tactical control of these big mining districts, and also utilizing their solid State Federation of Labor connections with Arizona AFL crafts unionists, the Globe-Miami men briefly dominated the entire Arizona AFL. The men from Globe and Miami had achieved the goal to which President Charles Moyer in Denver headquarters had aspired in vain. They had completely integrated their portion of the WFM into an entire statewide organized-labor movement. They had, at last, the set of effective AFL connections which could win strikes.

The Arizona inclusionist majority, the Globe-Miami men and their allies, had left the pre-1903 version of WFM radicalism far behind. The IWW's 1915–16 western radicalism resembled that of the 1894–1903 WFM. It resembled the radicalism of Coeur d'Alene, Cripple Creek, and Leadville. The new, 1915 Arizona version of working-class *activism,* if not radicalism, emphasized immediate working-class power. Using the leverage provided by their Arizona power base, the Miami men prepared to challenge Charles Moyer's grip on the national WFM. Their tactics, at least, were in the mainstream of WFM tradition. WFM ethnic-racial inclusionists had always been as much concerned with power as with issues of ideology. With a momentarily united, confident, and well-financed chunk of western organized labor behind him, Miami's George Powell was about to campaign to take the WFM presidency away from Charles Moyer.

◄ 10 ►

LABOR, MANAGEMENT, AND THE FEDERAL GOVERNMENT STRUGGLE IN ARIZONA, 1916–1917

Arizona organizing was the only WFM success story during the union federation's dismal First World War years. Following a succession of strike losses, and after the destruction of the WFM's flagship local, Butte Number 1, morale fell to abysmal depths, except in Arizona. Members' letters to *Miners' Magazine* editor John M. O'Neill became increasingly angry. By February, 1916, the letter writers were demanding new leadership. They complained about strike failure, financial weakness, and "The principal complaint . . . is our failure to make progress in organizing our industry."[1]

Globe and Miami separatists led a WFM "new blood" movement against Charles Moyer. The new blood movement divided the faltering union confederation still further. George Powell was the new blood candidate for the WFM presidency. Moyer's partisans considered him a traitor.[2] At the national convention in June, Moyer defeated Powell by a relatively close 3-to-2 margin.[3]

By the summer of 1916, the WFM was fading fast. Moyer described his union as penurious and "practically dismembered," and he recommended "every possible retrenchment," including the "temporary suspension of all organizers and field work." For the future, Moyer recommended "time contracts" (that is, standard union recognition agreements), and he recommended that the Western Federation be converted into a "business institution."

While the national WFM declined, the Arizona State Federation of Labor came into its own. The State Federation had begun in 1912. Phoenix building tradesmen created the State Federation, but some of its original members were veterans of the Arizona Labor Party, an influential force at the 1910 Arizona Constitutional Convention. Phoenix men dominated the early ASFL. In 1914, the Arizona Federation was chartered by the national American Federation of Labor. The newly created WFM Clifton, Morenci, and Metcalf locals were forced to relinquish their WFM charters shortly after the strike; but the Clifton-area men quickly reaffiliated with the ASFL. The combined influx of Miami-sponsored Ray and Clifton-Morenci-Metcalf members made their Miami and Globe sponsors the most powerful force within the ASFL. After George Powell's June 1916 election loss to Charles Moyer, the Miami and Globe men informally separated themselves from national WFM leadership. Globe and Miami candidates won most of the important ASFL offices later in the year and they dominated the annual ASFL convention. By late October 1916, the Globe-Miami men were, in effect, running a union confederation of their own, controlling four tributary miners' union locals whose first allegiance was probably to Miami Local 70, and also commanding the allegiance of most of Arizona's non-mining AFL unions. Between 10 and 20 percent of the entire national membership of the WFM (now generally called the Mine-Mill Union) was probably allied with the Miami men by late 1916.[4]

In Denver, President Charles Moyer and his Executive Board supporters resented the Arizona men, but were unable to stop them. But the Arizona State Federation of Labor was "a local organization without its International standing," and "like a lone fish in the ocean."[5] WFM men had used the inclusion tactic for the last time in the wartime West. The Miami and Globe men who momentarily represented the cutting edge of a new working-class activism had also created, unknowingly, the means for their own destruction. Western mining companies interpreted the basic weakness and division in western unionism as a fine opportunity for a counterattack. IWW leaders in eastern states saw their moment of opportunity too. Neither copper-company management nor the Wobblies wasted any time in mobilizing for action.

IWW national headquarters began planning a western copper-country offensive early in 1916. The enthusiastic success of the IWW's 1915 Agricultural Workers' Organization provided the inspiration. The planned copper-organizing drive was to be selective. Bingham, Ely-McGill, and several other regions were initially adjudged too difficult to organize; Arizona was to be the prime target.[6]

175

In January 1917, the IWW drive began. Grover H. Perry, bringing money and supported by field organizers, went from New York City to Phoenix, where a minimal town workers' IWW local still functioned.[7] From Phoenix, half-trained and newly recruited IWW organizers slipped quietly into Bisbee and about a half dozen other mining communities and began the IWW version of talking union. The communities selected were those adjudged most susceptible to the IWW appeal.[8]

Once again, and for the last time, it is worth considering the IWW's commitment to helping the western states' Mexicans, Mexican Americans, Spaniards, Spanish Americans, Italians, Greeks, and South Slavs—and even Finns and Japanese. The question is: Did the IWW offer western ethnic and racial minorities an inclusive, egalitarian, just relationship with their fellow workers during 1917–18? Did the IWW offer *more* to ethnic-racial minorities than the WFM/IUMMSW or their own mutualistas and benefit societies were offering?

Grover H. Perry, who directed the Arizona campaign, promoted a single idea above all others. He promoted the six-hour workday, and all other demands were subordinated to that. The six-hour day was unique to the IWW in Arizona.[9] A. S. Embree of the IWW's Bisbee local, which had formerly been the WFM Bisbee Miners' Union, insisted that potential recruits "cannot grasp" the idea of a six-hour day, and pleaded with Perry to be "revolutionary" and promote class struggle instead. Perry refused—the six-hour day had become part of his litany. It was to be six hours and a six-day week, for a $6.00 daily wage.[10]

Perry meant what he said, and most Arizona recruits joined for the six-hour day and related demands, and not because they wanted to participate in revolutionary unionism. Historiographical controversy on this point obscures the basic transaction then taking place. According to Melvyn Dubofsky's explanation, Grover Perry's demands were a continuation of the successful bread-and-butter pragmatism begun by Walter T. Nef for the IWW's Agricultural Workers' Organization in 1915: "a better deal today—not revolution tomorrow."[11] However, recent writing which argues for the importance of IWW radicalism suggests instead that the Wobblies had a culture of revolution. Salvatore Salerno's *Red November Black November* postulates a consciousness-raising IWW, in which "The priority . . . was agitation."[12] Even when the agitation failed to produce any concrete concessions from management in strikes like the Mesabi iron range conflict in late 1916, some IWW stalwarts could still maintain that "we have no cause for complaint for we have accomplished something vastly more important

. . . we have awakened the slaves of the iron industry."[13] But the Arizona copper industry's slaves had long since been awakened. "Agitation," or revolution by implication, was inappropriate for Arizona, where the mining workers were taking the six-hour campaign literally, ignoring Grover Perry's ultimate intent. Six hours attracted attention and outbid the WFM/ IUMMSW, which offered a set of standard eight-hour and Miami-scale demands.

This was labor activism, but it was not revolutionary. Elsewhere in the United States, IWW leaders had been first to bring a real egalitarian spirit to labor relations. The IWW's *Industrial Union Bulletin* had explicitly opposed all forms of racial prejudice at least as early as 1909.[14] Officially expressed IWW ideology also favored, specifically, the recruitment of Mexican workers.[15] But the big Arizona membership drive was very different from real ethnic recruitment. In 1917 Arizona, the IWW had no plan for "recruitment of the unemployed and unskilled workers in job categories over which existing craft unions had declined jurisdiction."[16] In Arizona, the choicest targets were the men in the most heavily Anglo-Irish mining districts, and the Wobblies went after them first.

Even before the coming of the IWW, the Bisbee Miners' Union had been refusing to pay dues to Denver IUMMSW headquarters, and the BMU had tried to obtain an ASFL charter from the Globe-Miami men. The Miami leaders, at the same moment, were beginning to lose their way. They were unsure of whether or not to encourage dissident activity in Arizona, because IWW infiltration was beginning, and labor-union dissidence was likely to assume epidemic proportions. The Miami men refused to charter Bisbee as an ASFL local. At the same time, they suggested to Grover Perry that the ASFL and IWW might develop arrangements for mutual support. Sensing weakness and extraordinary opportunity, IWW men had begun slipping into Bisbee even before Grover Perry reached Phoenix.[17]

Local 106, the Bisbee Miners' Union, had had Anglo-Irish officers. Early in 1917, the BMU became, in fact but not in name, an IWW-controlled union organization. But, the advent of IWW influence in the local did not change its Anglo-Irish character. When Executive Board nominees were selected for the new Metal Mine Workers Union Number 800 (IWW) branch in Bisbee on June 17, 1917, one nominee who won election was Finnish-surnamed, and one of the losing candidates was Spanish-surnamed. Fourteen Anglo-Irish candidates were nominated. Only one other Spanish surname even appears in the Bisbee convention's records.[18] However, Mexican employees at the Copper Queen mine eagerly signed up at the Metal Mine Workers' Bisbee headquarters—that is, until the second week of July 1917, when the Bisbee Deportation drove the Metal Mine Workers out of town.

By early July 1917, Grover Perry was reporting that three hundred of the total of about three hundred and fifty Mexican employees at the Copper Queen had joined the IWW in Bisbee. Why did they join? Because, as even A. S. Embree, the man who preferred revolution to the $6.00 wage, was willing to admit, "The Mexicans are a sure bet, as we are demanding a minimum of $5.50 for all topmen," and practically all of the Mexican miners at the Queen were topmen. They also joined because Cochise County Sheriff Harry Wheeler was harassing Mexicans even before the notorious Bisbee Deportation. Sheriff Wheeler made plans to stop a putative "uprising" of local Mexicans that spring, an uprising that was probably a product of his own imagination. (Wheeler was to take action against another dubious Mexican "revolt" three years later.) The Bisbee IWW was not necessarily offering Mexican workers complete equality. The IWW would demand $6.00 for underground mining workers, none of whom was Mexican, and $5.50 for Mexican topmen.[19] The Mexicans in Bisbee were joining because of a special set of circumstances. Mexican workers were being harassed at the same moment that they were being offered the chance for an extraordinarily high wage, and the only functioning miners' union group in Bisbee, the former WFM/IUMMSW local, now part of the IWW Metal Mine Workers Number 800, wanted them as members.

The IWW's 1917 Metal Mine Workers Number 800 local was not especially revolutionary in its approach to Mexican and other Hispanic workers in Arizona, but it was definitely opportunistic. The Metal Mine Workers' drive was planned in the East. There was little or no planning in Arizona itself, where Number 800 was a purely adventitious creation.

The IWW was associated with a Spanish-language newspaper, *El Rebelde,* but *Rebelde* belonged to the Propaganda League of Mexicans in Los Angeles, and the League refused, at first, to move the newspaper to Phoenix. *Rebelde* was in short supply in Arizona. "If you have a few copies of Spanish paper send them along," wrote one organizer. *Regeneración,* the Partido Liberal Mexicano newspaper, was also infrequently seen in Arizona. There was only one kind of Spanish handout literature available at the crucial Globe office of Number 800, along with many other handouts written in English and some in other languages. *El Rebelde* only became the official voice of Number 800 belatedly, in June 1917, and immediately afterward, on July 1, it was moved along with 800's offices and Grover Perry himself, to 800's new Salt Lake City headquarters. Why would Number 800, in the middle of a gut-wrenching Arizona campaign, have suddenly left Bisbee and moved to Salt Lake City, eight hundred miles away?[20]

Utah workers were not the reason for the big move. The IWW did not even publish newspapers in the Greek or Serbo-Croatian languages in mid-1917, so a major Utah and Nevada campaign was not even being contemplated.[21] Perhaps the IWW intended to obtain a pivotal position for itself midway between the 1917 Arizona labor trouble and the big contemporaneous strike at Butte.[22] But this is an improbable reason for the big move because Salt Lake City was too far from *both* Arizona and Montana to allow Grover Perry to have supervised either strike directly, while the Arizona labor action included at least half a dozen constantly shifting battlegrounds which badly needed constant attention and centralized direction. Instead, it seems probable that Grover Perry and other IWW leaders abruptly moved their headquarters because they had received advance warning about the approximate date and scope of the Bisbee Deportation. James Byrkit's *Forging the Copper Collar* describes the general mood in Bisbee as having been antagonistic to labor activism and conducive to anti-IWW retaliation for weeks before July 12, when the actual Bisbee Deportation occurred. Planning for the Deportation, which included hundreds of armed men conducting a massive roundup in a small city, could not have been kept entirely secret from everyone associated with the IWW.[23]

Shortly before the Deportation, there had been a sense of haste underlying the IWW drive. One IWW organizer wrote that he expected to finish the major part of his work in "a few short months." Mexicans and other Hispanics were the most numerous element among workers that the Wobblies might hope to recruit in Arizona. At least three hundred Mexican members did sign on in Bisbee, as mentioned, and some Spanish-surnamed recruits joined at Copper Hill, near Globe. But Mexican and other Hispanic recruitment had low priority in IWW plans. "Kimball got hold of a good man for organizer among the Mexicans and he is on the payroll," wrote A. S. Embree to Perry. Haphazard arrangements like these were pervasive. A planned campaign among Mexican and other Hispanic communities would have included the dispatch of a corps of trained Spanish-speaking organizers from Los Angeles or Phoenix, along with Spanish-language literature. Instead, the eager IWW men mostly proselytized the Anglos and Irish. The IWW's Golconda organizer discussed Anglo-Irish hot prospects all over Mohave County, including the "white miners" of the Kingman vicinity, without mentioning Mexican miners at all. Another organizer told Grover Perry that "now is the time for us to strike into the crafts as hard as possible." He meant that he wanted to recruit skilled men, few of whom were Hispanic.

Meanwhile, the highly visible Mexican, Spanish, and Spanish American populations of Clifton, Morenci, and Metcalf were barely touched by the IWW drive.[24]

Copper-company-inspired vigilante groups forcibly ejected over a hundred suspected Wobblies from Jerome in the Jerome Deportation on July 10, and over a thousand men were forced out of Bisbee on July 12.[25] The U.S. government began its campaign of anti-IWW repression in the autumn of 1917. The Wobblies' main thrust in Arizona had been blunted by the end of the year.

At Clifton-Morenci, the Mexican and other Hispanic workers had become increasingly assertive without IWW help. "No matter what the outcome of the present strike is," wrote the *Arizona Republican*'s Clifton area correspondent in 1915, "working conditions in the district are almost certain to be improved. . . . The companies will adopt a different attitude toward their employees."[26]

They certainly would. The Clifton-Morenci strikers voted to return to work on January 24, 1916, and they signed a contract with the copper companies there in March. Wages rose as much as 60 percent for some unskilled workers, and continued to rise because of the newly adopted sliding Miami wage scale. A new Clifton District Labor Council organized four thousand workers by early 1916.[27] But the strike settlement brought only a momentary pause in the Clifton-Morenci labor-management war. Angry Mexican workers precipitated a series of incidents in 1916–17. Men who had previously been living quietly with their bitterness became forceful and frequently aggressive.

A series of arguments between shift bosses and unskilled workers, mostly about relatively minor work rules and job-control issues, began after the March 1916 strike settlement.[28] The issues were argued through the newly established grievance-committee procedure. One typical instance involved a personality clash between a Spanish-surnamed timberman and a shift boss, in which the timberman was laid off for two weeks "for flagrant breach of instructions." After unsuccessful processing through the grievance committee, the timberman's grievance evolved into a strike by 2,500 men, in which mining operations ceased for two weeks.[29] Nine moderately large strikes and many smaller ones occurred during the fifteen months following the 1916 strike settlement. Some of these were accompanied by major acts of sabotage. On one occasion, "thousands of feet of steel was buried in the stope-filling and the company not only put to great expense, but its operations hindered until an additional supply could be obtained."[30] It was also reported that, "On three occasions . . . attempts have been made to burn

District Grievance Committee of the Clifton-Morenci-Metcalf miners' unions and national officers of the WFM, probably taken at Clifton, 1916. In the top row, WFM President Charles Moyer is second from left, and Miami organizer Henry S. Mc-Cluskey is third from left. In the bottom row, the three men crouching in the center are, from left, Canuto A. Vargas, Pascual M. Vargas, and Luis Soto, all local union officers. Courtesy of Department of Archives and Manuscripts, Hayden Library, Arizona State University, Tempe.

the mines in this district." The damage was severe: one of the mines had to be closed entirely for some weeks.[31] There were more strikes and walkout action at Clifton-Morenci-Metcalf during the fifteen-month period following the 1915–16 strike settlement than there had been during the entire preceding two decades. Mexicans and other Spanish-surnamed men and women called the many small strikes *strikitos*.[32]

The strikitos, the larger work stoppages, and the repeated acts of sabotage all indicated a general malaise. They were initiated by Mexican workers, and to a lesser degree, by Spanish and Italian immigrant workers. Much of the labor action was begun by relatively young, recently hired men.[33]

The copper companies continued to observe the general terms of the 1916 strike settlement, according to *Miners' Magazine* in late 1916. The labor troubles during these months were not directly related to specific wage and job discrimination issues, as the 1903, 1907, and 1915–16 Clifton-Morenci strikes had been.[34] Instead, they were indications that the continuing struggle between unskilled labor and management had reached a new plateau: the workers were demanding increased control over their everyday work situations, equivalent, ultimately, to an enhanced sense of social equality. Management reported that "when one of their number has been discharged for any cause, such action has in numerous cases been followed by a walkout. . . . Common operating orders are ignored or resented. Taunts of inability to dismiss are made by the men, with the veiled and sometimes open threat of consequences. Discipline is forgotten. Timbermen and shift bosses are intimidated if they attempt to give orders."[35]

The mine managers reported that the men were dictating their own work standards: "In one case . . . they actually installed a wholly unnecessary track and car which involved extra labor for them, but permitted them to measure the standard day's work!"[36] According to Norman Carmichael of Arizona Copper, his employees had "assumed an attitude of independence amounting to arrogance which has made it exceedingly trying and exasperating to those in authority." "Discipline" underground had become impossible and "insubordination was rife," complained Carmichael.[37]

The Globe and Miami Anglo-Irish WFM/IUMMSW men were amazed at the rapid progress of their erstwhile pupils. The patron-and-client relationship between Globe-Miami and Clifton-Morenci seemed to disappear after the 1915 strike. Also, the 1916–17 Clifton-Morenci Mexicans' and Spanish Americans' job actions were more radical, even more revolutionary, than most of what was performed or even proposed by the contemporaneous IWW. Large-scale radical job action, complete with an ideology of equality, fairness, and justice, had begun in the Southwest. The IWW-sponsored version of 1917 radicalism followed in the train of the far more potent Clifton-Morenci variety.

Labor-management war broke out across Arizona during the spring and summer of 1917. Beginning in July and August and on into the autumn, a combined counterattack by copper-company management and government took hold, and ultimately throttled union-led and nonunion workers' movements throughout the state.

The 1917 strike wave had begun at the Humboldt smelter in Prescott, south of Jerome. Two IWW activists, Frank Little and Pedro Coria, led the strike there, and the companies settled by offering their employees an average 12^1/$_2$¢ daily wage increase. A Jerome strike came next. Frank Little drew up a set of Jerome demands in April, and readjusted them in May. He demanded a flat rate of $6.00 a day (although not necessarily a six-hour

day) for underground workers. He wanted bonuses and contract work eliminated, a free hospital, two men for each Leyner (drilling) machine, no discrimination against strikers, and a joint IWW and IUMMSW grievance
committee. The IUMMSW and many individual Jerome mining workers
wanted wages raised to the Miami scale, which was 75¢ higher than the
Jerome wage scale. The International Mine-Mill union (IUMMSW) added
demands for a contract, a union shop, and a union dues checkoff system.[38]
The contract, union shop, and checkoff may have seemed especially urgent
necessities to the slumping IUMMSW because of its increasingly difficult
fight against the IWW.

The IWW originally offered to conduct a joint strike effort with the
IUMMSW at Jerome. The Wobblies' offer, if sincere, was generous. The
IWW was willing to concede the six-hour day, and it had offered to eliminate the two-men-on-one-machine demand, the hospital demand, and even
the flat-rate demand in favor of the International's Miami-standard sliding-
scale demand. The IWW, of course, did not favor union-shop arrangements, which would have excluded them.[39]

The Wobblies' first tactic—that of announcing a program of action
which was both distinctive and radical—would have attracted those workers who were most prone to striking. The initial IWW demands, especially
the six-hour day, were too extreme to be negotiated through compromise
with copper-company management. The announcement of an extreme set
of demands provided workers with a sharp contrast between the IWW and
the IUMMSW. The IWW was willing to bargain away its demands after it
had gained a sufficient number of adherents, since it actually did not hope
to totally eliminate the IUMMSW in Jerome. The IWW essentially predi-
cated its original set of strike demands upon the Mine-Mill Union's responses. Its main strategic concern at Jerome was that of successful organizational growth, not strike demands; and the growth was intended to be
parasitic.

The IUMMSW refused the offer. During the course of the ensuing
struggle, the IWW was to announce that it had won away about half of
the International Mine-Mill Union's membership.[40] Even as the strike was
in progress, and while Wobbly organizers were still trying to attract
IUMMSW collaboration, the Wobblies learned that the "State Federation
of Labor [the ASFL] was trying to get the mining companies of Arizona to
sign a contract with the WFM [IUMMSW] and thus drive the IWW out of
the mines."[41]

The Jerome companies conceded the Miami scale early in the strike.[42]
The final settlement was also to include an acceptance of shop grievance

committees (composed of employee representatives from each of the various sections of mine and mill operations), reemployment of strikers without discrimination, a guarantee of the right to union affiliation, and a pledge to reduce living expenses through utility and rent reductions and arrangements with local merchants. The binding union shop arrangements which would have given the IUMMSW institutional status were denied it by the terms of the settlement.[43] There was some strikebreaking and some violence, but the first phase of the strike was over in less than two weeks.[44]

In July, when local IWW members began a second strike at Jerome, there was no longer any possibility of collaboration between the IWW and the International Mine-Mill union, and local IUMMSW officials worked to destroy their rivals. The Jerome Deportation was accomplished with IUMMSW assistance.[45]

There had also been a strike at Ajo, Arizona. The New Cornelia Copper Mining Company at Ajo had just begun large-scale operations in 1916—it was the newest large copper area in Arizona. Electricians began the Ajo strike in November 1916, but it spread quickly to a thousand other workers who were "Mexicans, [Papago] Indians, and white" men. Neither the IUMMSW nor the IWW was yet in Ajo. The Ajo strike was "in the first place a popular uprising or rather a spontaneous combustion against the rate of wages paid by the New Cornelia Copper Company." A skilled-crafts union, the Structural Iron Workers, went back to work, and the strike ended on January 19, 1917.[46] Ely-McGill had a strike in early 1917.[47] There would probably have been a strike at Bingham Canyon, except for the extensive and thoroughgoing repression by local government and management there, which lasted through 1918.

One reason for the labor organizing activity of 1917 was that the cost of living had been rising rapidly, climbing about 30 percent between late 1915 and mid-1917, and wages had not kept pace with the increased living costs.[48] Management was almost certain to offer resistance to wage demands during 1917–18 because of the perpetual uncertainty and the short-term character of upward price shifts in the wholesale copper market. The Utah Copper Company's reported profit margins, in fact, actually declined from a 14.22¢ per pound of copper profit in 1916 to 13.23¢ in 1917, and to 8.50¢ in 1918.[49]

The International Mine-Mill confederation blamed the copper corporations, more than it did the IWW, for deliberately initiating the 1917 Arizona labor trouble. According to the International, the employers began an anti-union campaign, which the union called a "great spring drive," at Globe-Miami in April.[50] The International claimed that long-time union members were being discharged at Globe-Miami, and that nonunion men were being hired to replace them.[51] An early strike statement listed [anti-union] "discrimination" as the most important complaint, and explained that it was raised because "it had been reported over and over again that men were discharged without any adequate cause, and those developing any great activity on account of unionism were not only discharged, but blacklisted." The union's list of detailed allegations of discrimination was persuasive.[52] The Globe-Miami companies themselves described their new springtime employment policy as "the step of dropping from their employ those individuals whose words and actions branded them as disloyal to the United States."[53] If this was a great spring drive to reverse labor's gains, the Globe-Miami area—the old "center of labor agitation in the Territory," the home of the "best paid labor in Arizona" and the Miami scale, and the only effective IUMMSW organizing area in the southwestern copper industry—was the logical place for the copper companies to initiate it.

The International's Globe-Miami strike demands also included provisions for recognition of bargaining agents, for allowing organizers on company property, and for "equal representation on the Board of Control of the hospital." The IWW, of course, had its own list in Globe-Miami, including complaints about discrimination (against "any" union men in the IWW version), about hospital control, demands that men work in twos rather than working alone on some machines, that contracts and bonuses for special mining operations be terminated, that the rustling card system (which was a potentially devastating means of discrimination) be discontinued, and that the sliding scale be replaced by minimum flat rates of $5.50 for surface and $6.00 for underground mining workers.[54]

Even before the strike actually began, the companies at Globe and Miami had enlisted a set of allies which had previously been unavailable to them. The United States had just declared war on Germany. In a confused declaration about loyalty and patriotism in April 1917, part of the Globe conservative AFL labor community and Globe businessmen constituted themselves as the Globe Council of Defense, committing themselves to direct opposition to the IUMMSW. Two years earlier, the same kinds of tradesmen and small businessmen had *supported* the 1915 Miami strikers.[55] When the IUMMSW strike began on July 2, the Globe Engineers' Union and the Globe Electricians' Union were among the Mine-Mill's former allies who now turned against it, and a zealot "organization of about three hundred armed citizens" began patrolling the streets.[56]

The potential for a mining war developed at Globe's Old Dominion Mine, and first recently elected Governor Thomas Campbell, then a detachment of the United States Seventeenth Cavalry, and finally, newly chosen U.S. mediators George W. P. Hunt and John McBride (both of whom were sent by the U.S. Department of Labor) interposed their collective authority between the two sides.[57] The companies refused to "meet with the men and talk things over," wrote Hunt in early July—"they do not want a concilia-tor."[58] Later he wrote, "They will not recognize the grievance committee nor allow one of the men on the hospital Board . . . as they say they are go-ing to run their own property in their own way without any interference."[59]

The federal troops stayed on in Globe. Hunt felt that they ought to re-main in order to prevent another mass deportation of strikers such as those which had already occurred at Jerome and Bisbee.[60] Although there was no deportation, Lieutenant-Colonel George B. White's Seventeenth Cavalry conducted joint operations with Globe and Miami Loyalty League leaders and with the local sheriff, and assisted in the general harassment of Wob-blies during July.[61] Then, at the beginning of August, White announced that the Seventeenth Cavalry would protect any men who wished to break the strike at the Old Dominion, which promptly resumed operations.[62] Ex-governor Hunt wrote to Secretary of Labor Wilson that "Col White is act-ing as employment agent for the Old Dominion Mining and Smelting Co." "I supposed he was here to enforce the law against all violence and to pro-tect property and not to induce strike breakers to return to work under the protection of the government."[63]

The World War provided a fine opportunity for the copper companies to wrap themselves in the flag. Company men helped assemble new, anti-union coalitions of small town "patriots" to refight the local battles that had been lost to the WFM/IUMMSW during the previous several years, and to recover as much power as possible from immigrant and Hispanic employ-ees and the unions that represented them.

On August 11, all three major operating companies at Globe and Miami informed federal conciliator John McBride by letter that

> In the event the strike is called off in the next few days the companies will not discriminate against members of the IUMM&SW or other crafts union men. BUT IN THE FUTURE THE COMPANIES WILL ONLY EMPLOY MEN WHOSE CHARACTER AND PAST RECORD ARE SUCH AS WILL INSURE THEIR BEING LOYAL TO AMERICAN PRINCIPLES AND GOOD LAW-ABIDING MEMBERS OF THE COMMUNITY OF WHICH THEY ARE A PART.
>
> In other words, THE COMPANIES RESERVE THE RIGHT TO REFUSE EMPLOYMENT TO ANY MAN WHO DOES NOT CON-FORM TO THIS STANDARD. [original emphasis][64]

The copper companies also announced that they would not deal with IWW men and that they intended to attract "the best class of American workmen" in the future.[65] The companies' use of the term *American* may have originally been intended to refer to issues of patriotic loyalty, but in July, an exceptionally large number of South Slavic miners in Globe and Miami were being arrested and charged with having committed strike-related offenses.[66] In September, the company identified crafts-union nonstrikers as American workmen, in contradistinction to "Austrian" strikers: "Thus were loyal American citizens who were doing their duty in their own country, beaten and stoned by a mob consisting largely of Austrians."[67] In October, mining-company management again declared that "this was to be made an 'American camp'—no more foreigners with their violence and strikes and un-American practices and purposes." According to IUMMSW sources, "This is directed against the Mexicans, many of whom are of mixed descent, but their loyalty to unionism and their understanding of economic conditions have completely surprised the employers who brought them here in the first place to make a strike of the miners either impossible or ineffective."[68]

The copper corporations at Globe-Miami and elsewhere were trying to control their workers more effectively during 1917. The corporations disregarded any potential labor-supply problems. They asserted their power to exclude conservative unionists, radical unionists, and immigrant unionists. They were assured of success because their efforts were increasingly supported by both the federal government and by skilled AFL men in the mining communities.

In July, in Globe-Miami, some of the skilled and semiskilled English-speaking men began separating themselves from the unskilled Mexicans', Hispanics', and South Slavs' strike. On July 21, a group of Globe-Miami English-speaking men met to discuss a possible strike settlement. According to its organizers, the meeting was held only for the benefit of "the American citizens of this district, and especially the American workingmen who before the strike were employed in the mines, mills, and smelters. Members of the IWW are not welcomed, nor will any aliens who are not citizens be permitted to attend."[69]

In August, a list of union negotiators included four employees each from the Inspiration, Miami, and Old Dominion companies. At least eleven of the twelve union negotiators were men of English, Irish, or old-immigrant descent.[70] The Miami carpenters, electricians, and steam and operating engineers all returned to work during August.[71]

Besides the Seventeenth Cavalry, of course, the U.S. Government was represented by Hunt and McBride, the federal commissioners of conciliation. The commissioners tried to play the same sort of noncoercive, concil-iatory role which had worked so well at Clifton-Morenci in 1915–16. But the corporations themselves were no longer amenable to persuasion by the commissioners. Governor Hunt was correct: the copper companies did not want him there. Copper-corporation management was effectively using the Seventeenth Cavalry as its cat's paw, and the federal commissioners were superfluous.

As early as April 29, the Globe Miners' Union had met "To protest against the proposed importation of One Million Asiatics." In May, it was reported that the Council of National Defense was recommending the im-portation of large numbers of Mexican nationals because of a developing labor shortage. Both the Council and the burgeoning local Loyalty Leagues were beginning to prove very helpful to copper-company management.[72] The Council, with the approval of Secretary of Labor Wilson, intended to freeze working conditions and wages (allowing, however, for inflation-related wage increases) at the early 1917 level for the duration of the war.[73]

At least two other Arizona copper camps were subjected to federal po-lice action during 1917. Troops were sent to Ray. Since there was no strike at Ray, the troops were there simply to maintain the venerable southwestern tradition of "keeping down the Mexicans."[74] There was also some federal policing during the Bisbee strike.

The principal phase of federal government intervention in the 1917 strikes began when the President's Mediation Commission was created, in September. The commission was created by presidential proclamation. William B. Wilson, the Secretary of Labor, was its chairman, and its mem-bers were intended to represent "both labor and capital."[75] The commission was somewhat similar to the federal conciliators and to the Council of Na-tional Defense which had preceded them in the Southwest: it was nominally an investigative body. In practice, however, it was able to effectively impose its arbitration awards.[76] Soon, it would do so.

The Bisbee and Jerome "deportations" triggered an orgy of vigilante action and official deportation, with U.S. government assistance, in the latter part of 1917. On July 24, U.S. Immigration Service officials began investigating the status of Mexicans at Bisbee and in the Columbus, New Mexico, Bisbee deportees' camp, in order to deport (to Mexico) those who were illegal aliens.[77] Phelps Dodge, the owners of Bisbee's Copper Queen, deported eighty men from its Gallup-American Coal Company mines in Gallup, New Mexico, on July 31. "Vagging"—the arresting and occasional deporting of men on the questionable grounds of vagrancy—continued through August at Globe, Miami, and Clifton-Morenci.[78] On September 5,

1917, U.S. raids began against IWW local offices in thirty-three cities.[79]

The Clifton-Morenci-Metcalf strike was the least publicized and the least obtrusive of the Arizona strikes in 1917. It began on July 1. The strikers demanded the standard items which the International had listed at Jerome and Globe-Miami, with the addition of demands for time-and-a-half and overtime pay and a demand that a seniority rule be used in hiring and firing. The strike was called by the Arizona State Federation of Labor's leadership.[80] It was the first big, formally organized IUMMSW strike in which a preponderant majority of the strikers, nearly 90 percent, were Mexican.

The copper corporations reacted as though they were ready to conduct a "great spring drive" at Clifton-Morenci too. Norman Carmichael, the Arizona Copper Company's manager, immediately offered a wage increase, but threatened to lock out and eliminate committed unionists if his wage proposition was refused.[81] On July 13, it was reported that "It is no secret that the mine managers of the district are making preparations for a long shut down."[82] The strike was reported "dragging listlessly" on July 19.[83] At the beginning of August, corporation management announced that for the time being, they would not reopen the mines. They would only reopen if they could enforce improved "discipline" upon the men, and if they could discharge whomsoever they chose: they "could not tie [themselves] . . . up with any promise regarding re-employment."[84] In late September, the corporations threatened to "shut down indefinitely," unless the men reported for work immediately, without a prior strike agreement.[85]

The new links which had been forged between skilled and unskilled labor at Clifton-Morenci during 1915–16 were strained to the breaking point during 1917. The stationary engineers' local was lukewarm about the strike.[86] Several other crafts groups were unhappy with the strike, although the consensus seemed to be that "until those grievances had been satisfactorily adjusted, the craft members were legally and morally bound to support the miners." A rumor circulated in September that a secret vote had taken place among a group of skilled Anglos and Irish about whether or not they ought to withdraw altogether from the IUMMSW.[87] Although the proposition was defeated, the episode signified the increasing trouble between skilled and unskilled men, and between the English- and Spanish-speaking men.

Ethnic relations had deteriorated during the Clifton-Morenci strikitos. During the 1917 strike, fights erupted and threats were exchanged between mostly Anglo-Irish company loyalists and some Spanish-surnamed workers.[88] During the course of the strike, a large group of Mexicans was arrested on the charge of "rioting and planning a march on Clifton to attack and 'clean out the whites.'"[89] A group of Spaniards were arrested and charged with attempting to assassinate the Metcalf Mine's superintendent.[90] As the strike neared its end, a statement was signed by "seven hundred American citizens of all classes, protesting against the hasty and ill advised action of the alien element . . . in calling the strike."[91] Yet, after the strike, the IUMMSW praised the Spanish-surnamed mining workers and claimed that the relationship between them and the English-speaking workers had become closer than ever.[92] Although that was doubtful, some of the cohesion between the English-speaking men and Mexicans and other Hispanic unionists had endured.

The Clifton-Morenci strike ended, with the assistance of the federal Mediation Commission, in October 1917.[93] The "Decision and Order of the President's Mediation Commission" was prefaced by imperious phrasing about patriotism and high purpose. Because of the loftiness of the war aims, "No grievances on the part of the men, whether well-founded or imaginary, must be allowed to result in the stoppage of production." The Commission's plan wore an aspect of even-handedness, but considering the years of conflict which had preceded it, it was clearly one-sided.

According to the agreement, the copper corporations were to receive the disciplined, efficient job performance to which they were supposedly entitled. There was to be no discrimination against union members. The Commission was to investigate the company's hospital and make recommendations. The Commission would also investigate wage scales and "promulgate" new wage scales, if necessary.[94] The Commission would decide all otherwise unresolvable grievances, and its decisions would bind both parties. Otherwise, work rules in existence since the 1915–16 strike agreement would continue in effect. There was to be no union recognition, and grievances would be argued first with the foremen, as had been previous practice. Finally, if a new and higher wage scale was to be promulgated, "the President's Mediation Commission shall recommend to the President that such company shall be permitted to obtain an increased selling price" for its copper.[95]

If grievances were to be argued in individual shops, then union oversight of the copper companies' work forces would be impeded. Shop grievance committees were susceptible to being captured by "company men." The workers' side could not force resolution of shop grievances, according to the agreement. Complainants could only hope for Mediation Commission intervention. The workers gained essentially nothing from the 1917 Mediation Commission order. The increased wages that were eventually offered were contingent upon an increased, government-guaranteed price for copper, and were only a temporary wartime expedient. The use of an administrator to arbitrate grievances was also intended to be temporary. The enhancing of "discipline" and continuing importance of the foreman in work routines would favor the company. But the Clifton-Morenci Mexican and Hispanic copper workers' ten-week-long strike could have been effective. If the strike had continued, the strikers probably could have forced a genuine concession of power from the copper corporations, just as the 1915–16 strikers had done.

No more strikes or lockouts were to be allowed for the duration of the war.[96] Similar agreements were signed at Globe-Miami and at Bisbee. At Globe-Miami, the corporations were implicitly allowed to continue excluding union activist employees. The situation was covered by a clause which required the arbitration committee to "secure a place for . . . [them] at some of the other operations in the district."[97] At Bisbee, "Claims of discrimination against union members have been particularly insistent." "Such discriminations are hereafter prohibited, and the enforcement of the prohibition is vested in the United States administrator."[98] Again, work rules remained generally the same, but union power had been checked. In its place, there was the power of the government administrator—but only for the duration of the war.

◄ 11 ►

CONCLUSION, 1917–1918

The copper-mining corporations probably intended to nudge the wholesale price of copper upward during the First World War. Management and New York market traders extensively manipulated copper prices, costs, and labor supply during 1917.[1] The companies' willingness to delay negotiations, particularly at Globe-Miami and Clifton-Morenci, and even to hint of lockout tactics, helped enlist government on their side and helped boost the fixed copper price. The price of copper was fixed by the War Industries Board in mid-1917.[2]

The federal government's fixed copper price did not end the mine, mill, and smelter workers' demands for higher wages. Clifton-Morenci workers subsequently asked the War Industries Board to increase the copper price so that their wages could be raised in mid-1918.[3] The federal government fixed wages for the Anaconda Corporation employees at Butte in July. Anaconda announced that it had received a price increase, which "will be consumed in paying the increase in wages and in freight rates."[4] At Jerome in August, the federal arbitrator, Hywel Davies, "explained that the copper companies would derive no benefit whatever from the raise of price from $23\frac{1}{2}¢$; the difference being wholly consumed in additional labor, transportation, and refining charges."[5] By late 1918, Secretary of Labor Wilson and Felix Frankfurter, then Chairman of the War Policies Board, were considering the creation of new fixed wage scales, and planned to take action against labor transiency—apparently because the copper corporations had asked them for more help.[6]

Federal intervention did not end the mining workers' complaints. The companies at Globe were continuing to fire active union members during December 1917. Some of the discharged unionists had more than ten years' service and were Globe homeowners.[7] In late 1917 and early 1918, the IUMMSW reported general dissatisfaction at several Arizona camps centering around the same issues which had caused the 1917 strikes.[8] Organizer Henry McCluskey was reporting that the corporations had failed "to comply with the spirit of settlement arrived at by and through the United States Government mediators."[9]

The International Mine-Mill Union remained weak and could not force the federal government to respond to any of its concerns. As IWW pressure eased in the southwestern copper areas, the IUMMSW fought on alone against the mining corporations. The International began representing itself as patriotic. "Our organization, if permitted to do so, can keep the metal mines of America producing the maximum amount," said Charles Moyer. He also announced that his union would be willing to "discipline its members."[10]

Discrimination against unskilled copper mining and processing workers in Arizona, Utah, Nevada, and West Texas had been of two kinds. First, unskilled men generally had not been allowed to attain skilled status, and had not been offered entry-level employment with skilled status potential. European and Mexican immigrant and Spanish American workers generally had been offered dead end jobs. There had been a large difference in pay between unskilled and skilled men, and the unskilled had been subjected to frequent abuse by foremen. Second, although relatively few Anglo-Irish employees had worked at unskilled and semiskilled jobs, those few who had worked at them had received higher wages than wages paid to the immigrants and Spanish Americans. Anglo-Irish miners and timbermen and some unskilled and semiskilled smelter workers had been paid more than immigrants and Spanish Americans doing the same work.[11] Joseph Park's study, which measured the difference in wages between workers he categorized as Anglo-American and Mexican, indicated a wage gap which was wider in 1910 than it had ever been before, and which was steadily increasing.[12]

By 1918, that pattern had been reversed. The discrimination which had existed before the 1915 Clifton-Morenci strike had definitely diminished. There were still few European immigrant, Mexican, or Spanish American skilled men, and there were generally no helpers of non-Anglo-Irish ethnicity either. But the jobs with differential wage rates based on ethnicity were gone. Timberman was the only mining job held by significant proportions of both Anglo-Irish and non-Anglo-Irish in 1918. Although there were still two common wage rates for timbermen in 1918, timbermen's wages were no longer directly related to their ethnicities. Also, the skilled and unskilled wage gap which Park described as widening through 1910, and which probably continued to widen until 1915, was narrowing in 1918. For instance, muckers (who were generally unskilled Mexican or Spanish American laborers) earned $2.03 in June 1915, and $3.30 in June 1918. Most carpenters, who were generally skilled English-speaking men, earned $4.08 in June 1915 and $5.60 in June 1918. The muckers' wage had been slightly less than 50 percent of the carpenters' wage in 1915, but it had become approximately 59 percent of the carpenters' wage by 1918. The wage gap between muckers and mine timbermen had narrowed even more.[13]

At Bingham Canyon, the gap between skilled and unskilled workers' pay narrowed by about 5 percent between mid-1915 and mid-1918. At Bingham, too, the pattern had been reversed; until 1915, the gap between skilled and unskilled wages had been widening. The Utah Copper Company frequently increased wages after 1915. Wages rose six times (and fell once) between August 1915 and July 1918 for the unskilled pitmen, dumpmen, and trackmen at the Bingham Canyon mines. Hours of work decreased from ten to nine.[14] In March 1918, the Utah Copper Company announced that it would be paying employees semimonthly, instead of once every thirty days. Two paydays a month meant that workingmen and their families could "operate more on a cash basis," avoid costly credit indebtedness to local stores, and thus increase the discretionary portion of their spending and possibly save money.[15]

The tendency toward greater equality in wages and working conditions continued into 1918. A mining engineer, reporting on "the Southwest Copper Field" in 1918, wrote that there was still a difference between Hispanic and Anglo-Irish wages in some areas, and that the Mexicans were still dissatisfied about it. However, he wrote things were changing. "In some places . . . [Mexicans and other Hispanics] are paid the same as white men."[16] The Phelps Dodge Copper Queen mine in Bisbee, a venerable source of wage discrimination, began paying many of its IUMMSW employees $5.35 per day, "without regard to length of service or relative competency."[17] Mine managers at Clifton-Morenci had been pleading their inability to match Miami-scale wages because special circumstances rendered their operations less profitable than those at Globe-Miami. In 1917–18, however, the standardized Miami scale was being extended all over Arizona, and it finally came to Clifton-Morenci in April 1918.[18]

Individual wartime success stories in the mining communities can convey a misleading impression. Some mining workers enlisted and fought in Europe; some, deported from Jerome, Bisbee, or from the coal mines near Gallup, New Mexico, spent days or weeks out in the desert, and some left mine, mill, and smelter jobs for other reasons. Previously, especially in 1903, mining workers' level of job retention had been measured in mere months. Men had begun retaining their jobs longer in 1915, before the 1915 Clifton-Morenci strike began. During wartime, perceived job transiency became an explicit employer concern. "A large migratory working force is economically an intolerable waste. Socially it is a disintegrating element in society." "Labor turnover" was described as "an evil which can be substantially reduced if not wholly eliminated."[19] From 1915 through 1920, a small sample study of unskilled, low-wage Clifton-Morenci employees indicates that, from 1915 through 1920, workers did not necessarily retain their jobs long enough to experience the positive workplace changes made within that period. Of twenty-eight men who were employed by the Arizona Copper Company in June 1915, including nineteen with Spanish surnames, five Italians, and four with English and Irish surnames, seventeen were still working there two years later (in June 1917). But at the end of five years (in June, 1920), only three of the original twenty-eight, two Italians and one Spanish-surnamed man, were still employed by the Arizona Company. The Anglo-Irish had left first, and married men had persisted somewhat longer than the single men had. Essentially, transiency had been reduced during 1915–17, but it increased markedly again thereafter.[20]

The frequency with which mine, mill, and smelter workers quit work during these turbulent years meant that only an atypical Mexican, Spanish American, European immigrant, or Anglo or Irish employee would have been able to experience an extended series of wage increases and on the job improvements during 1915–20. *Collective* change occurred, although the changes only partially affected *individual* workingmen's lives.

The most obvious changes occurred among Spanish American, Spanish, and Mexican mining workers. Discussing the strikitos of 1916–17, Norman Carmichael, the Arizona Copper Company's superintendent, expressed astonishment and outrage over the hostile and extraordinarily assertive behavior of his unskilled and semiskilled employees: "The rank and file of our employees are of Mexican, Spanish, and Italian origin, and since the strike of 1915 have been strongly unionized but their idea of unionism is that they must have everything their own way, that they need not obey orders, they do not have to do any more work than *they* think sufficient and that they cannot be fired."[21] Carmichael said that management had gained only one doubtful advantage from the post-1915 situation. "Hidden grievances," he said, had been converted into readily visible grievances.

The result was the greatest mass of overt labor trouble ever experienced in the Clifton-Morenci district.[22] According to Carmichael, one of the three men who had been laid off told his boss, " 'Well, if I don't get work in the morning underground nobody will go to work in the mine.' . . . [The shift bosses] were pretty well used by now to that sort of talk. On the following morning, Tuesday the 13th, the men did not go to work, demanding that the three roustabouts who had been laid off should be given work."[23] Superintendent Carmichael also indicated management's newfound, albeit grudging, respect for the power wielded by non-Anglo-Irish employees. Carmichael and the other superintendents who offered testimony at the Department of Labor hearings in late 1917 did not attempt to resurrect the pre-1915 legend of ignorant foreigners duped into mischief by evil Anglo-Irish unionists. Carmichael's own seething hatred directed against his obviously knowledgeable and assertive Hispanic employees had replaced his pre-1915 version of the dynamics of labor conflict.[24]

The International Mine-Mill Union's Guy Miller told a hearing board inquiring into the 1917 labor conflict in Bingham Canyon that the copper workers there had come to consider *autonomy* more important than wages.[25] And the President's Mediation Commission, summarizing the 1918 Arizona copper conflicts, wrote:

> The men demanded the removal of certain existing grievances as to wages, hours, and working conditions, but the specific grievances were, on the whole, of relatively minor importance. The crux of the conflict was the insistence of the men that the right and power to obtain just treatment were in themselves basic conditions of employment, and that they should not be compelled to depend for such just treatment on benevolence or uncontrolled will of the employers.[26]

The WFM locals at Clifton, Morenci, and Metcalf which had briefly disbanded as a part of the 1915–16 strike settlement were recreated in 1917, but their 1917 officers were Spanish-surnamed. The leading spokesman of all the Clifton-Morenci strikers during the big 1917 strike there was Pascual M. Vargas, the Morenci local's president. At least ten of the thirteen Clifton district delegates to the 1917 Arizona State Federation of Labor convention were Spanish-surnamed.[27] At least half of the Arizona Federation's total constituent membership was Mexican, Spanish American, or Spanish in 1917, as was one of the state federation's vice-presidents. One of the two Miami Miners' Union representatives to the national IUMMSW convention was Spanish-surnamed in 1917 and both of the representatives were Spanish-surnamed in 1918.[28] One of two Jerome Miners' Union convention representatives was the much-traveled Lázaro Gutiérrez de Lara, who soon afterward became a vice-president of the Arizona State Federation of Labor. Canuto A. Vargas of Metcalf, a $3.52-a-day mucker at Morenci in 1916, became the Morenci Miners' Union's secretary, and by late 1917 was co-editing a national American Federation of Labor Spanish-English newspaper. During 1918, he became the Spanish language secretary of the AFL-sponsored Pan-American Federation of Labor in Washington, and Vargas was still secretary of the PAFL credentials committee in 1927.[29] Pascual M. Vargas was appointed to the seven-member Arizona Council of Defense in January, 1918.[30] Pascual Vargas, Canuto Vargas, and several other Arizona Mexican mining workers were the majority of the U.S. delegation to the Pan-American Federation of Labor's first International Labor Conference in 1918. Both Pascual and Canuto Vargas were nominated for the post of conference chairman, although both declined in favor of Samuel Gompers, then president of the American Federation of Labor, who somewhat grumpily accepted the chairmanship.[31] An impressive series of individual Mexican and Hispanic successes had begun with the big Ray and Clifton-Morenci strikes of 1915.

New copper-mining and processing complexes were created in the West during the World War. The Guggenheim combine developed a new smelter area at Hurley, in Grant County, New Mexico, near its Santa Rita copper mine. Despite all of the recent immigrant and Spanish American activism, despite all of the labor conflict, despite the Ludlow Massacre and the Mexican Revolution, the Guggenheim's Chino Mines Division smelter area was created to be a racially segregated replica of an earlier era.

The Chino Mines Division's Hurley smelter area living arrangements emphatically reasserted copper-company power prerogatives at a time when corporate power over work-force ethnic issues was being seriously challenged across the Southwest. Hurley was planned as an Anglo-and-Irish community together with a much larger other side of the tracks (a term that was used literally in Hurley) community for Mexican immigrants adjacent to, and strictly separate from the Anglo-Irish. Hurley was arranged to be like the older Guggenheim company smelter towns of McGill in Nevada, part of the Murray smelter area in Utah, and also like the more recently created company towns of Hayden, Arizona, near Ray, and Ray, including Sonora and Barcelona. Hurley's racial segregation owed nothing to custom; racist residential policy was built into the new community as a means of creating, from the beginning, a socially divided work force. Hiring and job placement at Chino Mines (Hurley and Santa Rita) were at least as racially discriminatory, if not more so, than hiring and placement practices at other, big western mining areas.[32] New Anglo employees hired at Chino Mines between 1910 and 1926 were generally untrained young men. Some of them had never previously worked for an employer. One man in a sixteen-man sample who had previously been a cowboy began work as an assistant fireman at Chino. Four years and two promotions later, he was a power-plant engineer. Another Anglo employee who began as a teamster's helper was an ore sampler, truck driver, and fireman shortly thereafter. A man hired as a switchtender became a sampler three days later. An entry-level warehouse clerk was managing the warehouse four years later. A 1910 new hire began as a carpenter and soon became a security policeman. A 1917 newly hired laborer was promoted within one week, and had become a mill foreman by 1924. Mexican employees were neither hired nor promoted in this fashion.[33]

The New Cornelia Copper Company at Ajo, Arizona, was another big wartime creation. Ajo was also begun with a racially segregated residential area carefully planned by its creator, John C. Greenway. Greenway's Ajo was contemporaneously described as a "model" set of mining communities. During the first year of full operations at the New Cornelia mine, a major nonunion strike had begun. Ajo's wages were significantly below those of other, older Arizona mining districts. Anglo-Irish electricians were the first to walk off their jobs, and Mexican and Papago Indian mining workers soon joined them. Before a group of Anglo-Irish structural iron workers helped to break the strike, a thousand racially diverse nonunion men had struck together at the newly expanded mine.[34]

Copper-company management forcefully reasserted its prerogatives over its work forces during 1917–18. The newest of western mining operations resorted to the oldest methods of dividing and manipulating their workers. Latent exclusionists and racially hostile Anglo-Irish workers still paid their dues and helped influence labor union policy during 1917–18. No egalitarian missionary effort had ever converted southwestern and Utah and Nevada exclusionists into inclusionists. But the racially and ethnically inclusionist sentiment developed during the previous years was also present, and potent, in 1917–18. Even at nonunion Ajo, three different racial-ethnic groups of newly arrived unskilled and skilled men had struck together, an event that earlier Arizona, Utah, Nevada, and West Texas labor trouble had made possible.

National IUMMSW anti-immigrant bias had not been extinguished. Delegates to the International's 1918 convention felt threatened by the Mexican nationals who were entering the United States and taking copper-mining jobs. IUMMSW delegates feared that "unless they are organized, they will be open to ruthless exploitation by the companies of Arizona, and will be a menace to all the men in the copper industry."[35] This was a re-statement of the "Mexican peons" problem, phrased almost the same way as it had been phrased at the 1914 WFM convention. But at the same 1918 convention, the two Miami delegates, both Spanish-surnamed, and the Anglo-Irish-surnamed delegates from Globe, Clarkdale (near Jerome), and Bisbee proposed increasing cooperation between Mexican nationals and U.S. labor; and they also proposed "organizing the miners of northern Mexico."[36]

The following year, members of the Pan-American Federation of Labor (whose delegates, pledged to furthering international cooperation, should have known better) inveighed against renewed immigration, the "human avalanche from Europe." Into the 1920s, some Arizona unionists continued to promote anti-alien legislation and restrictive quotas on Mexican immigration in newspaper articles which appeared practically alongside Spanish-language articles intended for working-class readers in the mining communities.[37] Contemporary readers apparently understood the distinction being made between resident immigrant workers and potential immigrants from Mexico and Europe, who were still being portrayed as a menace in the 1920s.

Did workplace change cause corresponding change in the southwestern and central western mining communities? Indices of community change in an historical setting are many and varied, and their utilization is frequently controversial. Yet there are answers.

The town of Bingham appeared to be even less egalitarian after 1917. The Bingham immigrant workers suffered through an orgy of wartime repression. A labor-organizing campaign had begun in Bingham in the autumn of 1917, and the Utah Copper Company retaliated. A Finnish mining worker reported that "when it was feared that a strike was brewing, in be-half of officers of the vigilance committee he made a house-to-house canvas of every Finnish home in the camp and ascertained the fact that every Finn here would oppose a strike should one be attempted. And this information he said he delivered to the [vigilance] committee."[38] Also, members of the Brotherhood of Locomotive Engineers and the Brotherhood of Locomotive Firemen warned the immigrant workers at Bingham not to organize, threatening them with dire consequences if they tried to replicate the events of 1912.[39] IUMMSW organizer Ben Goggin reported that during a visit to the Bingham area in October, a committee, including two Utah Copper Company white-collar men, a plumber, a banker, and a doctor, all of whom were members of a "Citizens' Protective Association," told him that he, Guy Miller, and a local area union organizer named Matt Alfirevich ought to quit organizing and leave Bingham Canyon quickly, before they were all lynched. E. G. Locke, who had been a union officer at Bingham since before 1903, was also threatened.[40] In early 1918, the Bingham Town Board decided that "no undesirables will be harbored in the camp, but those who cannot prove a definite place of employment will be asked to leave town or will be locked up."[41] Bingham town authorities, together with company officials, also conducted a thoroughgoing repressive campaign against unskilled employees.[42] The town of Bingham was in full cry against wartime "slackers" and "undesirables" throughout the last year of the World War.

Chino Mines Division's Hurley had an exceptionally thorough system of racial segregation. When the town's only motion picture theater opened, it was located in Anglo-Irish Hurley, and a Mexican resident from the other side of the tracks was only allowed to attend the theater if he or she was chaperoned by an Anglo-Irish resident. There was only one crossover location at which residents were allowed to go from El Otro Lado (the Mexican community) into Anglo Hurley. The crossover point was located behind the Chino company store and a town meat market, and eventually, it was guarded.[43]

At least a third of the Globe and Miami stores which served ethnically mixed clienteles had non-Anglo-Irish owners as early as 1912. Most of these owners were South Slavs, but a few of the owners were Jewish, Syrio-Lebanese, and Italian. Society news and holiday celebration coverage in Miami newspapers included, albeit infrequently, Serbians, and an occasional Hispanic, Italian, or Chinese resident as early as 1915. In 1915 also, the union-sponsored *Free Press* newspaper recommended editorially that residents attend a new night school which featured classes in Spanish for English speakers.[44] But, also in 1915, the town of Globe forced black residents to send their children to a separate elementary school and Mexican and other Hispanic residents to send their children into another, separate school. Miami planned to initiate segregated schooling in 1915. The Miami Cooks and Waiters' Union demanded that other Miami union men help them in eliminating Chinese restaurants from the town, and in early 1916, a newspaper reported that "The war of the whites against the Chinese goes merrily on in Miami." Four years later, the Miami YMCA opened a new, segregated building "for the Mexicans and other foreigners."[45] By 1918, life at the mines, mills, and smelters had become more ethnically tolerant; but generally, life in the communities near them had not.

Unskilled and semiskilled, mostly European immigrant, Mexican immigrant, and Spanish American mining workers saw great workplace changes at western mines, mills, and smelters. Significant change began in 1912. Massively organized immigrant opposition to management came close to success at Bingham Canyon and Ely-McGill during that year, and in 1915–16, combined Arizona Anglo-Irish and Mexican, Spanish, and Spanish American working-class activism succeeded in securing both better working conditions and a partial transference of power. Immigrant and Spanish American wages, hours, and working conditions improved, when compared with Anglo-Irish skilled and semiskilled wages, hours, and conditions of work. In the Southwest, an added increment of equality, opportunity, and ethnic-racial toleration which had developed during 1913–16 endured through the vicissitudes of wartime repression and xenophobia.

If there was comparable change in the communities adjacent to the western mines, mills, and smelters, it was either not susceptible to measurement or quantitatively insignificant. Wartime xenophobia certainly discouraged western ethnic toleration, but the war ended at last, in November 1918. Eventually, of course, some young Mexican American men and women would marry some Irish- and English-American men and women, some young Greek-American men and women would marry some young Irish-, English- and some Mexican American men and women, their children would eventually attend some of the same schools together, and all would eventually appear, more often, on the newspaper sports and society pages together. In the years ahead, increased ethnic tolerance at work might catalyze increased ethnic tolerance in the community.

Does the fact of great social change initiated by labor unions, mutual societies, and spontaneous employee groups require a drastic revision of conventional thinking? Perhaps so. As indicated at the beginning of this narrative, William Kornblum's exceptionally thorough treatment of political and sociological change in Chicago's Steeltown neighborhoods demonstrated the same phenomenon—that attitudes derived from and related to the workplace helped initiate the process which eventually changed community attitudes on race and ethnicity. But the ideas expressed in Kornblum's 1974 *Blue Collar Community* have generally been ignored by historians who specialize in the current popular issues of ethnicity, race, class, gender, work, and community. Workplace rather than community emphasis is still historiographically problematic.

No social movement dedicated to racial and ethnic toleration existed in the Southwest, Utah, or Nevada during 1896–1918. No groups worked explicitly for the ideology of inclusion. Great statements of national policy, whether emanating from the IWW, AFL, WFM, or nationally organized ethnic societies had little direct effect upon western mining communities' history. Social change occurred primarily because of *local* WFM, IWW, mutual-benefit society, and strike-connected ethnic-society activism. Events, individuals, and groups specific to particular Arizona, West Texas, Nevada, Utah, and New Mexico copper areas made changes occur. There was no natural process of change in western labor relations. Even after two decades of struggle, backsliding toward community xenophobia and discrimination was thoroughly possible.

The great ideologies of the Industrial Workers of the World or of the Partido Liberal Mexicano and the Mexican Revolution had relatively little effect upon the course of events in the copper areas. The specific cultural behavior of Greeks, South Slavs, Italians, Irish, Mexicans, Spaniards, and Spanish Americans has not been a significant part of this story, either, because it too was generally irrelevant to the outcomes of the workingmen's struggles. Most of this book has been about joint, blended union and ethnic-group activism.

In the war between men promoting ethnic inclusion and those opposing it, factions promoting inclusion won some of the battles, and exclusionist factional elements won others. Neither inclusion nor exclusion was permanently vanquished in the many copper-camp battles; and after each defeat, men of each persuasion retired to tend to the wounds, repair their weapons, and prepare for the next encounter. But by the end of the span of years discussed in this study, the ethnic inclusionists were winning the war.

Inclusion had begun as little more than a tactic which turn-of-the-century WFM radicals used because it offered them a potential means to achieve power in union locals. But eventually, when attached to Mexican, Spanish, Italian, Greek, and South Slavic notions of ethnic-racial justice, fairness, and equality, inclusion became a potent ideology as well. After 1912, there were enough ideological inclusionists to make a difference. Even John M. O'Neill, *Miners' Magazine* editor and doughty warrior for the cause of miners' unionism, came to genuinely like the idea of creating a multiracial fraternity of working people. In early 1917, he wrote a cheerful description of the striking Ajo, Arizona, nonunion work force. O'Neill knew full well that the IUMMSW would not be making a major recruiting drive among Papago Indians in the near future. But O'Neill admired the nonunion strike effort in Ajo because "while the Mexican and white man have fought the good fight for labor's cause before in this state and have stood shoulder to shoulder in it, never before has our Indian brother joined us in the battle for labor's progress."[46] Momentarily, at least, O'Neill was sharing the ideology that had changed things for the better in the Southwest, Utah, and Nevada during the early twentieth century.

NOTES

Introduction

1. Boyce was the WFM's president from 1892 to 1902; Gompers presided over the AFL during 1886–95 and 1896–1924; and Mitchell was UMWA president during 1898 and 1899–1908.

2. The Western Federation of Miners changed its name to the International Union of Mine, Mill, and Smelter Workers (IUMMSW) at its 1916 annual convention.

3. Some historians argue otherwise. Mark Wyman, for instance, explains that "the makeup of Western metal-mining labor" was "ultimately changed" by a large influx of native-born and generally Anglo-American miners, beginning in about 1896. Wyman claims that many of the new men were Missouri strikebreakers who stayed on in the West. The claim, for instance, that Missouri Anglo strikebreakers replaced Mexican workers in communities along the Mexican border is patently absurd. Wyman's analysis is not actually western, but regional. Most of his conclusions are apparently based upon a limited amount of Idaho and Colorado information (Mark Wyman, *Hard Rock Epic: Western Miners and the Industrial Revolution, 1860–1910* [Berkeley: University of California Press, 1979], 166–67; also see 55–56).

4. Charles A. Siringo, *Two Evil Isms: Pinkertonism and Anarchism* (Austin: Steck-Vaughn Co., 1967, a facsimile reproduction of the original 1915 volume, which was privately published), 109.

5. H. B. Pulsifer, "The Metallurgy of Lead," *Salt Lake Mining Review,* 30 September 1912, 20.

6. Copper miners predominated in the Butte local. Butte was a small city with a settled, old-resident Irish population whose influence was pervasive in town politics and community life, as well as at the workplace. Butte was unique in this respect. The Irish did not control any of the major copper camps, towns, or cities south of Butte. For a thorough study of Butte, see David M. Emmons, *The Butte Irish* (Urbana and Chicago: University of Illinois Press, 1989).

7. Nonselective mining operations processed low-grade ore containing as little as 1 or 2 percent copper. For an explanation of the transition to nonselective copper mining, see Oris Clemens Herfindahl, *Copper Costs and Prices: 1870–1957* (Baltimore: The Johns Hopkins Press, 1959). Also, more recently, George Hildebrand and Garth L. Mangum, *Capital and Labor in American Copper: 1845–1990* (Cambridge: Harvard University Press, 1992), 61–93.

8. There were few African Americans employed in western hard-rock mining areas during 1896–1918.

9. Emmons, *Butte Irish;* Andrea Yvette Huginnie, "'Strikitos': Race, Class, and Work in the Arizona Copper Industry, 1870–1920" (Ph.D. dissertation, Yale University, 1991); Gunther W. Peck, "Crisis in the Family: Padrones and Radicals in Utah, 1908–1912" in Dan Georgakas and Charles C. Moskos, eds., *New Directions in Greek-American Studies* (New York: Pella Press, 1991).

10. Detroit Copper Mining Company, "Payroll" and "Time Book" records for mine and ore-processing facilities, 1902–4, at Special Collections, University of Arizona Library, Tucson.

11. Mexican immigrants, who were a work-force majority in many southwestern mining areas, frequently returned to Mexico and sometimes reappeared at the mines in Arizona. A 1919 study of men and women crossing into Mexico from the United States at El Paso, Texas, many of whom had probably spent some time in southwestern mining areas, found that 54 percent had spent less than five years in the United States (Servando I. Esquivel, "The Immigrant from Mexico," *The Outlook* 125 [19 May 1920]:131, cited in Emilio Zamora, *The World of the Mexican Worker in Texas* [College Station: Texas A & M University Press, 1993], 14).

12. Some work has been done in amassing individual mining workers' biographical information, especially through state- and county-centered oral-history programs, but little work has yet been done in synthesizing it.

13. "Gunsmoke," purportedly the story of "the hard-living citizens of old Dodge City," actually began on radio, and then moved to television. For a classic description of the real Dodge City, with high transiency rates and a constantly changing group of leading citizens and law enforcement personnel, see Robert R. Dykstra, *The Cattle Towns* (New York: Knopf, 1968), especially 74–132, 355.

14. Patricia Nelson Limerick's *The Legacy of Conquest: The Unbroken Past of the American West* (New York: W. W. Norton and Company, 1987) is perhaps the best-known recent volume of historical essays about western subject matter. Her treatment of late-nineteenth and early-twentieth-century western working-class history includes a mismatched and chronologically homogenized blend of Industrial

Workers of the World and Western Federation of Miners information which blurs sequential cause-and-effect relationships during the crucial 1905–16 period (117–22). Alan Derickson's *Workers' Health, Workers' Democracy* (Ithaca: Cornell University Press, 1988) also blends IWW and WFM information, and generally offers topical essays about western mining areas based on combined data from geographically and chronologically unrelated western areas; see esp. 161. A recent book edited by William J. Cronon, George Miles, and Jay Gitlin, *Under an Open Sky: Rethinking America's Western Past* (New York: W. W. Norton and Company, 1992) includes a chronologically nonspecific essay by Sarah Deutsch, "Landscape of Enclaves: Race Relations in the West, 1865–1990," whose statements about "hegemony," "enclavement," the IWW, the AFL, and *mutualista* activity are accurate enough when applied to some times and places, and completely erroneous when applied to other portions of her century-and-a-quarter-long time sequence (118–23). Similarly, statements about western "radicalism," "political apathy," and the western IWW during a forty-year-long period which appear in Michael E. McGerr's essay in the same book are true of some times and places and incorrect when applied to others ("Is There a Twentieth-Century West," in Cronon, Miles, and Gitlin, op. cit., 249–50). Current examples of chronological blurring in non-western general essays about late-nineteenth and early-twentieth-century labor history include Walter Licht, *Getting Work: Philadelphia, 1840–1950* (Cambridge: Harvard University Press, 1992); and James R. Barrett, "Americanization from the Bottom Up: Immigration and the Remaking of the Working Class in the United States, 1880–1930" in *Journal of American History* 79, no. 3 (December 1992), esp. 999.

15. Ira Katznelson, *City Trenches* (New York: Pantheon Books, 1981), 51–58, 58–61, 11; Emmons, *Butte Irish*, 134; Charles Stephenson and Robert Asher (eds.) *Life and Labor: Dimensions of American Working-Class History* (Binghamton: State University of New York Press, 1986), 79–80; John Bodnar, Roger Simon, and Michael Weber, *Lives of Their Own: Blacks, Italians, and Poles in Pittsburgh, 1900–1960* (Urbana: University of Illinois Press, 1982), 130, 143–44.

16. Vincent DiGirolamo writes that the 1913 Wheatland hop workers' strike in California was "sparked" by "female consciousness" rather than IWW organizing ("The Women of Wheatland: Female Consciousness and the 1913 Wheatland Hop Strike," *Labor History* 34, nos. 2–3 [spring–summer, 1993]:237). Colleen O'Neill claims that the Bisbee Deportation was not, primarily, "a male affair" ("Domesticity Deployed: Gender, Race, and the Construction of Class Struggle in the Bisbee Deportation," *Labor History* 34, nos. 2–3 [spring–summer, 1993]:258–59). Women who were neither actually *in* the workplace nor directly organizing among the men in it sometimes lent significant support to strike efforts, as in the Lawrence, Massachusetts strike of 1912, as Mari Jo Buhle explained in a 1989 essay ("Gender and Labor: History," in *Perspectives on American Labor History,* ed. J. Carroll Moody and Alice Kessler-Harris, 65–66 [DeKalb, Ill.: Northern Illinois University, 1989]). However, this was certainly not the case in Bisbee in 1917.

17. William Kornblum, *Blue Collar Community* (Chicago: University of Chicago Press, 1974), 219–28. The gulf between the ethnic and racial groups in Gary and South Chicago was bridged through an appeal to class, rather than race, at work, according to Kornblum. "Union politics," Kornblum wrote, presented "the greatest potential for change in blue collar communities," and the first generation of ethnic leaders, particularly those in the South Chicago Mexican and Mexican American community, was composed of the men who had become union leaders at the steel plants. See also 81, 84, 102, 105.

18. James R. Barrett, *Work and Community in the Jungle* (Urbana: University of Illinois Press, 1987), 136–42; Zamora, *World of the Mexican Worker,* 210, also see 196–98.

19. The one exception is the El Paso smelter strike of 1913, discussed later.

20. There are no agreed-upon definitions for most ethnic categories, which makes direct historiographical comparisons among ethnic studies dubious at best. Definitions of culturally Hispanic, ethnically Hispanic, and Hispanic-via-geographic-nativity populations in the United States include those of Sarah Deutsch, in *No Separate Refuge: Culture, Class, and Gender on an Anglo-Hispanic Frontier in the American Southwest, 1880–1940* (New York: Oxford University Press, 1987); Mario T. García, *Desert Immigrants: The Mexicans of El Paso, 1880–1920* (New Haven: Yale University Press, 1981); and those employed in a recent article by Jeanette Rodda, "'A Little Bit Better': William Andrews Clark and Welfare Work in Arizona," in *Montana* 42, Number 4 (autumn, 1992); and in Huginnie, "Strikitos." Deutsch favors the use of the term *Chicanos,* and avoids distinguishing between long-resident Spanish Americans and the several cohorts of more recent Mexican immigrants; and she applies her "Chicanos" rubric to Hispanic people in "New Mexico, Texas, California, and Colorado"; she unaccountably omits Arizona (*No Separate Refuge,* 6–7). García explicitly refuses to categorize the various recognizable types of Hispanic populations separately (*Desert Immigrants,* 2). His terminology of choice—"Mexican," "Mexican American," and "Spanish surnamed"—is overlapping: an individual Hispanic person could have been all three, simultaneously, using García's definitions. Jeanette Rodda specifically discusses "Hispanos" (that is, U.S.-born persons with some discernible connection to Hispanic culture and/or nativity). But the population of Jerome, Arizona, the subject of her article, was partly Spanish immigrant and partly Mexican immigrant as well. She solves this "problem" by carefully conflating the word *Hispano* with *Hispanic* in her discussions of Jerome population groups (42–43). Huginnie, similarly aware of the existence of several "Hispanic" populations in early-twentieth-century Arizona, uses *Mexicans* and *Mexican Americans,* and *Spaniards* and *other immigrants* interchangeably and nonspecifically in a melded variety of different situations (esp. 6, 172–75, 179–80). A more careful, limited, and effective use of terminology in explaining South and East Texas in the early twentieth century is that of Emilio Zamora, who employs the term *Mexican,* along with, on occasion, specific information about nativity, and acknowledges the descriptive limits of his terminology

(*World of the Mexican Worker,* xi–xii). South Slavs, an important population in Bisbee, Arizona at the time of the 1917 Deportation, are defined into oblivion by Colleen O'Neill. O'Neill states, "I am using the term 'white' to characterize people with European heritage." Many Mexicans, Anglo-Americans, Irish Americans, and South Slavs can, of course, claim some measure of "European heritage." The South Slavs are implicitly described as "other people" on one page of the article, as the "40%" of the deportees who "were from Eastern Europe" in a nearby section, and as "white workers," indistinguishable from Anglos and Irish, elsewhere in the article. O'Neill also offers her own, adventitiously crafted definition of Bisbee-area "Mexicans" ("Domesticity Deployed," 256–73). South Slavs were generally labeled "Austrians" by unknowing Anglo-Americans in early-twentieth-century accounts. They are similarly labeled in Ronald C. Brown's general study of western mining (*Hard-Rock Miners: The Intermountain West, 1860–1920* [College Station: Texas A & M University Press, 1979], 132).

21. Gunther Peck, "Padrones and Protest: 'Old' Radicals and 'New' Immigrants in Bingham, Utah, 1905–1912," *Western Historical Quarterly* 24, no. 2 (May 1993); Peck, "Charles Moyer and 'New' Immigrants: The Politics of Race and Ethnicity in the WFM, 1910–1912," a paper presented at the Western History Association's annual conference, 19 October, 1991; O'Neill, "Domesticity Deployed"; Huginnie, "Strikitos." David Emmons's study of the Irish working-class community in Butte similarly avoids discussion of comparable ethnic groups in comparable circumstances by defining Butte as an industrial city, and all of the other, contemporary western mining and metal-processing communities in the intermountain West and Southwest as "camps" rather than cities. Using Emmons's definition, the "camps" were not directly comparable with the "city" of Butte or its working people. Bisbee and Globe, Arizona, Bingham, Utah, and arguably, several other relevant incorporated political entities in western mining areas are conventionally described as towns and cities everywhere except in Emmons's book (*Butte Irish,* esp. 36, 190, 235, 247).

Chapter 1

1. Ralph Mann, *After the Gold Rush: Society in Grass Valley and Nevada City, California, 1849–70* (Stanford: Stanford University Press, 1982), 184, 187–88, 216; Arthur Cecil Todd, *The Cornish Miner in America* (Truro, England: D. Bradford Barton, 1967), 165–66; Gwendolyn Rachel Mink, *Old Labor and New Immigrants in American Political Development: Union, Party, and State, 1875–1920* (Ithaca: Cornell University Press, 1986), 53. The Cornish-Irish alliance was not invariably nativist, according to Ralph Mann. Ronald Brown, citing an older study of Comstock (Nevada) mining, argues against Cornish-Irish alliances, even in the 1890s (*Hard-Rock Miners,* 132).

2. The terms *Cornish, Irish, Scotch,* etc. do not appear on material written at the workplace, such as time sheets, payroll records of other kinds, "company ground" records, etc., after 1900. Also, those ethnic categories do not appear in company-

generated information sources, nor in most newspaper interviews with company administrative personnel after 1900. The terms *American, foreign, Italian,* and *Mexican,* however, were included in the company's vocabulary during the early twentieth century. Nowhere in the western copper communities south of Montana did copper-company management distinguish between its northwest European employees in assigning wage rates; but everywhere, company management distinguished between employees of northwest European descent as against all of the other ethnic groups in their work forces.

3. Helen Zeese Papanikolas, "Magerou, The Greek Midwife," *Utah Historical Quarterly* 38, no. 1 (winter 1970):53.

4. George S. McGovern and Leonard F. Guttridge, *The Great Coalfield War* (Boston: Houghton Mifflin, 1972), 47; Victor S. Clark, "Mexican Labor in the United States," *Bulletin of the United States Bureau of Labor Statistics,* no. 78 (Washington, D.C.: U.S. Government Printing Office, 1908), 516. Many of the "Mexican" strikebreakers in Colorado during 1903 were probably Americans of Spanish or Mexican descent rather than Mexicans. This group remained a frequently recognizable although decreasing proportion of the southwestern copper industry work force after 1903.

5. Hildebrand and Mangum, *Capital and Labor,* 109–13.

6. Clark, "Mexican Labor," 466, 486, 492, 512. Clark's study followed a study of Mexican workers in Mexico by Professor Walter F. Weyl several years earlier. Weyl called Mexican labor "cheap, inefficient, unintelligent, and untrustworthy." "The most salient characteristic of native [that is, Mexican] labor is apathy" (Walter E. Weyl, "Labor Conditions in Mexico," *Bulletin of the U.S. Department of Labor* 34–38, no. 38 [January 1902]:12, 88).

7. Huginnie, "Strikitos," 14–17; Loren B. Chan, "The Chinese in Nevada: An Historical Survey, 1856–1970," *Nevada Historical Society Quarterly* 28, no. 4 (winter 1982):270–71, 280.

8. José Ignacio Torres, "The Globe Strike (Lockout?) of 1896," typescript at Arizona State University, Tempe, dated "1974 or 1975," 6, 7; *Arizona Silver Belt* (Globe), 4 June 1896, 2. Further research could reveal even earlier examples of Mexican-and-Anglo ethnic replacement at small industrial and mining facilities.

9. Torres, "Globe Strike," 7–10.

10. Ibid., 10–18.

11. Ibid., 9–10.

12. Ibid., 18, 21.

13. Ibid., 13.

14. *Arizona Silver Belt,* 4 June 1896, 2.

15. Torres, "Globe Strike," 10, 11, 16–18; *Arizona Silver Belt,* 11 June 1896, 3. There was a miner's union in Globe in 1884. It was associated with the miner's-union movement at Virginia City, Nevada, and several other western camps. This group of unions became the Western Federation of Miners in 1893, but the Globe union had apparently disintegrated during the nine-year interim. It was, in effect,

resurrected by the events of 1896 (Vernon H. Jensen, *Heritage of Conflict* [Ithaca: Cornell University Press, 1950], 17).

16. *Arizona Silver Belt,* 11 June 1896, 3; Torres, "Globe Strike," 14, 15.

17. Torres, "Globe Strike," 14, 15.

18. Edward Boyce, "Travel Diary," 1896 entries, in Edward Boyce Papers, 1881–1941, at Cheney Cowles Museum, Special Collections, Eastern Washington State Historical Society, Spokane.

19. Boyce, "Travel Diary," 1896–1902 entries; *Jerome Mining News,* 23 July 1900, 2; Brown, *Hard-Rock Miners,* 12; WFM, *Proceedings . . . 1903,* 88–89; WFM, *Proceedings . . . 1905,* 204–8; WFM, *Proceedings . . . 1906.*

20. *Arizona Daily Citizen* (Tucson) 2 February 1900, 1; Michael Casillas, "Mexicans, Labor, and Strife in Arizona, 1896–1917" (M.A. thesis, University of New Mexico, 1979), 39. Casillas extensively researched Arizona territorial newspapers to find antecedents to the 1903 Clifton-Morenci strike, and to find the earliest Arizona mining strikes conducted by Mexican workers. The interpretation offered here differs from Casillas's, and is based upon newspaper accounts.

21. *Arizona Daily Citizen,* 2 February 1900, 1.

22. Ibid., 3 February 1900, 1.

23. Ibid., 30 October 1901, 3; *Arizona Republican,* 2 November 1901, 3.

24. *Arizona Republican,* 2 November 1901, 3.

25. *Jerome Mining News,* 25 August 1902, 1.

26. Ibid.

27. Correspondence to United Verde Copper Company from W. E. Giese, Manager, Thiel Detective Service Company, dated from 13 September 1903 to 21 December 1903 and also including a letter of uncertain vintage (but probably 1903), in Box 45, Folder 1, United Verde Copper Company Collection, Special Collections, Northern Arizona University, Flagstaff; WFM, *Proceedings . . . 1903,* 84.

28. United Verde correspondence, letter dated 22 August 1903.

29. Ibid., date unknown but probably 1903.

30. The union affiliation (or lack of it) of the one or more men who dynamited the bridge near Jerome Junction cannot be determined, but it seems likely that he or they were anti-Hispanic and associated with Jerome-area unionism.

31. See the discussion of the August–October 1902 Globe strike later.

32. *Arizona Silver Belt,* 25 September 1902, 1 and 9 October 1902, 2; James David McBride, "Organized Labor in Globe: Building a Gibraltar in the Desert, 1884–1912," (paper presented at the annual meeting of the Arizona Historical Society, Globe, 4 May 1991), 11–12.

33. WFM, *Proceedings . . . 1903,* 230–31. Several other big WFM locals, including Butte Number 1, and Tonopah, Nevada's Number 220, are known to have had contracts with copper-company management during 1907. The 1907 contracts may have been inspired by Globe's action five years earlier. For an explanation of some of the circumstances surrounding the writing of the Butte contract, see

Emmons, *Butte Irish*, 241; for Tonopah, see *Tonopah Sun*, 19 January 1907, 2.

34. WFM, *Proceedings . . . 1903*, 230–32. The Globe contract, the Globe Union's exclusionist activities, and the men who sponsored both were still a subject of contention in 1907. In that year, Ed Crough, a young organizer for national WFM headquarters, went to Globe and again argued with the local's members about the contract. Crough wrote in his notebook that he had convinced the local's leaders to submit the contract to a referendum of the membership. He hoped that the referendum would bring about the elimination of the Globe contract, but his proposition failed, in a close vote (Edward Crough Notebooks, held by the Crough family, Phoenix, Arizona, entry dating from 1907).

35. WFM, *Proceedings . . . 1903*, 230–31; McBride, "Organized Labor in Globe," 11. The maintenance of a consistent floor under wages paid for particular mining jobs had a long history in western metal-mining unionism. The notion of maintaining a set of standard wages in particular mining districts was in no sense "radical" in the West. It was traditional. Wage-scale maintenance before 1900 is best explained in Richard E. Lingenfelter, *The Hardrock Miners: A History of the Mining Labor Movement in the American West, 1863–1893* (Berkeley: University of California Press, 1974), 163–65, 196–201.

36. James McBride ("Organized Labor in Globe," 12) quotes a hostile statement that appeared in the *Arizona Silver Belt* shortly after the boycott against that newspaper ended, to the effect that the GMU's conservative majority was overwhelmingly large. Since the conservatives themselves had been unable to control the union local only a few weeks earlier, this seems unlikely.

37. McBride, "Organized Labor in Globe," 10.

38. WFM, "Report of the Executive Board," in *Proceedings . . . 1903*, 95–96. I am indebted to Professor James Foster for suggesting the relevance of this information. Also, *Jerome Mining News*, 23 July 1900, 3.

39. WFM, *Proceedings . . . 1903*, 95–96, 224, 265; Ibid., *Proceedings . . . 1902*, 5.

40. WFM, *Proceedings . . . 1903*, 96.

41. Ibid., 265.

42. *Jerome Mining News*, 1 September 1902, 3. The Western Federation of Miners, of course, was part of "organized labor," but not part of the American Federation of Labor. When the two national union organizations had parted company in 1897 they had not parted as friends. In Arizona, however, there are strong indications that the WFM and the AFL skilled-trades unions worked together for the eight-hour day, and that they worked together in politics and continued to do so through the 1910 Constitutional Convention as well. For a discussion of that Constitutional Convention and labor's role in it, see chapter 4. Bingham Canyon, Utah's WFM Local Number 67 also consistently collaborated with the Salt Lake City AFL labor movement throughout this period, as explained in chapter 5.

43. WFM, *Proceedings . . . 1903*, 18, 142.

44. *Arizona Silver Belt*, 27 March 1902, 4; 10 April 1902, 1.

45. C. L. Sonnichsen, *Colonel Green and the Copper Skyrocket* (Tucson: University of Arizona Press, 1974), 119–21; *Arizona Silver Belt,* 8 May 1902, 1.

46. *Arizona Silver Belt,* 1 May 1902, 5.

47. The price of copper began to fall in January, 1902, because the Amalgamated Copper Company, a Standard Oil affiliate and a major producer, had been restricting output, and had ceased restricting it in December 1901 (Herfindahl, *Copper Costs and Prices,* 80–82).

48. *Jerome Mining News,* 1 September 1902, 3.

49. Ibid., 11 May 1903, 3.

50. Joseph F. Park, "The History of Mexican Labor in Arizona During the Territorial Period" (M.A. thesis, University of Arizona, 1961), 254.

51. *Arizona Silver Belt,* 12 August 1902, 1; 12 February 1903, 1.

52. WFM, *Proceedings . . . 1903,* 230.

53. Ibid., 25; Russell R. Elliott, *Nevada's Twentieth-Century Mining Boom* (Reno: University of Nevada Press, 1966), 206–8; Jack Fleming, *Copper Times* (Seattle: Jack Fleming Publications, 1987), 75–77.

54. *Arizona Silver Belt,* 28 May 1903, 2.

Chapter 2

1. Anonymous, "Morenci," published in *El Obrero* (Morenci, Arizona), 4 July 1903, 1.

2. Jensen, *Heritage of Conflict,* 96 159; *Arizona Republican* (Phoenix), 11 June 1903, 2; *Arizona Silver Belt,* 5 March 1903, 1.

3. A thorough discussion of the Eight Hour Movement at its zenith and of the labor-management conflict which was associated with it appears in George G. Suggs, Jr., *Colorado's War on Militant Unionism: James H. Peabody and the Western Federation of Miners* (Detroit: Wayne State University Press, 1972). Many veterans of the Colorado struggle later found work in Nevada mines.

4. *Arizona Silver Belt,* 23 January 1902, 4; 27 February 1902, 1; 14 August 1902, 1; 4 June 1903, 1, 2.

5. *Copper Era* (Clifton, Arizona Territory), 18 June 1903, 2.

6. Park, "History of Mexican Labor," 189–90.

7. Roberta Watt, "The History of Morenci, Arizona" (master's thesis, University of Arizona, 1956), 38.

8. Clark, "Mexican Labor," 468; U.S. Bureau of the Census, manuscript returns for 1900 labeled "Graham County, Arizona Territory," and specifically, "Morenci," "Clifton," and "Metcalf."

9. James Monroe Patton, "The History of Clifton, Arizona" (master's thesis, University of Arizona, 1945), 47–48; personal interview with Al Fernandez, an early-twentieth-century and current Clifton resident, in Clifton, 21 May 1991.

10. Quoted in Park, "History of Mexican Labor," 256. The actual difference in wage rates, while significant, was much less than 50 percent in 1903.

11. *Arizona Republican,* 11 June 1903, 1, 8.

12. J. H. Bassett, "Notes dictated for the Arizona Archives while He was in the Arizona Pioneers Home, 15 March 1936" (Arizona State Archives, Phoenix), typescript version, 1.

13. Photographs from LaMoine Collection, Arizona Historical Society Library, Tucson.

14. Detroit Copper Mining Company, "Payroll" and "Time Book" records, 1902–4, at Special Collections, University of Arizona Library. Subsequent references to Detroit and Arizona copper company payroll records and time sheets are styled "DCC" (Detroit Company), and "ACC" (Arizona Copper Mining Company), and are specific as to payroll and time-sheet dates. Where particular mine or smelter payrolls were used, they are indicated. In most instances, the information is derived from several, or as many as several dozen payroll sheets for a given mine or date. Some of the payroll records at the University of Arizona Library used by this writer were subsequently destroyed by the Library. This writer used the original handwritten pay and time records. Microfilmers inadvertently destroyed the handwritten material from years preceding 1903 without microfilming them.

15. James Foster, "The Ten Day Tramps," *Labor History* 23, no. 4 (fall 1982): 608–23; Todd, *The Cornish Miner in America*, 237. Because of the overwhelming western residential and occupational transiency rates and the frequency of Italian, Greek, and Mexican recidivism, meaningful ethnic population estimates must be directly tied to contemporary events. Discussions of 1903 work-force population must be confined to 1903 and the months immediately preceding and following 1903; or they must be measured in intervals of *months,* rather than years, from 1903 events. Decennial censuses provide precise measures, but they are almost useless when measuring early-twentieth-century western mining area work-force populations in noncensus years. Despite this, some studies of non-decennial-year events use the decennial census for their population estimates. These studies tend to compensate for the inherent inaccuracy of their population information by generalizing about "decades" and "patterns," and avoiding the specific dynamics of month-by-month and year-by-year change in western mining areas.

16. U.S. Bureau of the Census, manuscript returns for 1900.

17. Comparative information which correlates the work histories of mining-company employees with the purchase and sale of their homes is compiled from many sources: Greenlee County, Arizona, Recorder's Office, *Incorporations,* Greenlee County, Book 1 (Transcribed record of Graham County incorporations); ibid., *Bills of Sale,* Books 1, 2; ibid., *Miscellaneous Records,* Book 2; ibid., *Index to Mortgages and Mortgagees,* Book 1; Greenlee County, Arizona Assessor's Office, "Original Assessment Roll of Graham County, 1902"; visual observation of old Morenci and Metcalf housing; and miscellaneous photographs entitled "Morenci home" and "Morenci dwelling," dates estimated as 1904–5, at Arizona Historical Society Library, Tucson.

18. Accumulated property and other forms of material wealth are arguably the most important determinants of community social class and community-ascribed

status, as explained in an essay by Stuart Blumin, quoted in an article in the *Journal of Social History*. That is, real estate ownership, more than job status or earnings, may have made these Clifton-Morenci families "middle class," or "settled," in a strictly local community context (Stuart Blumin, quoted in "Economic Growth and Occupational Mobility in Nineteenth Century Urban America: A Reappraisal," by Michael Weber and Anthony Boardman, *Journal of Social History* 2, no. 1 [fall 1977]:52–74).

Several studies ascribe "deeply conservative tendencies" to married, regularly employed homeowners. The Clifton-Morenci workingmen of 1903 fit the specifications, but not the image. They were not deeply conservative. For the conservative interpretation, see Stephenson and Asher, *Life and Labor,* 79–80; John Bodnar, *Workers' World: Kinship, Community, and Protest in an Industrial Society, 1900–1940* (Baltimore: Johns Hopkins University, 1982), 166, 177, 185; Bodnar, Simon, and Weber, *Blacks, Italians, and Poles,* 119, 153–54. Bodnar discusses frame homes in Pittsburgh owned by lower-income Italian workers during 1900–24. The average purchase price of these homes was $2,585. Workers' homes in Morenci and Metcalf often sold for between $100 and $200 (Bodnar, Simon, and Weber, *Blacks, Italians, and Poles,* 173).

19. DCC, "Payroll" and "Time Book" records, 1903–3. The copper company records generally did not distinguish between Mexicans, Mexican Americans, Spanish Americans, and Spaniards.

20. Ibid.

21. Ibid.

22. An estimated four hundred Spaniards lived in the Clifton-Morenci area during these years (Al Fernandez interview).

23. Ibid. In comparable circumstances, also during the early twentieth century, the Oliver Mining Company at the Mesabi iron range in Minnesota stated openly that its promotion policy discriminated in favor of American-born men (Michael G. Karni, "Finnish Immigrant Leftists in America: The Golden Years 1900–1918," in Dirk Hoerder, ed., *Struggle a Hard Battle: Essays on Working-Class Immigrants* [DeKalb: Northern Illinois University Press, 1986], 206).

24. As previously indicated, there are no thorough monographic studies of the 1903 Clifton-district strike, although many historians have alluded to it in general discussions of western labor and ethnicity. The strike was presented to public-television viewers in 1991 and 1992 in the videotape "Los Mineros" (Galán Productions, Incorporated of Austin, Texas, and television station WGBH, Boston, 1990). Typically, "Los Mineros" carefully avoided discussion of Spanish American and Italian strike participation in favor of a chauvinistic all-Mexican-immigrant story.

25. Similar evidence of ethnically combined local activist societies appears in Charles van Onselen's study of Rhodesian (Zimbabwean) mining workers and unionism in the teens and 1920s. Van Onselen writes that Rhodesian miners often joined workers' groups regardless of their own tribal affiliations. Van Onselen says

that Rhodesian miners' associations "tended to stretch beyond the more limited horizons of tribalism," and that the African miners joined the associations "as *workers* [his emphasis], rather than as ethnically-defined individuals" (van Onselen, *Chibaro: African Mine Labour in Southern Rhodesia, 1900–1933* [Johannesburg: Ravan Press, 1980], 202–3).

26. DCC, "Payroll" and "Time Book" records, May 1903; *Arizona Republican,* 13 June 1903, 1; 14 June 1903, 1; 25 June 1903, 2; *Copper Era,* 25 June 1903, 2.

27. Park, "History of Mexican Labor," 255.

28. *Arizona Republican,* 12 June 1903, 1; *El Obrero,* 4 July 1903, 2. The English approximation of "Weneslado" is "Winslow."

29. *Phoenix Gazette,* 9 June 1953, n.p., scrap in Arizona State Archives files, Phoenix. In 1903, the temporary headquarters of the Western Federation of Miners' creation, the American Labor Union, was in Chicago.

30. "Three Fingered Jack" was the name given the most famous associate of Joaquín Murieta, in 1850s California. "Jack" was, by reputation, a brutal killer (John Rollin Ridge, *The Life and Adventures of Joaquín Murieta, The Celebrated California Bandit,* edited by Joseph Henry Jackson [Norman: University of Oklahoma Press, 1955]); letter from Weneslado Laustaunau, Jr. to Weneslado Laustaunau, Sr. dated 29 November 1905, written at Territorial Prison, Yuma, Arizona (copy provided by the late Edward Laustaunau).

31. *Arizona Republican,* 12 June 1903, 1; the description of Laustaunau as a Romanian and as a possible assassin's accomplice appears in several accounts, but there is no indication of how these tales originated.

32. *Arizona Republican,* 5 June 1903, 3.

33. Greenlee County, Arizona, *Incorporations,* Book 1.

34. Ibid.

35. Ibid.; Isidro Fabela, *Documentos Históricos de la Revolución Mexicana,* Vol. 11 (Mexico City: Editorial Jus, 1960), 133. There is no clear evidence of the Alianza's active involvement in this strike, or even of its inspiring "resistance" at Clifton-Morenci. The unproven notion that the Alianza could have been a frequent participant in early-twentieth-century southwestern labor activism is suggested by events at Yuma, Arizona Territory, cited in Rodolfo Acuña, *Occupied America: A History of Chicanos,* 3rd ed. (New York: Harper and Row, 1988), 96–97.

36. Fabela, *Documentos Históricos,* 133.

37. Greenlee County, Arizona, *Incorporations,* Book 1.

38. Zamora, *World of the Mexican Worker,* 70, 72, 88, 90–92, 131–32, 149–51, 205; Roberto Calderón, "Mexicano Mutualistas and Labor Activity in Early Texas History," a paper presented at Western History Association's Annual Conference, Tulsa, Oklahoma, 15 October 1993. Other, more general studies of mutualistas include Mario Barrera, *Beyond Aztlan: Ethnic Autonomy in Comparative Perspective* (New York: Praeger Publishers, 1988), esp. 13–15; Jose Amaro Hernández, *Mutual Aid for Survival: the Case of the Mexican American* (Malabar, Florida: Robert F. Krieger Publishing Company, 1983), esp. 34–40; Kaye Lynn Briegel, "Alianza

Hispano-Americana, 1894–1965: A Mexican American Fraternal Insurance Society" (Ph.D. dissertation, University of Southern California, 1974). All of these studies suggest connections between the mutualistas and 1900–10 labor conflict, but none of them explains precisely how the mutualistas and labor were interrelated. A general statement about the origins of other southwestern mutualistas without any specific claims to labor activism appears in Deutsch, *No Separate Refuge*, 26. David Corbin's study of eastern coal miners suggests a paucity of precise information about grass-roots, local-level worker social organizations during the early twentieth century, combined with a plethora of unsubstantiated conclusions. Corbin writes that "Little is known about the role of social clubs and fraternities in the lives of the black miners in the company towns" but then he promptly concludes that "it must have been significant" (David Alan Corbin, *Life, Work, and Rebellion in the Coal Fields: The Southern West Virginia Miners, 1880–1922* [Urbana: University of Illinois Press, 1981], 74–75).

39. Zamora, *World of the Mexican Worker*, 108–9, 115, 189–93.

40. Van Onselen's study of East African miners in about 1920 suggests that social and mutual societies were "the logical precursors of a trade union movement." One Rhodesian union, the Industrial and Commercial Workers' Union, actually used an ethnic society as its operational base, but it was an exception. Most Zimbabwean workers were not able to create combined mutual societies and unions because they were too poor to pay for the potential costs of activist labor unionism (van Onselen, *Chibaro*, 203).

41. Zamora, *World of the Mexican Worker*, 88, 90, 92.

42. Philip Frank Notarianni, "Tale of Two Towns: The Social Dynamics of Eureka and Helper, Utah" (Ph.D. dissertation, University of Utah, 1980), 95; David Montgomery, "Nationalism, American Patriotism, and Class Consciousness among Immigrant Workers in the United States in the Epoch of World War I," in Hoerder, *Struggle a Hard Battle*, 331.

43. See chapter 8. Emilio Zamora mentions an early-twentieth-century cement workers' strike on the outskirts of San Antonio which was begun by a fraternal lodge chapter, the Woodmen of the World of Cementville, Texas (*World of the Mexican Worker*, 75).

44. *Arizona Republican*, 13 June 1903, 1; Fabela, *Documentos Históricos*, 133.

45. *Arizona Republican*, 12 June 1903, 1.

46. Ibid, 13 June 1903, 1.

47. Ibid., 12 June 1903, 1.

48. Letters from C. E. Mills, Superintendent, to Professor James Douglas, President, Detroit Copper Mining Company, from Morenci, dated 30 July 1903, in Lewis Douglas Collection, AZ 290, Box 12b, Special Collections, University of Arizona Library.

49. *Arizona Republican*, 13 June 1903, 1.

50. "Register and Descriptive List of Convicts in the Territorial Prison, Arizona," entries listed as "Graham County," "miner," and "Riot," 1903; at Arizona

State Archives, Phoenix. Surnames which "look" Spanish and Italian are not a reliable means of assigning probable ethnic origin for persons in historical accounts under *present* circumstances; but there is a much greater likelihood of reliability in dealing with early-twentieth-century surnames. Conjectural evidence for ethnic origins of working people in the West and Southwest during the late nineteenth and early twentieth centuries has become conventionally acceptable; perhaps too much so, as Weneslado Laustaunau's name might indicate. Immigrants from Spain itself and men who came from Spain by way of Mexico were a measurable component in the work force of several big southwestern mines; and they are practically "lost" too, just as Laustaunau's ethnic origins almost were. Frequent movement from job to job and the absence of 1890 census materials, together with a paucity of corroborating evidence, combine to create this uncertainty about surnames and ethnicity during that period. The historians' custom of assigning apparent ethnicity based primarily upon surname is followed here.

51. Available sources do not show the national origins of the other five men. U.S. Bureau of the Census, manuscript returns for 1900; Fabela, *Documentos Históricos,* 133. There is no evidence that the Mexican Americans involved in this strike were significantly less disaffected than were the Mexicans at Clifton, Morenci, and Metcalf. The two groups generally lived in the same residential areas, and they were thoroughly intermingled in the almost exclusively Spanish-surnamed sections of Metcalf in 1900. In fact, the proportions of 1900 Mexicans and Mexican Americans who were literate in English were surprisingly similar. The Mexican Americans do not appear to have been a class of knowledgeable Americanized intermediaries, in comparison to the Mexicans (U.S. Bureau of the Census, manuscript returns for 1900, pages labeled "Metcalf").

52. Letters from Cecelia A. Hall, Banning, California to this writer, dated 6 March 1981; 13 May 1981; the late Edward Laustaunau, Riverside, California (Edward Laustaunau was Weneslado Laustaunau's nephew), personal interviews in 1981 and 1990; "Territorial Prison at Yuma, A. T., Description of convict William H. Laustaunau" [*sic*], typescript from Yuma Territorial Prison State Park, Yuma, Arizona.

53. Edward Laustaunau, personal interviews; *Arizona Republican,* May, June, 1903, passim. "El Mojo" does not translate into "The Crippled Hand," and the newspaper reports on this nickname must have been in error. Laustaunau was more probably "El Cojo," "The Cripple."

54. U.S. Bureau of the Census, manuscript returns for 1900; Greenlee County, Arizona, Assessor's Office, "Original Assessment Roll of Graham County, 1903."

55. Greenlee County, Arizona, *Recorder's Bills of Sale, Greenlee County,* Book no. 1 (Transcribed from Graham County records); Greenlee County, "Original Assessment Roll of Graham County, 1903"; U.S. Bureau of the Census, manuscript returns for 1900.

56. U.S. Bureau of the Census, manuscript returns for 1900, manuscript returns for 1910; Greenlee County, Arizona, "Original Assessment Roll of Graham County,

1903." However, Maxemilo Arilo is listed as a strike leader in other source material. The assessment roll lists a lumber house, valued at $75, standing on Arizona Copper Company land in 1903, belonging to Maximo Avalos. Recordkeeping being what it was, "Avalos" may have been "Arilo."

This does not, however, suggest that the new arrivals were necessarily exceptionally young, or that they were newly arrived in the United States. Some may have worked at other American mines or on railroads, or may even have been previously employed at Clifton-Morenci-Metcalf.

57. *Copper Era,* 18 June 1903, 3. Copies of the injunction have since disappeared from court records and archives.

58. Territorial Prison at Yuma, A.T., "Description of Convict" typescripts.

59. Ibid.

60. *Arizona Republican,* 12 June 1903, 1; Watt, "History of Morenci," 57.

61. *Arizona Republican,* 9 June 1903, 4.

62. *Bisbee Daily Review,* 5 June 1903, quoted in Park, "History of Mexican Labor," 257.

63. *Arizona Republican,* 5 June 1903, 3. Most of the Spaniards in the Clifton-Morenci area lived above the Shannon "incline" tramway in Morenci, and were employed at dangerous, skilled work by the Shannon Copper Mining Company. Shannon was a relatively small, independent operator, and not yet connected with Phelps Dodge. Most of the Shannon strikers were probably Spaniards (Al Fernandez interview).

64. *Arizona Silver Belt,* 25 June 1903, 3.

65. Watt, "History of Morenci," 58; *Arizona Republican,* 11 June 1903, 1, 8; 12 June 1903, 1; *Tucson Citizen,* 9 June 1903, 5.

66. *Arizona Republican,* 7 June 1903, 1; 10 June 1903, 1.

67. Ibid., 10 June 1903, 1; 11 June 1903, 1.

68. Ibid., 11 June 1903, 1.

69. *Copper Era,* 18 June 1903, 2 (editorial).

70. *Arizona Republican,* 11 June 1903, 2 (editorial).

71. *Copper Era,* 18 June 1903, 2 (editorial); *Weekly Republican,* 11 June 1903, 1.

72. *Copper Era,* 11 June 1903, 3.

73. *Arizona Republican,* 12 June 1903, 1.

74. Ibid., 12 June 1903, 1; 13 June 1903, 1; 15 June 1903, 8.

75. Ibid., 13 June 1903, 1.

76. Ibid., 14 June 1903, 1; 15–30 June 1903, passim.

77. Ibid., 13 June 1903, 1.

78. DCC, "Payroll" and "Time Book" records, 1903–4.

79. Western Federation of Miners, *Executive Board Minutes,* Western History Collection, University of Colorado, dated June 1903, 71.

80. *Tucson Citizen,* 9 June 1903, 5.

81. *Arizona Republican,* 13 June 1903, 1.

82. DCC, "Payroll" and "Time Book" records, 1902–4.

83. *Miners' Magazine,* 1903–15.

84. DCC, "Payroll" and "Time Book" records, 1903–4.

85. *Copper Era,* 17 August 1905, 3; *El Obrero,* 4 June 1903, 4.

86. Fabela, *Documentos Históricos,* 105.

87. Territorial Prison at Yuma, A.T., "Description of Convict" typescripts; miscellaneous prison records described by Yuma Territorial Prison State Park personnel during telephone interview, 5 July 1990; Cecelia A. Hall letter; Edward Laustaunau interviews; letter from Weneslado Laustaunau, Jr., dated 29 November 1905.

88. Weneslado Laustaunau, letter; *Morenci Leader,* 8 September 1906, 1. One of the other prisoners, Francisco Gonzales, also died in Yuma prison, but prison authorities reported that he was in "bad physical condition upon entering prison" (Territorial Prison at Yuma, A.T., "Description of Convict" typescripts; telephone conversation with John King, director of Yuma Territorial Prison State Park, 16 July 1990).

89. *Graham Guardian* (Safford, Arizona Territory), 28 September 1906, n.p., article retyped by Yuma Territorial Prison State Park staff.

90. *Copper Era,* 10 May 1906, 3.

91. Ibid.

92. Juan Gómez-Quiñiones, *Sembradores: Ricardo Flores Magón y el Partido Liberal Mexicano: A Eulogy and a Critique* (Los Angeles: Aztlán Publications, 1973).

93. W. Dirk Raat, *Revoltosos: Mexico's Rebels in the United States, 1903–1923* (College Station: Texas A & M University Press, 1981), 43–44. For more about Salcido's subsequent revolutionary career, see also 94, 137–42, 151–52, 156.

94. Rodolfo Acuña discusses several other western strikes involving Mexican workers in 1903. Acuña lists two California agricultural workers' labor actions, one of which was a cooperative Mexican and Japanese strike, and also a seven-hundred-worker Pacific Electric Railway strike in Los Angeles. The strikes Acuña lists were unconnected to one another and also unconnected to the strike at Clifton-Morenci (Acuña, *Occupied America,* 154–55).

95. WFM, *Proceedings . . . 1903,* Executive Board Report, dated 25 June 1903, 224; *Weekly Republican* (Phoenix), 11 June 1903, 1.

96. WFM, *Proceedings . . . 1903,* Executive Board Report, dated 25 June 1903, 224.

97. *Miners' Magazine,* March 1903, 35; WFM, *Proceedings . . . 1903,* Executive Board Report dated 25 May 1903, 123. The full convention adopted this recommendation (WFM, *Proceedings . . . 1903,* 260). David Thomas Brundage maintains that national WFM leadership *had* made up its mind, and had decided to actively recruit non-English and non-Irish ethnic workers even before 1900. According to Brundage, "the increasingly conscious manipulation of ethnic and racial divisions by Denver employers forced labor activists at last to embrace a full

internationalist approach" (Brundage, "The Making of Working-Class Radicalism in the Mountain West: Denver, Colorado, 1880–1903" [Ph.D. dissertation, University of California, Los Angeles, 1982], 220). The Denver smelter trouble may have temporarily convinced WFM leadership about the necessity for ethnic inclusion in the late 1890s, but inclusion was again an open question in the spring of 1903, at the WFM's annual convention.

98. WFM, *Proceedings . . . 1903*, 262–69.

Chapter 3

1. Hildebrand and Mangum, *Capital and Labor*, 98–100, 107–8.

2. Paul Frederick Brissenden, *The I.W.W.: A Study of American Syndicalism,* Studies in History, Economics and Public Law, vol. 83, no. 193 (New York: Columbia University, 1919), 41.

3. *Solidarity,* 28 May 1910, 3; Kenneth Ross Tooele, "A History of the Anaconda Copper Mining Company: A Study in the Relationships Between a State and Its People and a Corporation, 1880–1950" (Ph. D. dissertation, University of California, Los Angeles, 1954), 154–55.

4. WFM, *Proceedings . . . 1903*, 270; Melvyn Dubofsky, *We Shall Be All; A History of the I.W.W.* (Chicago: Quadrangle Books, 1969), 60. Despite the generous language, Boyce, at least, had no intention of inviting Asian workers to step through his open portals. Shortly before resigning the WFM presidency, Boyce reminded miners at a meeting in Tuscarora, Nevada, to maintain their boycott of local Chinese business establishments (Edward Boyce, "Personal Diary," entry dated 20 February 1902, in Edward Boyce Papers). At about the same time, Charles Moyer was speaking in opposition to ethnic recruitment, even as he theoretically supported the interests of *all* unskilled men. Working as an organizer during 1902, Moyer reported that WFM Anglo and Irish miners at the Congress, Arizona, gold camp were losing their jobs to "greasers" (a racial epithet which referred to Hispanics). Moyer said that the English-speaking miners should have fought for "their rights" against the Congress Mining Company and the Mexican mining workers (WFM, *Proceedings . . . 1902*, 141).

5. John H. M. Laslett, *Labor and Left: A Study of Socialist and Radical Influences in the American Labor Movement, 1881–1924* (New York: Basic Books, 1970), 197. Men of English and Irish descent, recently immigrated Europeans, and African Americans probably competed for the same jobs in the coal mines, which was not generally the case in the copper mines. Thus, necessity may have compelled the coal miners to choose between general cooperation or especially brutal competition for jobs.

6. George S. McGovern and Leonard F. Guttridge, *The Great Coalfield War* (Boston: Houghton Mifflin, 1972), 47, 49; WFM, *Proceedings . . . 1906*, 124–25.

7. WFM, *Proceedings . . . 1904*, 75, 78.

8. *Miners' Magazine,* January 1903, 56–59.

9. WFM, *Proceedings . . . 1904*, 5; WFM, *Proceedings . . . 1905*, 10.

10. WFM, *Proceedings . . . 1905,* 124–25; *Miners' Magazine,* 22 February 1906, 9. This was not a plan for "raiding" UMWA territory, but for organizing former union miners.

11. *Miners' Magazine,* 4 January 1906, 15; WFM, *Proceedings . . . 1906,* 77–91; *Proceedings . . . 1907,* 188, 192.

12. WFM, *Proceedings . . . 1906,* 222.

13. WFM, *Proceedings . . . 1907,* 364–66, 874–75.

14. Ibid., 154; *Miners' Magazine,* 7 February 1907, 13.

15. In 1906, the IWW split into factions led by DeLeon, Trautmann, and St. John on the one hand, and Sherman and the WFM on the other, because of a series of disagreements partly related to President Charles O. Sherman's malfeasance in office. IWW radicals opposed moderates and conservatives, and most of the WFM men shunned the IWW thereafter.

16. Jensen, *Heritage of Conflict,* 160–88.

17. WFM, *Proceedings . . . 1907,* passim; Jensen, *Heritage of Conflict,* 188–89, 193–94.

18. WFM, *Proceedings . . . 1904,* 176.

19. WFM, *Proceedings . . . 1905,* 254–57.

20. Crough Notebooks; personal interview with William Crough, Edward Crough's son, Phoenix, Arizona, 25 May 1991.

21. *"Justicia"* was not literally justice, in the U.S. sense. James Sandos, in a current book on Partido Liberal Mexicano (PLM) politics and the Plan of San Diego, describes justicia precisely as an "implied redress for past wrongs," rather than egalitarianism. Justicia "promised that the given social hierarchy, with its specific roles and rewards, would be returned to normal" (James A. Sandos, *Rebellion in the Borderlands: Anarchism and the Plan of San Diego, 1904–1923* [Norman and Lincoln: University of Oklahoma Press, 1992], 24–25). Justicia combined with igualdad, however, suggests a complaint about basic unfairness, and a demand that equal treatment and basic fairness be either restored or created.

22. Rodney D. Anderson, *Outcasts in Their Own Land: Mexican Industrial Workers, 1906–1911* (DeKalb: Northern Illinois University Press, 1976), 110, 114–16, 198, 212, 315–26.

23. Esteban Baca Calderón, quoted in John M. Hart, *Anarchism and the Mexican Working Class, 1860–1931* (Austin: University of Texas Press, 1978), 91.

24. Salcido and de la O, as explained previously, were two of the four Mexican leaders of the 1903 strike who survived incarceration at Yuma Prison.

25. Salcido was forced out of the Clifton district during 1906, as explained in chapter 2.

26. WFM, *Proceedings . . . 1906,* 136.

27. WFM, *Proceedings . . . 1905,* 253–54; David M. Pletcher, *Rails, Mines, and Progress: Seven American Promoters in Mexico, 1867–1911* (Ithaca: Cornell University Press, 1958), 237.

28. *Miners' Magazine*, 1903–6; 8 March 1906, 3; 15 March 1906, 13; 12 April 1906, 3; WFM, *Proceedings . . . 1906*, 220.

29. An entirely different interpretation of WFM support for Hispanic labor is offered by W. Dirk Raat in his book *Revoltosos*. He posits a steadily growing Anglo-American commitment to both southwestern non-Anglo labor and to revolutionary politics. Raat dates the growth of solid WFM backing for Mexicans from 1905, because of the increased number of Arizona locals, and the fact that some included Mexicanos and Navajo Indians. He maintains that those locals had sent organizers to work among Mexicans working at Bisbee, Cananea, and Nacozari (a medium-sized Sonora copper area) in 1906. Raat also ties the WFM securely to the Mexican revolutionaries, beginning with the arrest and detention of five PLM leaders in late 1907, but his arguments lack any evidentiary basis. From 1907 on, according to Raat, "the PLM cause became one with that of the American Left" (45–46). The evidence stressed herein indicates no more than a tentative WFM commitment on both issues. Also, WFM organizing work in areas which included mixed work forces did not necessarily indicate mining organizing among the entire work-force population as Ed Crough's work, described previously, demonstrates. That is, WFM organizing in Arizona Territory was not necessarily, and not usually, organizing of Hispanics.

30. *Bisbee Daily Review*, 14 April 1907, 2.

31. Fleming, *Copper Times*, 143–44.

32. *Morenci Leader*, 2 June 1906, 1.

33. Ibid., 19 May 1906, 2.

34. Juan Gómez-Quiñiones, "The First Steps: Chicano Labor Conflict and Organizing, 1900–1920," *Aztlán* 3, no. 1 (1972):28; *Morenci Leader*, 18 May 1907, 1; 27 July 1907, 1; 3 August 1907, 1.

35. WFM, *Proceedings . . . 1907*, 148.

36. Ibid., 6, 148.

37. *Miners' Magazine*, 9 January 1908, 15.

38. Carmen Acosta and the Metcalf local survived the strike. He was still an official in the Metcalf local in mid-1910, and was still a popular local labor leader there during the First World War years. Ibid., 14 April 1910, 15; *El Rebelde* (an IWW-affiliated Los Angeles Spanish-language newspaper), 1916–17, passim.

39. DCC, "Payroll" and "Time Book" records, May-August, 1908.

40. *Bisbee Daily Review*, April 6, 1907, 5.

41. *Morenci Leader*, 18 May 1907, 1; 15 June 1907, 2.

42. Ibid., 15 June 1907, 2; WFM and International Union of Mine, Mill, and Smelter Workers, *Official Charter Book of the Western Federation of Miners and the International Union of Mine, Mill, and Smelter Workers*.

43. *Morenci Leader*, 27 July 1907, 1.

44. Ibid.

45. Ibid.

46. *Miners' Magazine,* 27 August 1908, 8.

47. *Morenci Leader,* 3 August 1907, 1.

48. Ibid., 3 August 1907, 1; 9 November 1907, 1. Since the strike was failing, the strikers might have expected reemployment soon afterward. A depression was already beginning and so jobs were relatively scarce. Consequently, the fact that many strikers left the area late in the strike is remarkable: it seems to defy economic common sense. Quitting, in this instance, appears to have been the strikers' final action in the strike itself.

49. *Miners' Magazine,* 27 August 1908, 8. Frank Little readily admitted the inadequacy of his organizing efforts at Clifton. In an explanation of his work made to the 1907 WFM Convention, Little spoke of the "few members we have," and added that "we haven't very much of an organization" (WFM, *Proceedings . . . 1907,* 680).

50. DCC, "Payroll" and "Time Book" records, May–August, 1908.

51. *Miners' Magazine,* 27 August 1908, 8.

52. Fabela, *Documentos Históricos,* 61–62, 105.

53. Ibid., 56–59, 75, 97, 109–15, 117, 133. Juan Gómez-Quiñiones, utilizing U.S. Department of State correspondence, wrote that a "Unión de Obreros Libres" was founded at Morenci by Praxedis Guerrero in 1907. (Juan Gómez-Quiñiones, *Sembradores,* 30; idem, "The First Steps," 28.) A "Sociedad Unión de Obreros" already existed at Morenci in 1903, and so the State Department's correspondent may have been in error—that is, the Unión de Obreros may have predated Guerrero's arrival. (*El Obrero,* 4 July 1903, 4.)

54. *El Obrero,* 4 July 1903, 4; Fabela, *Documentos Históricos,* 106.

55. *Graham Guardian* (Safford, Arizona Territory), 28 September 1906, n.p. Retyped clipping from Yuma Territorial Prison State Park files.

56. *Morenci Leader,* 27 July 1907, 1; 3 August 1907, 1.

57. Thomas E. Sheridan, *Los Tucsonenses: The Mexican Community in Tucson, 1854–1941* (Tucson: University of Arizona Press, 1986), 84–85.

58. U.S. Bureau of the Census, manuscript returns for 1900; DCC, "Payroll" and "Time Book" records, May-August, 1908; Fabela, *Documentos Históricos,* 72, 130, 133; Juan Gómez-Quiñiones, "The First Steps," 28; *Miners' Magazine,* 6 February 1908, 11.

Chapter 4

1. WFM, *Proceedings . . . 1907,* 894.

2. *Bisbee Daily Review,* 6 March 1907, 1; George F. Leaming, "Labor and Copper in Arizona: Origin and Growth," *Arizona Review,* April 1967, 15.

3. Lewis Douglas, "Autobiographical Recollections," V, typescript version of diary, Lewis W. Douglas Papers, AZ290, Box 2, University of Arizona Library, Tucson, 23; *Jerome Mining News,* 10 March 1906, 1.

4. *Bisbee Daily Review,* 6 March 1907, 1; 17 March 1907, 1.

5. Emmons, *Butte Irish,* 183–84, 190–94, 221–23, 228–30, 233.

6. A. L. Rowse, *The Cousin Jacks: The Cornish in America* (New York: Charles Scribner's Sons, 1969), 390–91; Emmons, *Butte Irish,* 145, 239. Despite their anti-union and anti-Irish reputation (which was, in many instances, richly deserved), the "Cousin Jacks" (Cornish) sometimes organized unions, and even co-operated with Irish mining workers when severely pressed, as indicated in chapter 1. A group of pro-union Cornish was working at the Ishpeming, Michigan iron mines in 1906–7 (Mann, *After the Gold Rush,* 187–88; WFM, *Proceedings . . . 1907,* 157).

7. *Bisbee Daily Review,* 13 February 1907, 1; 14 February 1907, 1; 15 February 1907, 1; 26 February 1907, 1, 3, 8.

8. Ibid., 8 April 1907, 1; 10 April 1907, 1.

9. WFM, *Proceedings . . . 1907,* 194–95; *Bisbee Evening Miner,* 11 April 1907, 1.; 15 April 1907, 1; *Morenci Leader,* 13 April 1907, 1; 27 July 1907, 1.; *Bisbee Daily Review,* 16 April 1907, 1; Crough Notebooks, n.d., n.p.

10. *Bisbee Daily Review,* 26 April 1907, 6.

11. *Bisbee Evening Miner,* 15 April 1907, 1.

12. *Bisbee Daily Review,* 23 April 1907, 1, 8; 30 April 1907, 8; WFM, *Proceedings . . . 1907,* 194.

13. *Bisbee Daily Review,* 10 March 1907, 1. The situation was probably more complex than the contemporaneous accounts indicated. The immigrant workers included small numbers of other nationality groups. For instance, at a late April WFM meeting, of the seven new members initiated into the union, three were "Slavonians" (that is, South Slavs), one was an American, and three were "Swedes"—who may have been Finns (Ibid., 23 April 1907, 8).

14. Ibid., 17 April 1907, 1.

15. Ibid., 2, 8; Crough Notebooks.

16. *Morenci Leader,* 13 April 1907, 1; *Bisbee Evening News,* 12 April 1907, 1. On the Union-at-Large, see James Foster, "Ten Day Tramps." Some of the men at the Bisbee meetings had probably come north from Cananea, Sonora as well (WFM, *Proceedings . . . 1907,* 195).

17. *Morenci Leader,* 13 April 1907, 1; *Bisbee Evening News* 23 April 1907, 1. An instance in which some former WFM members had ceased paying dues but were able to disrupt Bisbee organizing appears in Crough Notebooks, entry dated 6 May 1908.

18. *Bisbee Daily Review,* 26 April 1907, 6; Bingham Miners' Union No. 67, *Minute Books,* in Box 2, Record Group C-25, Western Federation of Miners and International Union of Mine, Mill and Smelter Workers collection, Cornell University, 93 (4 January 1908).

19. As David Montgomery has observed, "The dominance of the skilled crafts blended all too easily with a national ideology that proclaimed the supremacy of the white race" (*The Fall of the House of Labor* [Cambridge: Cambridge University Press, 1987], 46).

20. Crough Notebooks, entry dated 1907.

21. *Morenci Leader,* 20 July 1907, 2 (editorial).

22. Jensen, *Heritage of Conflict,* 361–63.

23. Letter from Joseph D. Cannon, Jerome, Arizona, to Charles H. Moyer, dated 5 July 1909, in Arizona Collection, Arizona State University, Tempe, 3, 4.

24. Proportionately fewer skilled mining workers were being employed as most big western mines shifted to "nonselective" mining: the mining and processing of low-grade ore deposits using mostly unskilled workers.

25. Letter from Joseph D. Cannon, Jerome, Arizona, to Charles H. Moyer, dated 5 July 1909, 9.

26. Ibid.

27. Ibid., passim.

28. *Industrial Union Bulletin,* 18 May 1907, 3; 28 September 1907, 1; WFM, *Proceedings . . . 1912,* 284.

29. WFM, *Proceedings . . . 1906,* 220, 267. The statement about Globe's "revolutionary" character was made by Marion W. Moor, a member of the WFM Executive Board, in a convention report.

30. WFM, *Proceedings . . . 1907,* 100–1. One of the major, typical votes on the IWW-versus-WFM issue lost by a 239$^{1}/_{2}$-to-114 margin.

31. Ibid., 660–62, 699.

32. *Industrial Union Bulletin,* 5 October 1907, 2.

33. Ibid., 24 October 1908, 3.

34. Crough Notebooks. As noted in chapter 1, contracts were a serious WFM issue. Radical delegates to the 1907 WFM national convention argued against contracts and similar "time agreements," and moderates and conservatives argued *for* them. The unions at Butte, Globe, and Tonopah, Nevada had contracts, and at least a few other locals, including the old goldfield local at Grass Valley, California, had signed agreements with mining-company management which were probably contracts too (WFM, *Proceedings . . . 1907,* 308–12).

35. WFM, *Proceedings . . . 1907,* 148.

36. Robert B. Riell, "An Introduction to Globe, Arizona," typescript in Clara Woody Collection, Arizona Historical Society Museum, Tucson, 20; McBride, "Organized Labor in Globe," 5.

37. *Industrial Union Bulletin,* 27 February 1909, 1, 3.

38. *Miami Silver Belt,* 28 October 1910, 8; WFM, *Executive Board Minutes,* 3 August 1910, 48.

39. Ibid.

40. Park, "History of Mexican Labor," 265, 267–80.

41. Tru Anthony McGinnis, "The Influence of Organized Labor on the Making of the Arizona Constitution" (M.A. thesis, University of Arizona, 1930), 37–38, 83–85. The most recent scholarly treatment of Arizona's 1910 Constitutional Convention and its labor component appears in Huginnie, "Strikitos," 236–57. Huginnie's treatment of the convention's labor voting is derived from both Park and McGinnis.

42. *Morenci Leader,* October 1907; James H. McClintock, *Arizona: Prehistoric, Aboriginal, Pioneer, Modern: The Nation's Youngest Commonwealth,* 3 vols. (Chicago: S. J. Clarke Publishing Co., 1916), 2:430; *Arizona Silver Belt,* June 1908, passim.

43. Jensen, *Heritage of Conflict,* 247–48; WFM, *Proceedings . . . 1907,* 188, 892, passim; Patrick Renshaw, *The Wobblies: The Story of the Syndicalism in the United States* (Garden City, N.Y.: Doubleday, 1967), 114–15.

44. Renshaw, *Wobblies,* 114–15; Joseph H. Cash, *Working the Homestake* (Ames: Iowa State University Press, 1973), 88–96.

45. *Solidarity,* 1 June 1910, 3.

46. Brissenden, *I.W.W.,* 269; *Solidarity,* 27 August 1910, 1.

47. Jensen, *Heritage of Conflict,* 238–43.

48. Ibid., 110. Vernon Jensen suggested that doctrinal differences between the AFL's Left and the WFM were not great, and that in fact the WFM hoped to ally itself with a relatively powerful socialist element within the AFL (Ibid., 237–38). John Laslett quoted a *Miners' Magazine* editorial which argued unconvincingly for the continuity of WFM radicalism and implied that the WFM would "bore from within" the AFL until industrial unionism had been achieved. Laslett, however, felt that the union's leaders were deceiving themselves—that the union made necessary compromises with conservatives in order to reenter the AFL (Laslett, *Labor and Left,* 268–69)

49. *Solidarity,* 9 July 1910, 2; 6 August 1910, 2.

50. *Miners' Magazine,* 30 January 1908, 10–22; 20 February 1908, 11; 2 April 1908, 10; 14 May 1908, 5; 21 May 1908, 8; 15 October 1908, 5; 5 November 1908, 11; 17 December 1908, 11; WFM, *Proceedings . . . 1908,* 272, 275, 282, 371.

51. Brissenden, *I.W.W.,* 269, Appendix VIII. Juan Gómez-Quiñiones credits the Wobblies with some degree of influence in several California strikes before 1915 ("The First Steps," 28); *Solidarity,* 21 May 1910, 4.

52. *Solidarity,* 17 September 1910, 2.

53. Ibid., 10 September 1910, 1.

54. Ibid., 17 September 1910, 2. Number 13 may have been the Gas Workers' local.

55. *Miners' Magazine,* 9 January 1908, 2.

56. *Bisbee Daily Review,* 27 June 1910, 7.

57. WFM, *Proceedings . . . 1907,* 159. St. John subsequently became Secretary-Treasurer of the IWW.

58. *Solidarity,* 5 November 1910, 4.

59. *Industrial Union Bulletin,* 28 March 1908, 1; 18 April 1908, 2; *Solidarity,* 2 July 1910, 3; 9 July 1910, 1; passim. The IWW eventually began intensive southwestern organizing, in 1917, as explained later.

60. Leo Wolman, "The Extent of Labor Organization in the United States in 1910," in *Quarterly Journal of Economics,* 30 May 1916, 505.

61. WFM, *Proceedings . . . 1912,* 374–75.

62. Ibid, 130–37.

63. Ibid.

Chapter 5

1. Jensen, *Heritage of Conflict,* 263 (quoting an article in the *Engineering and Mining Journal*).

2. Beatrice Spendlove, "A History of Bingham Canyon, Utah" (master's thesis, Department of History, University of Utah, 1937), 1–2, 49.

3. Bingham Canyon Lions Club, "Bingham Canyon and Its Mammoth Copper Mine" (pamphlet), 4; Spendlove, "History of Bingham Canyon," 19.

4. Spendlove, "History of Bingham Canyon," 49, 106.

5. *Bingham Press-Bulletin,* 25 January 1918, 2.

6. *Deseret Evening News* (Salt Lake City), February–July, 1912.

7. Utah Copper Company, *Seventh Annual Report of the Utah Copper Mining Company,* dated 1911, i; *Kennescope* (a magazine published for employees of the Utah Copper Company), April 1956, n.p.

8. WFM, *Proceedings . . . 1903,* 26.

9. George G. Suggs, Jr., *Colorado's War on Militant Unionism,* 83.

10. WFM, *Official Charter Book, Western Federation of Miners and International Union of Mine, Mill, and Smelter Workers,* n.p.

11. Bingham Miners' Union No. 67, *Minute Books,* in Box 2, Record Group C-25, Western Federation of Miners and International Union of Mine, Mill and Smelter Workers collection, Cornell University, 4–5 (26 November 1904); 28 (28 January 1905). The *Minute Books* are hereafter styled BMU-MB, below.

12. Alan Kent Powell, *The Next Time We Strike: Labor in Utah's Coal Fields, 1900–33* (Logan: Utah State University Press, 1985), 34, 47, 232 (fn. 3).

13. Helen Zeese Papanikolas, "Magerou," 53; "The Exiled Greeks," in *The Peoples of Utah,* ed. Helen Zeese Papanikolas (Salt Lake City: Utah State Historical Society, 1976), 411–12.

14. Papanikolas, "Magerou," 53; *Solidarity,* 18 March 1911, 3.

15. WFM, *Proceedings . . . 1905,* 215.

16. Papanikolas, "Magerou," 53.

17. Papanikolas, "The Exiled Greeks," 412; Joseph Stipanovich, "Falcons in Flight: The Yugoslavs," in *The Peoples of Utah,* ed. Helen Zeese Papanikolas (Salt Lake City: Utah State Historical Society, 1976), 367. There are abundant examples of a coal-and-copper connection in early Utah labor history. Examples in BMU-MB include 22 April 1905, 72; 17 June 1905, 100. Richard Lingenfelter suggests that some of the organizational planning in metal-mining unionism may have originated in coal mining. He considers it likely that the Gold Hill, Nevada union constitution was probably modeled after an eastern state's coal mining union constitution. The Gold Hill Miners' Union and its constitution were part of the early ancestry of the Western Federation of Miners (Lingenfelter, *Hardrock Miners,* 45).

18. Although there is a wealth of detail about the weekly meetings of the Bingham Miners' Union in BMU-MB, there are no lists of union members, and there is no record of which members ceased paying dues and quit the union. Consequently, there is no means for determining how many mining workers of each ethnic group belonged to the local at any given moment. Also, heated discussions of the most controversial issues faced by Local 67 were generally noted rather briefly. Detailed transcription of a set of lengthy remarks during a discussion was probably beyond the capability of the local's recording secretaries.

19. The death of an Italian member was announced in late 1904 (BMU-MB, 17 December 1904, 13).

20. Ibid., 26 November 1904–17 December 1904, 1–12. Serbian, Croatian and Slovenian surnames are similar to one another, although not identical. To avoid possible confusion of one with the other, they are "South Slavic" here. There was one consistent, significant exception to BMU immigrant drives. No Japanese were initiated into the union local during 1904–8, the years included in the BMU-MB records.

21. BMU-MB, 14 January 1905, 24; 18 February 1905, 41; 2 September 1905, 145.

22. BMU-MB, 22 July 1905–30 September 1905 (pp. 116–171); 14 October 1905, 174; passim.

23. Ibid., July 1905, 116; 18 November 1905, 189.

24. Membership in the Bingham Miners' Union was 73 in 1903, 529 in 1905, and 585 in mid-1906. It rose and fell back to approximately the same level after abortive strike efforts in 1906 and 1907 (WFM, *Proceedings . . . 1907*, 137).

25. *White Pine News* (McGill, Nevada), 20 July 1907, 6; 14 August 1907, 4; 28 October 1907, 1; 27 November 1907, 2; 1907, passim; Russell R. Elliott, *Growing Up in a Company Town* (Reno, Nevada Historical Society, 1990), 25–26; *Great Falls Daily Tribune,* 9 April 1908, 4; *Ogden Standard* (Ogden, Utah), 9 April 1909, 2. Robert Wiebe also postulates increased anti-immigrant hostility, beginning, he claims, in 1908 (*The Search for Order, 1877–1920* [New York: Hill and Wang, 1967], 209–10).

26. Gunther W. Peck, "Crisis in the Family," 77–78; *Salt Lake Tribune,* 24 June 1908, 9.

27. *Salt Lake Tribune,* 18 June 1908, 10; 10 August 1908, 12; *Deseret Evening News,* 19 August 1908, 3.

28. *Salt Lake Tribune,* 11 July 1908, 18; 12 July 1908, 1; 13 July 1908, 1; 10 August 1908, 1; *Deseret Evening News,* 11 July 1908, 1; 14 July 1908, 2; 17 July 1908, 10; 13 August 1908, 5. Newspaper accounts which label many of these men "Greek Catholics" or "Roman Catholics," together with the apparent ethnicity implicit in their surnames, allows a historian to ascribe probable ethnicity to some of them. Most of the newspaper articles used here and in the previous discussion of Nevada and Montana xenophobia are transcribed typescripts of the originals

provided this writer by Helen Papanikolas from her collection of early-twentieth-century Utah and other central western manuscript materials.

29. WFM, *Proceedings . . . 1904*, 272. They eventually struck, in 1907 (WFM, *Proceedings . . . 1907*, 35); *Proceedings . . . 1907*, 273; *Proceedings . . . 1905*, 215–16.

30. BMU-MB, 21 January 1905, 26; 24 June 1905, 103; 1 July 1906, 106.

31. Ibid., 16 June 1906, 268, 270; 9 November 1907, 79; WFM, *Proceedings . . . 1907*, 139.

32. BMU-MB, 16 June 1906, 271; 30 June 1906, 277; 1 December 1906, 329.

33. Ibid., 14 July 1906, 283; 21 July 1906, 286; 4 November 1908, 189; 21 November 1908, 193–94. Utah's eight-hour law was passed in 1896 (Jensen, *Heritage of Conflict*, 97–100).

34. BMU-MB, 19 December 1908 (insert page near page 200). On this issue, also, Bingham was very different from Butte, Montana, where, according to David Emmons, Butte Miners' Union leadership was generally uninterested in questions of mine safety (Emmons, *Butte Irish*, 228–29).

35. BMU-MB, 21 October 1905, 176. Alan Derickson, in his recent general study of Western Federation of Miners/IUMMSW health and mine safety, notes that "After 1905 resolutions of condolence [expressed by WFM locals] began to comment on the causes of death." He cites two such resolutions which make mention of the "ruthless system" and the "insatiable greed of the exploiting class" (Derickson, *Workers' Health, Workers' Democracy*, 13; BMU-MB, 1 June 1907, 1–4).

36. WFM, *Proceedings . . . 1907*, 31.

37. BMU-MB, 18 August 1906, 298; 27 October 1906, 319.

38. BMU-MB, 16 February 1907, 353; 23 February 1907, 356; 2 March 1907, 359; April–September, 1907.

39. *Tonopah Sun*, 14 May 1907, 1.

40. BMU-MB, 20 April 1907, 20

41. Ibid., 20 April 1907, 20; 20 July 1907, 26, 27–28; 3 August 1907, 33; 17 August 1907, 41.

42. Spendlove, "History of Bingham Canyon," 66a.

43. *Deseret Evening News*, 16 August 1912, 7; *Miners' Magazine*, 3 September 1908, 10.

44. Again, it is worth noting that the BMU was not recruiting Japanese workers.

45. Spendlove, "History of Bingham Canyon," 66a.

46. *Miners' Magazine*, 3 September 1908, 10.

47. Ore-sorters in mines were paid less in some places, but there were relatively few of them. The Utah Copper Company's policy toward its unskilled employees apparently required simultaneous use of the carrot and the stick. The company began hiring Greeks as "gang bosses" (over other Greeks) around January 1908, but then paid them only $2.50 per day (Spendlove, "History of Bingham Canyon," 66a; *Miners' Magazine*, 3 September 1908, 10).

48. *Miners' Magazine*, 3 September 1908, 10; also see the discussion of the El Paso 1913 strike in chapter 7.

49. WFM, *Proceedings . . . 1908*, 278–279.

50. Ibid., August 1907, 50; 12 October 1907, 68.

51. Ibid., 11 April 1908, 128; 25 April 1908, 132; handwritten copy of a letter in Box 2, Record Group C-25, "Western Federation of Miners and International Union of Mine, Mill, and Smelter Workers collection, Cornell University, from Bingham Miners' Union, addressee unknown, written during September, 1908; BMU-MB, 28 November 1908, 196.

52. Quoted in Peck, "Crisis in the Family," 81.

53. Ibid.

54. BMU-MB, 1 August 1908 (pp. 158–60).

55. *Miners' Magazine*, 3 September 1908, 11. Immigrant workers were swindled by WFM-connected Anglos or Irishmen on other occasions, too. According to two 1906 reports, WFM men organizing in the Minnesota iron region probably cheated Italian and Finnish immigrant mining workers there (WFM, *Proceedings . . . 1907*, 156, 188).

56. Peck, "Crisis in the Family," 78, 79, 83–86.

57. BMU MB, 31 August 1908, 163; 28 November 1908, 196; 5 December 1908, 199.

58. *Miners' Magazine*, 4 November 1909, 12.

59. Ibid.

60. *Deseret Evening News*, 30 September 1909, 3; *Salt Lake Tribune*, 1 October 1909, 1; *Miners' Magazine*, 4 November 1909, 12.

61. Ibid.

62. Peck has discussed 1902–12 Bingham Canyon labor relations in "Crisis in the Family"; "Charles Moyer and the New Immigrants: WFM Politics, 1907–1912," a paper presented at the Western Historical Association's annual meeting, 19 October 1991; and "Padrones and Protest," 157–69, 174–77. Peck also chooses to ignore Greek transiency and recidivism, and treats the 1905–12 Greeks and Cretans as a constant entity, capable of growth and change; all of which enhances vague hypothesizing, as explained previously ("Padrones and Protest," especially 177–78). On South Slavic sickness-and-benefit societies, see Stipanovich, "Falcons in Flight," 370–71, 376.

Peck portrays the Bingham Canyon Greeks as a unique group of consciously radical workingmen who developed coherent plans for improving their wages, hours, and working conditions during the years before the great 1912 Bingham Canyon strike. Turning conventional explanation on its head, Peck blames the pro-immigrant BMU leadership for not finding enough Greeks to join their union. Without evidence about Greek organizational affiliation, Peck claims that Greeks were developing a "mutualistic culture." He hypothesizes the existence of a specifically Greek leadership and organizational structure which influenced the direction of Bingham Canyon labor activism before 1912. This hypothesis suggests the unique quality of Greek pre-strike activism because it ignores the existence of contemporaneous South Slavic activism and denies the Miners' Union's connections with the Bingham Canyon Greeks. This hypothesis would also mean that the Greeks, who in fact were among the *least* organized of Bingham Canyon's workers, were the *most* organized; and that the random series of violent incidents and walkouts explained here was actually a patterned mass of organized Greek activism.

63. For examples, see Clark, "Mexican Labor," 466–522; Don D. Lescohier and Elizabeth Brandeis, Vol. 3 of *History of Labor in the United States, 1896–1932,* ed. by John R. Commons (New York: Macmillan Company, 1935); Victor R. Greene, *The Slavic Community on Strike* (Notre Dame: University of Notre Dame Press, 1968).

64. Conventional interpretation of the Industrial Workers of the World holds that the IWW pioneered in ethnic and racial egalitarianism within organized labor. The Bingham Canyon IWW local definitely did not work for egalitarianism during 1905–8, nor did either of two other small Utah and Nevada IWW locals familiar to this writer. National IWW leadership certainly promoted ethnic inclusion, as did at least part of the Spokane IWW leadership after 1908, as indicated in the pages of the IWW's *Industrial Worker.* But the Bingham Canyon situation, rather than being an exception, was probably typical of small Utah and Nevada locals. For the conventional interpretation of IWW ethnic policy, see Philip S. Foner, *History of the Labor Movement in the United States* (New York: International Publishers, 1964–88), 4:123, 127; also Dubofsky, *We Shall be All.* For the interpretation suggested here, see Philip Mellinger, "AFL, IWW and WFM Coexistence in Bingham Canyon, Utah, 1905–8," a paper presented at the Southwest Labor Studies Conference, Stockton, California, March 22, 1991.

Chapter 6

1. Papanikolas, "The Exiled Greeks," 412, 414–15, 416; Telephone interview with Helen Z. Papanikolas, 4 January 1991; Stipanovich, "Falcons in Flight," 370–71, 376; Philip F. Notarianni, "Italianita in Utah: The Immigrant Experience," in *The Peoples of Utah,* ed. Helen Zeese Papanikolas (Salt Lake City: Utah State Historical Society, 1976), 30; Ivan Cizmic, "Yugoslav Immigrants in the U.S. Labor Movement, 1880–1920," in Dirk Hoerder (ed.), *American Labor and Immigration History, 1877–1920s: Recent European Research* (Urbana: University of Illinois Press, 1983), 182–83.

2. U.S. Commission on Industrial Relations, "Record of Hearings Before the Special Commission to Inquire into the Alleged Deportations from Bingham Canyon, Utah," (Washington, D.C.: GPO, 1918), dated 7–8 November 1917, 83.

3. WFM Executive Board, "Report of the Executive Board of the WFM to the Eighteenth Annual Convention of the WFM," dated 18 July 1910, 4.

4. WFM, *Executive Board Minutes,* 22 August 1911, 93; 14 January 1912, 70.

5. *Solidarity,* 19 November 1910, 1.

6. Letter from Mike Lakis and forty-nine other Greek immigrants, addressed to Utah Government, dated 12 February 1911, in *Papers of Governor William Spry, 1910–1912,* at Utah State Archives, Salt Lake City.

7. Ibid. Various estimates of the price of a job ranged as low as $20 and as high as $50. In 1912, $50 was nearly a month's pay at the commonest unskilled-labor wage (*Deseret Evening News,* 17 February 1912, 10–11; U.S. Commission on Industrial Relations, "Record of Hearings," 80). Japanese unskilled workers at Bingham had the same complaint, voiced against a Japanese labor agent. Other nationality groups also dealt with labor agents there (*Deseret Evening News,* 17 February 1912, 11; 24 September 1912, 2).

8. *Deseret Evening News,* 17 February 1912, 11; 20 September 1912, 3; 23 September 1912, 1–2.

9. *Salt Lake Tribune,* 20 September 1912, 1.

10. *Miners' Magazine,* 11 April 1912, 10. The only group of ethnically centered, organized Greeks in Bingham during 1912, according to Gunther Peck's study of the 1912 strike, was the Panhellenic Union, a promanagement group sponsored either by Skliris confederates, or, according to Helen Papanikolas, by the Greek government (Peck, "Crisis in the Family," 88; Papanikolas interview). Although Peck argues for a Greek spirit of "mutualism," his explanation of the mutualist phenomenon includes only commonplace shared living arrangements and visits to taverns and coffeehouses ("Crisis in the Family," 79).

11. *Miners' Magazine,* 5 May 1912, 1.; *Copper Ore* (McGill, Nevada), 18 April 1912, 1.

12. *Deseret Evening News,* 1 May 1912, 7. However, the Murray smeltermen worked only an eight-hour day.

13. Ibid., 16 December 1911, 51; 20 December 1911, 7; 12 February 1912, 7.

14. Ibid., 18 May 1912, 7; *Miners' Magazine,* 23 May 1912, 4; 27 June 1912, 4.

15. *Miners' Magazine,* 27 June 1912, 4; *Deseret Evening News,* 18 May 1912, 7.

16. *Miners' Magazine,* 23 May 1912, 4; 30 May 1912, 11.

17. *Deseret Evening News,* 17 May 1912, 1; 18 May 1912, 7; Helen Zeese Papanikolas, "Life and Labor Among the Immigrants of Bingham Canyon," *Utah Historical Quarterly* 33 (fall 1965):289–315.

18. Gunther Peck's recent article, "Padrones and Protest," offers an entirely different interpretation of strike planning, causation, and resolution. His interpretation stresses the importance of a specific ethnic group (the Greeks) rather than a labor union. Peck's interpretation is apparently based upon an incomplete reading of the Bingham Miners' Union *Minutes* and Western Federation of Miners convention proceedings. According to Peck, WFM leaders "maintained only marginal control of the strike movement," the strike was made possible because Greeks and Cretans "began organizing themselves," Serbian strikers were not major strike participants, and the Ely-McGill strike was practically insignificant ("Padrones and Protest," 157–73).

19. WFM, *Proceedings . . . 1914*, 8; *Deseret Evening News*, 17 September 1912, 1. Daniel Jackling was later to reply that the Bingham-area employees' wages were equivalent to wages paid to men working under similar conditions elsewhere in Utah, implying that Utah's coal mines, railroads, and metal mines, not the western copper industry as a whole, ought to be the criterion for judging the mining workers' wages (*Salt Lake Tribune*, 21 September 1912, 2).

20. Jensen, *Heritage of Conflict*, 264. Jensen does not indicate the source from which he obtained this information.

21. WFM, *Executive Board Minutes*, 30 July 1912, 93.

22. WFM, *Proceedings . . . 1914*, 133.

23. *Deseret Evening News*, 16 August 1912, 7; 12 September 1912, 1.

24. Ibid., 12 September 1912, 1; *Salt Lake Mining Review*, 15 December 1912, 21.

25. *Deseret Evening News*, 18 September 1912, 1.; 20 September 1912, 2.

26. *Miners' Magazine*, 3 October 1912, 8.

27. *Deseret Evening News*, 18 September 1912, 1; 20 September 1912, 2.

28. *Salt Lake Tribune*, 7 October 1912, 1. "Austrians," in these 1912 accounts, of course, were most often Serbians.

29. *Deseret Evening News*, 25 October 1912, 1.

30. *Salt Lake Tribune*, 22 September 1912, 2.

31. Salt Lake County, Utah, "Assessment Record for 1912, Book J." The sample excludes men of uncertain ethnic background (there were several) and joint owners of property. It is taken from listings in the Bingham area labeled "U.S. Mining Company Ground," "Yampa Mine Property," and "Highland Boy Property." Assessment records are correlated with names of known strikers from *Deseret Evening News*, September–November 1912; *Salt Lake Tribune*, September–November 1912; *Miners' Magazine*, September–November 1912.

32. *Miners' Magazine*, September–November 1912, passim.

33. Ibid. This estimate is based on the following calculation: $1.75 was a common daily wage rate. Men worked perhaps 300 days per year (which is possibly an underestimate during periods of full copper production), and had houses with assessed valuations of $75 each. Nineteenth-century Newburyport, Massachusetts homeowners, in Stephan Thernstrom's classic study, achieved "notable economic progress" through homeownership, along with stability, security, and "respectability." Seventy-five-dollar property ownership provided stability, but certainly not "notable economic progress" (Stephan Thernstrom, *Poverty and Progress: Social Mobility in a Nineteenth Century City* [Cambridge: Cambridge University Press, 1964], 132, 136–37, 188).

34. *Salt Lake Tribune*, 20 September 1912, 1.

35. *Deseret Evening News*, 20 September 1912, 3. Lescohier and Brandeis, in the old John R. Commons labor history study, reported a similar concern among Italian subway construction workers in New York City, in 1902. They struck, and "They did not ask for an increase in their wages of $1.35 for ten hours. They asked

only for the elimination of the padroni. This demand, if acceded to, would have increased their actual wages considerably by eliminating the extortions of the padroni" (*History of Labor in the United States, 1896–1932,* 3:ix).

36. *Deseret Evening News,* 20 September 1912, 1; 23 September 1912, 1–2.

37. Skliris, of course, had been driven out before.

38. *Deseret Evening News,* 2 October 1912, 1; Elliott, *Growing Up in a Company Town,* 25–49.

39. Ira B. Joralemon, *Romantic Copper* (New York: Appleton Century Co., 1936), 230. In 1910, Nevada was already the fifth largest copper-producing state (*Copper Ore* [McGill], 11 January 1912, 3).

40. *Salt Lake Tribune,* 24 September 1912, 3.

41. WFM, *Proceedings . . . 1903,* President's Report, 25–26.

42. *Salt Lake Tribune,* 24 September 1912, 3.

43. Charles D. Gallagher, "Memoir and Autobiography," Oral History Interview transcript, 63, Special Collections, University of Nevada, Reno Library; Thomas A. Michalski, "A Social History of Yugoslav Immigrants in Tonopah and White Pine County, Nevada, 1860–1920: (Ph.D. dissertation, State University of New York at Buffalo, 1983), 155.

44. *Miners' Magazine,* 1 November 1912, 8.

45. *Copper Ore,* 5 September 1912, 1; Michalski, "Social History of Yugoslav Immigrants," 138, 141–44.

46. *Copper Ore,* 18 January 1912, 1.

47. Ibid., 19 September 1912, 1.

48. Ibid.

49. Butte's terrible trouble during the 1912 contract season is explained in Jensen, *Heritage of Conflict,* 314–23; also see Emmons, *Butte Irish,* 268–75. Emmons explains that the Butte Miners' Union signed the 1912 contract without approval from WFM headquarters. Moyer had no excuse for making the Butte Miners' Union's achievements sound like his own (Emmons, *Butte Irish,* 269).

50. *Ely Record,* 27 September 1912, 1; 4 October 1912, 1; *Ely Weekly Mining Expositor,* 26 September 1912, 1; *Salt Lake Tribune,* 27 September 1912, 3.

51. Helen Z. Papanikolas maintains that padrones were, in essence, surreptitious contract labor agents ("The Exiled Greeks," 410).

52. Russell R. Elliott, *Nevada's Twentieth-Century Mining Boom: Tonopah, Goldfield, Ely* (Reno: University of Nevada Press, 1966), 258–59; *Copper Ore,* 5 October 1911, 1.

53. Elliott, *Nevada's Twentieth-Century Mining Boom,* 230–31, 254, 258–59, 263. The unionized portion of the Greek work force may have been much larger—13 percent is a minimal estimate.

54. Michalski, "Social History of Yugoslav Immigrants," 119, 136, 153, 156.

55. Elliott, *Nevada's Twentieth-Century Mining Boom,* 230–31, 254; *Copper Ore,* 2 November 1911, 2, passim.

56. *Copper Ore,* 26 September 1912, 1.

57. *Ely Weekly Mining Expositor*, 3 October 1912, 3. The two weeks' delay in striking at McGill may have been the result of Moyer's reluctance to involve McGill's Anglo-Irish in a primarily non-Anglo-Irish strike. There was considerable antistrike feeling in McGill, as discussed in this chapter.

58. *Ely Record*, 4 October 1912, 1; *Deseret Evening News*, 30 September 1912, 7.

59. *Copper Ore*, 3 October 1912, 4.

60. Ibid.

61. *Salt Lake Tribune*, 28 September 1912, 1.

62. *Miners' Magazine*, 31 October 1912, 7–8; WFM, *Proceedings . . . 1914*, 11.

63. *Deseret Evening News*, 20 September 1912, 1.

64. Ibid., 18 September 1912, 1; Ibid., 21 September 1912, 2.

65. Ibid., 18 September 1912, 1. The Utah National Guard was sent, later.

66. Ibid., 20 September 1912, 1.

67. *Salt Lake Tribune*, 18 September 1912, 1; 21 September 1912, 1; 22 September 1912, 2; 23 September 1912, 2; 24 September 1912, 10.

68. Ibid., 19 September 1912, 1; 20 September 1912, 1.

69. Ibid., 2 October 1912, 1.

70. *Deseret Evening News*, 4 October 1912, 2; 14 October 1912, 2; 15 October 1912, 2.

71. *Ely Record*, 18 October 1912, 1; *Ely Weekly Mining Expositor*, 17 October 1912, 1.

72. *Deseret Evening News*, 18 October 1912, 2; *Ely Record*, 18 October 1912, 1.

73. *Salt Lake Tribune*, 27 October 1912, 1.; *Miners' Magazine*, 30 October 1912, 8–9.

74. *Ely Record*, 18 October 1912, 1.; *Ely Weekly Mining Expositor*, 17 October 1912, 1.; *Salt Lake Tribune*, 27 October 1912, 1; *Miners' Magazine*, 30 October 1912, 8–9; *Deseret Evening News*, 29 October 1912, 2; *Ely Record*, 1 November 1912, 1.

75. *Salt Lake Tribune*, 6 October 1912, 28; 11 October 1912, 2.

76. *Deseret Evening News*, 16 December 1911, 51.

77. Salt Lake County, "Assessment Record for 1912, Book J."

78. The notion of "closed" and "open" western mining camps was discussed in George Stanley McGovern, "The Colorado Coal Strike, 1913–1914" (Ph.D. dissertation, Northwestern University, 1953), 49. In contemporaneous Carbon County, Utah, coal camps, "If the company found that a man had joined [the UMWA], he was promptly discharged and his belongings were put out of the company's house" (Dee Scorup, "The History of Organized Labor in Utah" [master's thesis, University of Utah, 1935], 126).

79. *Salt Lake Tribune*, 11 October 1912, 2. The shack homes, of course, were owned by the strikers. Salt Lake County collected assessment taxes from them. The searches and evictions may very well have been illegal. In fact, a later investigation

revealed that many of the "deputies" used in 1912 were never actually deputized (U.S. Commission on Industrial Relations, "Record of Hearings," 86).

80. *Deseret Evening News,* 12 October 1912, 1.

81. Ibid., 11 October 1912, 1.

82. *Salt Lake Tribune,* 1 October 1912, 16.

83. *Deseret Evening News,* 10 October 1912, 1; 11 October 1912, 1.

84. Ibid., 14 October 1912, 1.

85. *Salt Lake Tribune,* 15 October 1912, 3.

86. *Deseret Evening News,* 16 October 1912, 2; 25 October 1912, 1.

87. *Miners' Magazine,* 31 October 1912, 8; 28 November 1912, 12–13.

88. *Deseret Evening News,* 1 November 1912, 10.

89. Ibid., 29 October 1912, 2.

90. Ibid., 2 November 1912, 2; *Salt Lake Tribune,* 3 November 1912, 28; *Deseret Evening News,* 4 November 1912, 2; 2 November 1912, 2.

91. *Deseret Evening News,* 29 November 1912, 2.

92. Ibid., 28 November 1912, 1; *Miners' Magazine,* 20 February 1913, 9.

93. WFM, *Proceedings . . . 1914,* 12–13, 133–34.

94. Precisely as he had done in 1909, Leonidas Skliris probably returned to the Bingham area some time after the strike, and may have even resumed his previous relationship with the Utah Copper Company (*Deseret Evening News,* 18 October 1912, 14).

95. *Solidarity,* 27 June 1914, 4.

96. *Deseret Evening News,* 24 September 1912, 1.

97. Ibid., 27 September 1912, 2; *Miners' Magazine,* 3 October 1912, 8.

98. *Miners' Magazine,* 24 July 1913, 9; 7 August 1913, 3; 26 September 1912, 3; 3 October 1912, 8.

99. *Deseret Evening News,* 14 October 1912, 1–2; *Salt Lake Tribune,* 15 October 1912, 1.

100. *Deseret Evening News,* 23 October 1912, 2.

101. *Salt Lake Mining Review,* 15 October 1912, 22; *Ely Record,* 27 September 1912, 1; *Ely Weekly Mining Expositor,* 3 October 1912, 1.

102. Laslett, *Labor and Left,* 272.

103. The new AFL skilled-crafts connection was also carefully tested in at least one other WFM strike in 1912, at the new aqueduct construction project in Los Angeles County, California. At the Los Angeles Aqueduct strike, "several crafts walked out in support of the members of the WFM; and are still standing by them" (WFM, *Proceedings . . . 1912,* 277). I am indebted to Professor James Foster for pointing out the significance of the Los Angeles Aqueduct strike.

104. WFM, *Proceedings . . . 1914,* 11.

105. *Deseret Evening News,* 20 September 1912, 2.

106. WFM, *Executive Board Minutes,* 2 August 1912, 100.

107. *Chino Silver Enterprise* (Silver City, New Mexico), 3 May 1912, 4; 14 June 1912, 1.

108. *Miners' Magazine,* 28 November 1912, 6.

109. *Deseret Evening News,* 24 September 1912, 2.

110. *Miners' Magazine,* 28 November 1912, 6. As indicated previously, some steam-shovel men accepted the offer and signed individually with Nevada Consolidated.

111. WFM, *Proceedings . . . 1914,* 133.

112. *Chino Silver Enterprise,* 7 June 1912, 1.

113. Spendlove, "History of Bingham Canyon," 66a.

114. WFM, *Proceedings . . . 1914,* 9.

115. Ibid.; *Miners' Magazine,* 31 October 1912, 7–8; 28 November 1912, 13. But several railroad men participated in the big McGill antistrike meeting, as noted previously.

116. WFM, *Proceedings . . . 1914,* 11–12.

117. WFM, *Executive Board Minutes,* 8 January 1913, 106. The excuse of a "time contract," which would make strike support for fellow unionists difficult, was not at issue here, because the engineers and firemen had no contract. They were not, however, members of the AFL and thus they were not threatened by its potential retaliatory discipline. Carter was obviously being less than helpful.

118. *Deseret Evening News,* 10 October 1912, 1; WFM, *Proceedings . . . 1914,* 9.

119. *Deseret Evening News,* 7 October 1912, 1; *Salt Lake Tribune,* 18 September 1912, 2; 6 October 1912, 28; *Deseret Evening News,* 15 October 1912, 2.

120. *Deseret Evening News,* 20 September 1912, 2; 15 October 1912, 2.

121. *Miners' Magazine,* 28 November 1912, 13.

122. *Ely Record,* 20 December 1912, 1.

123. WFM Executive Board, *Report of the Executive Board of the Western Federation of Miners,* dated 17 July 1913, 1; WFM, *Proceedings . . . 1914,* 134.

124. WFM, *Proceedings . . . 1914,* 12.

125. *Salt Lake Tribune,* 19 September 1912, 2.

126. *Deseret Evening News,* 21 September 1912, 3.

127. Ibid., 4 October 1912, 2.

128. *Salt Lake Tribune,* 7 October 1912, 1, 3.

129. Ibid., 3.

130. *Deseret Evening News,* 9 October 1912, 1; 1 November 1912, 10; 29 November 1912, 2.

131. *Deseret Evening News,* 29 October 1912, 2.

132. *Miners' Magazine,* 31 October 1912, 9.

133. WFM, *Executive Board Minutes,* 3 November 1912, 101–2.

134. Ibid. The Nevada Consolidated later discharged many of the steam-shovel men (WFM, *Proceedings . . . 1914,* 13).

135. Ibid.; *Deseret Evening News,* 30 October 1912, 1.

136. Historian Gerald Rosenblum's argument that early-twentieth-century unskilled workers' threat to the skilled was "minimal if not non-existent" is certainly

incorrect in these instances. Similarly, Melvyn Dubofsky's notion that during the Progressive Era, ordinary workers actively sought "union recognition" was not true in the Utah and Nevada strikes (Gerald Rosenblum, *Immigrant Workers: Their Impact on American Labor Radicalism* [New York: Basic Books, 1973], 158; Melvyn Dubofsky, *When Workers Organize: New York City in the Progressive Era* [Amherst: University of Massachusetts Press, 1968], 56, 61, 101–2).

137. WFM, *Proceedings . . . 1914*, 21–22.

138. Salt Lake County, "Assessment Record for 1912, Book J."

139. Italian immigrants, of course, were active participants in *both* sets of strikes.

Chapter 7

1. IWW locals in Phoenix and Salt Lake City were exceptions. The Phoenix and Salt Lake locals were islands of urban IWW activity in a vast, inactive western mining region.

2. Herfindahl, *Copper Costs and Prices*, chart insert attached to the back cover.

3. Selig Perlman and Philip Taft, *Labor Movements*, vol. 4 of *History of Labor in the United States, 1896–1932*, ed. by John Rogers Commons (New York: Macmillan, 1935), 293–311.

4. Dubofsky, *We Shall Be All*, 228–29, 233–34; Donald Cole, *Immigrant City: Lawrence, Massachusetts, 1845–1921* (Chapel Hill: University of North Carolina Press, 1963), 179; *Solidarity*, 6 April 1912, 3.

5. Perlman and Taft, *Labor Movements*, 333.

6. Jensen, *Heritage of Conflict*, 249–55, 273–78, 302–35; Emmons, *Butte Irish*, 255–86.

7. Henry Pelling, for instance, discussed changes in hours and working conditions in terms of 1900–17, and in his discussion of labor-related legislation, his frame of reference is the prewar *decade* (*American Labor* [Chicago: University of Chicago Press, 1960], 120, 123). Foster Rhea Dulles wrote that labor unions grew until 1904, remained static until 1910, and then flourished between 1910 and 1917 (Foster Rhea Dulles, *Labor in America: A History*, 3rd ed, [New York: Thomas Y. Crowell, 1949], 204–5). An exception among older works is Philip S. Foner's *History of the Labor Movement in the United States*, which separates IWW and AFL history from one another and effectively subdivides the first two decades of the history of the AFL. The only major history of southwestern copper-industry labor relations, James Byrkit's *Forging the Copper Collar*, posits an era which began at the turn of the century, and which moved steadily toward its tragic denouement in the Bisbee Deportation of 1917 (James W. Byrkit, *Forging the Copper Collar: Arizona's Labor-Management War, 1901–1921* [Tucson: University of Arizona Press, 1982]).

8. Philip Taft, *The AFL in the Time of Gompers* (New York: Harper and Brothers, 1957), 233, 253–58; American Federation of Labor, *Report of Proceedings of the Thirty-Fourth Annual Convention of the American Federation of Labor*,

1914, 21, 109; Pelling, *American Labor*, 122; *Miners' Magazine*, 12 December 1912, 5–6.

9. Dubofsky, *We Shall Be All*, 225–26, 259, 287–88, 316.

10. WFM, *Proceedings . . . 1914*, 24–25, 35.

11. WFM, *Proceedings . . . 1907*, Executive Board Report, 148; *Industrial Union Bulletin*, 22 August 1908, 3; *Solidarity*, 21 May 1910, 4; Lowell L. Blaisdell, *The Desert Revolution: Baja California, 1911* (Madison: University of Wisconsin Press, 1962), especially 38–48, 70–71.

12. *Miners' Magazine*, 9 January 1908, 2; *Bisbee Daily Review*, 17 June 1910, 7; *Solidarity*, 10 September 1910, 1; 17 September 1910, 2; 5 November 1910, 4; 3 May 1913, 3; 13 September 1913, 4; Dione Miles, *Something in Common: An IWW Bibliography* (Detroit: Wayne State University Press, 1986), 493–95. *El Rebelde*, as explained later, carried IWW news, but was not an official IWW publication.

13. *Solidarity*, 20 October 1909, 1.

14. Quoted in Cole, *Immigrant City*, 180.

15. *Solidarity*, 17 September 1910, 2.

16. Ibid., 23 November 1912, 3.

17. Miles, *Something in Common*, 492–95; *Industrial Worker*, 29 April 1909, 4.

18. *Industrial Worker*, 20 May 1909, 1.

19. *Solidarity*, 23 August 1913, 3; *Arizona Republican*, 15 April 1907, 10. However, for a few months, Aurelio Vincente Azuara, Los Angeles-based *El Rebelde*'s editor, traveled for the IWW in Arizona (*El Rebelde*, 1916). Although some historians cite Louis Theos as a prototypical Greek IWW organizer, practically nothing is known about Theos's activities after he left northern Utah. If Theos was an IWW organizer, he was unique. No other Bingham Canyon or Ely-McGill Greeks are known to have organized for the IWW before 1918. Information about Louis Theos is derived from Peck, "Padrones and Protest," 175; telephone conversations with Dan Georgakas, July, 1991 and November, 1991.

20. *Arizona Republican*, 20 March 1915, 4; *Industrial Worker*, 24 September 1910, 4; Membership Lists and Appendices, Paul F. Brissenden Papers, IWW Files, Labor-Management Documentation Center, Cornell University.

21. By 1914, Charles Moyer had tested the fraternal proclivities of the AFL, and had found them wanting. Along with UMWA officials, he had asked President Gompers and the AFL Executive Council for an urgently needed levy to support the Colorado Fuel and Iron Company coal and Michigan copper strikes. The request was denied: lack of funds was offered as an explanation. Moyer was bitter about the outcome (*Solidarity*, 7 February 1914, 2).

22. Suggs, Jr., *Colorado's War on Militant Unionism*, 17; WFM, *Proceedings . . . 1904*, 249; *Proceedings . . . 1905*, 204–8; *Proceedings . . . 1907*, passim.

23. WFM, *Proceedings . . . 1912*, 415.

24. WFM, *Proceedings . . . 1911*, President Moyer's opening address, 37.

25. WFM, *Proceedings . . . 1914*, 37.

26. Kay Lynn Breigel, "Alianza Hispano-Americana, 1894–1965: A Mexican-American Fraternal Insurance Society" (Ph.D. dissertation, University of Southern California, 1974), 64–77.

27. James D. McBride, "The Liga Protectora Latina: A Mexican-American Benevolent Society in Arizona," *Journal of the West* 14, no. 4 (1975):82–83.

28. Mario T. García, *Desert Immigrants: The Mexicans of El Paso, 1880–1920* (New Haven: Yale University Press, 1981), 107.

29. Richard Medina Estrada, "Border Revolution: The Mexican Revolution in the Ciudad Juarez-El Paso Area, 1906–1915" (master's thesis, University of Texas at El Paso, 1975), 141.

30. *Industrial Worker*, 22 February 1912, 3; García, *Desert Immigrants*, 107–8. IWW recruiters traveled into Texas from three directions during 1905–18, but their El Paso campaigning originated entirely in Phoenix and Southern California. Emilio Zamora describes sporadic, albeit intense IWW activity only in South Texas (*World of the Mexican Worker*, 57–59, 136). James R. Green mentions ephemeral IWW locals in Mexico south of the Texas border, but there were few of these further north. Green also explains that after the failure of the IWW-Brotherhood of Timber Workers' 1912–13 organizing campaign in Merryville, Louisiana, "the IWW all but disappeared" west of Merryville (*Grass-Roots Socialism: Radical Movements in the Southwest, 1895–1943* [Baton Rouge: Louisiana State University Press, 1978], 11, 275–76).

31. *El Paso Herald*, 11 April 1913, 3; 15 April 1913, 8; *El Paso Morning Times*, 23 April 1913, 12; 24 April 1913, 1; *Miners' Magazine*, 8 May 1913, 9.

32. The strikers added a demand for a 35¢ increase later (*Texas Union* [El Paso], 18 April 1913, 1, 3; García, *Desert Immigrants*, 99–100; *Miners' Magazine*, 8 May 1913, 8; *El Paso Herald*, 10 April 1913, 1; *El Paso Morning Times*, 9 April 1913, 12; *Miners' Magazine*, 15 May 1913, 11). Mario T. García describes increased Mexican participation in El Paso's AFL unions as continuing through at least 1914, but he does not describe the 1910–14 accommodation phenomenon as a significant *process*. That is, according to García, there was no long-term tendency toward increasing ethnic-racial accommodation within the El Paso AFL's central labor body.

33. *Texas Union*, 18 April 1913, 1. Fifteen dollars, of course, was a pittance.

34. *Miners' Magazine*, 15 May 1913, 11.

35. *El Paso Herald*, 10 April 1913, 1.

36. García, *Desert Immigrants*, 100–3; *Texas Union*, April–June, 1913.

37. *Texas Union*, 20 June 1913, 1. Joseph Myers was soon to be a federal mediator in the much bigger First World War era strikes in Arizona. For earlier examples of CLU hostility to incoming Mexican workers, see Zamora, *World of the Mexican Worker*, 51.

38. *Miners' Magazine*, 15 May 1913, 11; *El Paso Morning Times*, 24 April 1913, 1.

39. An anti-IWW item appeared in the CLU's newspaper during June 1913 (*Texas Union*, 20 June 1913, 4).

40. WFM, *Proceedings . . . 1914*, 306–7.

41. El Paso had had a WFM local once before. WFM president Ed Boyce himself had made an organizing trip to El Paso in October, 1901. He had spoken to groups of workingmen in both El Paso and Ciudad Juarez, but claimed that he was unable to find an adequate interpreter on the Mexican side of the international border. Boyce had helped create an El Paso smeltermen's union before leaving El Paso, but it disappeared soon afterward (Edward Boyce, "Personal Diary," 28 October 1901 entry; "Travel Diary," 105).

42. *El Paso Morning Times*, 23 April 1913, 12; 24 April 1913, 1; WFM, *Proceedings . . . 1914*, 306–7.

43. Medina Estrada, "Border Revolution," 49.

44. *El Paso Morning Times* 23 April 1913, 12; 29 April 1913, 5; *Miners' Magazine*, 17 July 1913, 10.

45. *Miners' Magazine*, 17 July 1913, 10.

46. García, *Desert Immigrants*, 109. García's interpretation, the downplaying of "the role of agency and . . . combative spirit among working-class Mexicans" is specifically criticized in Zamora, *World of the Mexican Worker*, 207.

47. WFM, *Proceedings . . . 1914*, 34.

48. WFM, *Proceedings . . . 1900*, 24.

49. Leonor Lopez, *Forever Sonora, Ray, Barcelona* (privately published, 1984) in Arizona Room, Arizona State University Library, 3, 7, 8, 15, 16, 19; *Arizona State Business Directory*, 1915–16 (Denver: Gazeteer Publishing Company, 1914) 524–25; *Miami News*, June 29, 1912, 1.

50. Hildebrand and Mangum, *Capital and Labor*, 47.

51. U.S. Department of Labor, Records Group 174, *Records of the Commission on Industrial Relations, Records Relating to CIR Studies*, "Company Towns" file, U.S. National Archives, Washington, D.C.

52. Ibid., 2, 10. The Ray mining worker and part-time WFM organizer listed in the Commission on Industrial Relations interview files as "A. J. Marino" was probably E. J. Moreno.

53. Ibid., 14.

54. Ibid., 4.

55. Ibid., 2.

56. *Arizona Republican*, 20 August 1914, 1, 4; 21 August 1914, 1, 7; 22 August 1914, 1, 5; 23 August 1914, 1, 8; *Miami Silver Belt*, 13 January 1915, 2.

57. A headline accompanying the series of "Ray murders" stories reassured readers that the August events were "Not a Race War." Race war had been treated as a possibility in descriptions of similar sets of events at Clifton-Morenci, Ray, Christmas, and Globe, Arizona in previous years (*Arizona Republican*, 20 August 1914, 4).

58. Letter, from C. Harris, Phoenix, Arizona, to Roscoe Willson, dated 14 November 1955, in Roscoe Willson files, Arizona Historical Foundation, Tempe; *Arizona Republican,* 21 August 1914, 1, 7; 22 August 1914, 1, 5; 23 August 1914, 8.

59. *Arizona Republican,* 22 August 1914, 5. Gutiérrez de Lara had been organizing among southwestern Mexican immigrant workers during 1907 (see chapter 4).

Chapter 8

1. *Miami Silver Belt,* 11 January 1915, 1; 12 January 1915, 1; 15 January 1915, 1.

2. Ibid., 16 January 1915, 1; 18 January 1915, 4; 19 January 1915 1.

3. Ibid., January 1915, passim; 20 January 1915, 1.; 21 January 1915, 1; 23 January 1915, 1.

The sliding scale was not new in American industry. It had been used in steel mills in the East at least as far back as the late 1880s. The Butte, Montana, sliding-scale agreement dated from the time that Butte Local 1's power vis-à-vis management had begun to decline. While it had never been a very lively issue, the sliding-scale system had generally been proposed by companies and had never been popular with industrial workers because, especially in commodities-based industries, wholesale prices were about as likely to slide downward as they were to slide upward.

4. *Daily Silver Belt,* 14 January 1915, 1; *Bisbee Daily Review,* 3 January 1915, 1; 8 January 1915, 1.

5. Hunt Diaries, 1915, 64 (dated 30 June) at Arizona State University, Tempe. The version of the diaries at Arizona State University is a typed transcription of the original.

6. An example of how the Mexican revolutionary activity engendered Anglo-Mexican animosity was a report which circulated throughout Arizona during mid-1915 about a planned Mexican revolutionary uprising in Arizona, explained in chapter 9 (*Tucson Citizen,* 16 September 1915, 6).

7. *Miners' Magazine,* 5 August 1915, 3.

8. *Daily Silver Belt,* 29 June 1915, 4; 30 June 1915, 2; 9 September 1915, 1.

9. Ibid., 9 September 1915, 1.

10. This was probably less true of the Greeks in 1912 Ely and McGill, Nevada.

11. *Miners' Magazine,* 5 August 1913, 3; *Arizona Labor Journal,* 8 July 1915, 1, 3. Their demand went unheeded.

12. *Arizona Labor Journal,* 1 July 1915, 1; 8 July 1915, 1.

13. Mine Operators of the Globe-Miami-Superior Mining District, Arizona Chapter, American Mining Congress, "Conditions and Events Connected with Labor Strikes in Globe-Miami Mining District, Arizona, During Summer of 1917," pamphlet, dated September 1917, in Arizona State Archives, 2. Management's estimate was based on the 1917 Globe-Miami population, which was probably roughly similar. The total mining labor population in 1917 was estimated at about 5,000 men.

14. *Arizona Labor Journal,* 15 July 1915, 1, 4.

15. *Miners' Magazine,* 15 August 1915, 3.

16. *Arizona Labor Journal,* July 1915, passim.

17. Ibid., 1 July 1915, 1.

18. Ibid., July 1915, passim.

19. *Arizona Labor Journal,* 1 July 1915, 1, 4; 8 July 1915, 1, 3.

20. Ibid., 15 July 1915, 1, 4; McBride, "Liga Protectora Latina," 84.

21. *Miami Free Press,* 19 July 1915, 8; *Arizona Record* (Globe), 13 July 1915, 3; *Daily Arizona Silver Belt,* 9 July 1915, 1. This was actually the *third* Ray Miners' Union, counting from the pre-1910, pre-Guggenheim era at Ray. Andrea Yvette Huginnie argues that the Anglo-Irish WFM men colluded with Ray Consolidated to defeat the Ray strike. Her conclusions are apparently based upon an underutilization of sources ("Strikitos," 273–74).

22. Robert Bigando, *Globe, Arizona: The Life and Times of a Western Mining Town, 1864–1917* (Globe: American Globe Publishing Company, 1989), 69, 101, 104; *Arizona Record,* 10 January 1915, 3; 21 May 1915, 1; 22 May 1915, 1.

23. WFM, *Proceedings . . . 1904,* 6; *National Miner* (National, Nevada), 9 December 1910, 4; *Industrial Worker,* 7 March 1912, 3; WFM, *Proceedings . . . 1914,* 58; *Arizona Socialist Bulletin,* 11 July 1913, 4; *Arizona Labor Journal,* 21 October 1915, 6. The WFM, of course, had rejoined the American Federation of Labor in 1911.

24. James David McBride, "Henry S. McCluskey: Workingman's Advocate" (Ph.D. dissertation, Arizona State University, 1982), 3, 8–11, 15, 20, 26, 31.

25. WFM, *Proceedings . . . 1903,* 193; Globe City Directory, 1915.

26. WFM, *Proceedings . . . 1907,* 355, 746; IWW, "Locals chartered between September 1908 and April 1910," Paul Brissenden Collection, Cornell University; *Globe Leader,* 4 June 1913, 3; *Arizona Labor Journal,* 11 June 1920, 1.

27. Crough Notebooks, 1907 entry.

28. WFM, *Executive Board Minutes,* 16 January 1913, 123.

29. Ibid., 20 (dated 15 July 1915), 20–23.

30. Ibid., 29 (dated 26 November 1915), 23. President Moyer's denigrating references to "constitutional rights" and "a whole lot of other junk" were likely to have been an expression of personal hostility, rather than an accurate portrayal of the situation at Ray. The Miami union apparently presented a large body of evidence to indicate that discharges, threats, and general coercion of Mexican and Spanish workers were occurring at Ray. The WFM's *Miners' Magazine* seemed to concur with this in a discussion of Ray's problems a month later. Governor Hunt wrote to Labor Secretary William B. Wilson in December that "in some of the mining centers, particularly Ray, intolerable situations are existent," and that a federal investigation for publicity purposes was advisable (*Tucson Citizen,* 9 September 1915, 1; *Miners' Magazine,* 7 October 1915, 1, 5; letter from Governor George W. Hunt to U.S. Secretary of Labor William B. Wilson, dated 24 December 1915, in Hunt Collection, Arizona State University, Tempe).

31. WFM, *Executive Board Minutes,* 26 (dated 30 October 1915), 20–23.

Chapter 9

1. *Clifton Morenci Mining Journal,* 22 July 1915, 2. There is also evidence of organizational activity among the already-existing Mexican social organizations at Clifton-Morenci in 1915. Several of these rearranged their meeting places there between January and June (Greenlee County, Arizona, "Bills of Sale," 1915).

2. WFM, *Executive Board Minutes,* 20–23 (dated 15 July 1915); 23–24 (dated 23 August 1915, 2 September 1915); 25 (dated 11 September 1915).

3. Ibid., 21 (dated 23 August 1915); James H. McClintock, *Arizona: Prehistoric, Aboriginal, Pioneer, Modern. The Nation's Youngest Commonwealth* 3 vols (Chicago: S. J. Clarke, 1916), 2:423; *Tucson Citizen,* 29 September 1915, 4; *Arizona Republican,* 6 October 1915, 3; *Clifton Morenci Mining Journal,* 28 October 1915, 9; WFM, *Executive Board Minutes,* 25 (dated 12 September 1915).

4. WFM, *Executive Board Minutes,* 27 (dated 30 October 1915); *Outlook,* 2 February 1916, 251; *Arizona Republican,* 1 October 1915, 1.

5. *Clifton Morenci Mining Journal,* 23 September 1915, 4; *Outlook,* 2 February 1916, 250–52; *Miners' Magazine,* 7 October 1915, 7.

6. *Tucson Citizen,* 11 October 1915, 1.

7. Ibid., 5 October 1915, 3; *El Paso Morning Times,* 24 October 1915, 2; *Tucson Citizen,* 13 October 1915, 1, 3; ?? October 1915, 1.

8. Hunt Diaries, 1915, 64 (dated 30 June). Immediately after writing about the problems which the Ray miners were facing, Hunt wrote about Ludlow. The Ludlow Massacre occurred on April 20, 1914.

9. Typed memo, apparently quoted from an issue of *The Public* (Chicago), n.p., n.d., in Hunt Collection, Arizona State University Library, Tempe. A typescript in the same collection quotes a *New Republic* article dated 22 January 1916, n.p., as lauding the "absence of all those perversions or failures of government which accompanied the recent conflict in Colorado."

10. Barrera, *Beyond Aztlan,* 18–19; Sandos, *Rebellion in the Borderlands,* 81, 86–89. The raids associated with the Plan of San Diego ended in June, 1916; but the 1917 World War–connected Zimmerman Telegram reawakened Anglo suspicions of Texas Mexicans "as a potential internal enemy" (David Montejano, *Anglos and Mexicans in the Making of Texas, 1836–1986* [Austin: University of Texas Press, 1987], 123; Sandos, *Rebellion in the Borderlands,* 166). For a similar treatment which ascribes a larger portion of the raiding to Tejano (Texas) residents, see Linda B. Hall and Don M. Coerver, *Revolution on the Border: The United States and Mexico, 1910–1920* (Albuquerque: University of New Mexico Press, 1988), 22–25; also Charles H. Harris III and Louis R. Sadler, *The Border and the Revolution: Clandestine Activities of the Mexican Revolution, 1910–1920* (Silver City, N. Mex.: High-Lonesome Books, 1988), 76.

11. *Tucson Citizen,* 29 September 1915, 5.

12. Letter, from Colonel R. M. Tuthill, Commander of the Arizona National

Guard at Morenci to Governor George W. Hunt, dated 13 September 1915, in Hunt Collection; *Arizona Republican,* 12 October 1915, 1.

13. *Arizona Labor Journal,* 1 July 1915, 1–4.

14. Letter, from Fred A. Hill to Governor George W. Hunt, dated 22 June 1916, Governor's Office files, Special Subjects series, Box 8, Arizona State Archives, Phoenix.

15. *Tucson Citizen,* 13 October 1915, 3.

16. Ibid., 7 October 1915, 1, 2, 5.

17. Clipping, no name, 3 July 1915, from Hunt Collection, Scrapbook Number 16, Special Collections, University of Arizona Library, Tucson.

18. *Clifton Morenci Mining Journal,* 4 November 1915, 1; *Miami Free Press,* 2 August 1915, 1.

19. U.S. Department of Labor, "Transcript of the Proceedings of the President's Mediation Commission in Connection with the Investigation of Industrial Conditions at Clifton, Arizona," 25–30 October 1917, in Special Collections, University of Arizona Library, Tucson, 481, 484, 486–91; *Arizona Labor Journal,* 23 September 1915, 1.

20. Sheridan, *Los Tucsonenses,* 169–70, 172; clipping, no name, n.d., Hunt Collection, Scrapbook Number 16.

21. McBride, "Liga Protectora Latina," 83, 87.

22. Robert W. Bruere, "Following the Trail of the IWW," *New York Evening Post* reprint, 1918, 6.

23. Actually, both men were truly "wily." The governor's full name was George Wylie Paul Hunt.

24. Telegram from F. J. Perry to Governor George W. Hunt, dated 28 December 1914, in Governor's Files, 1905–16, Box 1A, Arizona State Archives, Phoenix; ibid., letter from J. F. Smith to Governor George W. Hunt, dated 6 December 1914; ibid., letter from Hunt to J. F. Smith, dated 9 December 1914; ibid., telegram from William B. Cleary to Hunt, dated 20 December 1914; ibid., telegram from Hunt to Cleary, dated 21 December 1914; ibid., letter from Cleary to Hunt, dated 23 December 1914; ibid., letter from Hunt to Cleary, dated 29 December 1914; ibid., telegram from Hunt to Editor, *New York Sun,* 9 December 1914; *Bisbee Daily Review,* 8 January 1915, 1; *Tucson Citizen,* 13 September 1915, 1; *Arizona Labor Journal,* 16 September 1915, 1.

25. Letter from Hunt to William C. G. Kruger, dated 17 December 1914, in Governor's Files, 1905–16, Box 1A, Arizona State Archives, Phoenix; telegrams from British Embassy and Italian Embassy to Hunt, dated December 1914, Governor's Files, 1905–16, 80% Law File, Arizona State Archives, Phoenix. The law seemed to threaten the livelihoods of both British and Italian resident alien workers in Arizona.

26. *Arizona Republican,* 14 October 1915, 7.

27. Lenore M. Kosso, "Yugoslavs in Nevada After 1900: The White Pine Community," *Nevada Historical Society Quarterly* 29, no. 3 (fall 1985):170.

28. M. James Kedro, "Czechs and Slovaks in Colorado, 1860–1920," *Colorado Magazine* 54, no. 2 (spring 1977):118.

29. Typescript, Information Department, dated 1912, Socialist Party Records, Reel 4, Special Collections, Duke University Library, Durham, North Carolina.

The ties between Socialist Party and Miners' Union activity were very close in some places. In 1913, Arizona Socialist membership totalled 603. Of those, 110 were in Globe, the largest Arizona Socialist local, and a Finnish local in Miami accounted for 22 more. The Bisbee local had 50 members. Calvin Rubush of Morenci, who was apparently the Socialists' presiding officer in Arizona during 1913, became the chairman of the Miami committee which organized support for the Clifton-Morenci strike two years later. George Powell, as mentioned previously, spoke about Bisbee labor conditions at a well-attended Socialist local meeting in Bisbee during 1913, a meeting which Governor Hunt attended (*The Arizona Socialist Bulletin,* 1913 fragments, Socialist Party Records, Reel 130; 11 July 1913, 4, Reel 130).

30. Information Department, "Immigration," a position paper by "B.N.O.," typescript, 1911, Socialist Party Records, Reel 4.

31. WFM, *Proceedings . . . 1911,* 37; *Proceedings . . . 1914,* 37.

32. "The Socialist Party Official Bulletin," Item Number 53, Socialist Party Records, Reel 130; Letter from Carl D. Thompson, Manager, Information Department, to A. James McDonald, 24 February 1913, ibid., Reel 4; "Bulletin, Information Department, Socialist Party," 8 March 1913, 3–4, ibid.

33. *Miners' Magazine,* 15 August 1915, 3; WFM, *Executive Board Minutes,* 20 (dated 15 July 1915); *Arizona Labor Journal,* 16 December 1915, 1; WFM, *Executive Board Minutes,* 23 (dated 11 September 1915).

34. WFM, *Proceedings . . . 1916,* 51.

35. Mink, *Old Labor and New Immigrants,* 52, 53, 68, 200, 266.

36. Aileen S. Kraditor, *The Radical Persuasion, 1890–1917: Aspects of the Intellectual History and the Historiography of Three American Radical Organizations* (Baton Rouge: Louisiana State University Press, 1981), 177–85.

37. Philip S. Foner, *The Industrial Workers of the World, 1905–1917, vol. 4 of History of the Labor Movement in the United States,* 123.

38. Nevada was a different story. The Wobblies were inconsequential in the White Pine County copper region, but they were, through 1907, briefly powerful and well organized in the gold and silver region in Nye and Esmeralda counties, Nevada, which included Tonopah and Goldfield.

39. *El Rebelde,* 16 September 1916, 4. Translated from Spanish.

40. *Miami Free Press,* 22 July 1915, 1; *Arizona Labor Journal,* 8 July 1915, 1; *Miami Free Press,* 2 August 1915, 1; Edward M. Steel, ed., *The Correspondence of Mother Jones* (Pittsburgh: University of Pittsburgh Press, 1985), 149–50.

41. For Rico's role in South and East Texas labor organizing work, see Zamora, *World of the Mexican Worker,* 171, 188.

42. Steel, *Correspondence of Mother Jones,* 150; U.S. Department of Labor,

"Proceedings of the President's Mediation Commission," 481, 483; Pan-American Federation of Labor, "Proceedings of the Pan-American Federation of Labor," typescript copy, 1918, 44; *El Rebelde,* 7 October 1916, 1; 12 November 1915, 2.

43. Herbert G. Gutman, "The Negro and the United Mine Workers of America," in *Work, Culture, and Society in Industrializing America: Essays in American Working-Class and Social History,* ed. Herbert Gutman (New York: Knopf, 1976), 122–24, 133–34, 140–41, 149, 151.

44. Corbin, *Life, Work, and Rebellion,* 65–68.

45. Joe William Trotter, Jr., *Coal, Class, and Color: Blacks in Southern West Virginia, 1915–32* (Urbana and Chicago: University of Illinois Press, 1990), 112–16.

46. Ronald L. Lewis, *Black Coal Miners in America: Race, Class, and Community Conflict, 1780–1980* (Lexington: University Press of Kentucky, 1987), 40–41, 136–37. On the same phenomenon in the late-nineteenth-century iron industry, David Montgomery writes that white workers "could no longer afford such disdain for black craftsmen" (*Fall of the House of Labor,* 27). Montgomery, however, does not credit the white workers with any semblance of democratic intent.

47. Lewis, *Black Coal Miners in America,* 164.

48. Bodnar, Simon, and Weber, *Blacks, Italians, and Poles,* 133. The hoisting engineers were being poorly paid. They joined a labor union which demanded union-scale wages for them. The employer, a building contractor, fired the black workers and replaced them with whites. The union accepted the firing and replacement.

49. Alexander Saxton, *The Indispensable Enemy: Labor and the Anti-Chinese Movement in California* (Berkeley: University of California Press, 1971), 270–71.

50. Brundage, "Working Class Radicalism," 220.

51. Yuji Ichioka, "Asian Immigrant Coal Miners and the United Mine Workers of America: Race and Class at Rock Springs, Wyoming, 1907," in *Amerasia Journal* 6 (November 1979):9–18.

52. Ibid.

53. Sign held by a Morenci striker, photograph c. 1915–16, in Henry S. McCluskey collection, Arizona Room, Arizona State University Library, Tempe.

54. *Arizona Labor Journal,* 2 September 1915, 2.

55. Clipping, no name, n.d., in Hunt Collection, Hunt Scrapbooks Number 14, University of Arizona Special Collections, Tucson.

56. *Clifton Morenci Mining Journal,* 21 October 1915, 5.

57. U.S. Department of Labor, "Proceedings of the President's Mediation Commission," 514.

58. John A. Fitch, "Arizona's Embargo on Strike-Breakers," *The Survey,* 36 (6 May 1916):144; Letter, signed by Miami Clifton Strike Committee, dated 28 January 1916, Number 34, in Hunt Collection, Scrapbook Number 19, (January–March 1916), Special Collections, University of Arizona Library, Tucson; *Clifton Morenci Mining Journal,* 28 October 1915, 8; *Miami Free Press,* 9 September 1915, 4; *Tucson Citizen,* 7 October 1915, 1; letter, from Joseph S. Myers and Hywel Davies, Federal Commissioners of Conciliation, to Governor Hunt, 10 February 1916, in

Governor's Office Collection, Hunt Collection, 1909–33, Box 8, Arizona State Archives, Phoenix.

59. DCC, "Payroll" and "Time Book" records, 1903.

60. Ibid., 1903, 1915.

61. Ibid.

62. Ibid.; ACC, "Longfellow Mine" payroll records, 1915.

63. ACC, "Longfellow Mine" payroll records, 1915; ACC, "Clifton," "New Smelter" payroll records, 1915; ACC, "Longfellow Rent Records," April 1912–June 1915; DCC, "Payroll" and "Time Book" records, 1903, 1915.

64. *Tucson Citizen,* 9 October 1915, 4; 25 October 1915, 4.

65. DCC, "Payroll" and "Time Book" records, 1903, 1915.

66. Tooele, "Anaconda Copper Mining Company," 164; Sumner H. Slichter, *The Turnover of Factory Labor* (New York: D. Appleton, 1921), 36, 46–51, 57; Wladimir S. Woytinsky, *Three Aspects of Labor Dynamics* (Washington, D.C.: Committee on Social Security, Social Science Research Council, 1942), 26–27; Paul Frederick Brissenden and Emil Frankel, *Labor Turnover in Industry* (New York: Macmillan, 1922), 156; DCC, "Payroll" and "Time Book" records, May 1902, May 1903, June 1915–June 1916.

As previously indicated, most of the immigrant Mexicans in the 1903 Clifton-Morenci-Metcalf sample group were relatively long-term residents: about two-thirds of them had lived in the United States for six years or more. In addition, there were many Spanish Americans and Spaniards in the Clifton area Spanish-surnamed population in 1903. A massive wave of Mexican immigration began in about 1912 and continued for several years thereafter, and these immigrants generally settled in communities like Clifton, Morenci, or Metcalf. Also, some Spanish immigrants began arriving at Clifton-Morenci after 1912 (Lawrence Anthony Cardoso, "Mexican Emigration to the United States, 1900 to 1930: An Analysis of Socio-Economic Causes" (Ph.D. dissertation, University of Connecticut, 1974), 66. Cardoso's information suggests that the national and ethnic origins of the Spanish-surnamed portion of the 1915 labor force were somewhat different from those of the 1903 group.

67. DCC, "Payroll" and "Time Book" records, 1903, 1915.

68. Ibid. Anglo-Irish and Italian immigrants took home approximately the same percentage of their paychecks in 1915 as they had taken home in 1903.

69. Ibid., 1903.

70. Ibid, June 1915.

71. ACC, "Longfellow Mine" payroll records, 1915. There were at least *eighteen* different pay rates for timbermen at the Longfellow Mine in mid-1915, and at least eight different rates for miners. (From Ibid.)

72. *Arizona Republican,* 1 November 1915, 19.

73. One-sixth or more of the total Clifton-Morenci-Metcalf mining-industry worker population was Anglo-Irish, as indicated previously.

74. *Tucson Citizen,* 11 October 1915, 1; *El Paso Morning Times,* 14 October 1915, 1; *Clifton Morenci Mining Journal,* 24 February 1916, 1; DCC "Payroll" and

"Time Book" records, June 1915. There were about fifteen recognized strike leaders in all.

75. Greenlee County, Arizona, *Original Assessment Roll,* A–O, 1913.

Chapter 10

1. *Miners' Magazine,* 3 February 1916, 1, 2, 5.

2. Steel, *Correspondence of Mother Jones,* 140–50.

3. Jensen, *Heritage of Conflict,* 371–77.

4. *Arizona Labor Journal,* 14 November 1915, 4; *Miami Free Press,* 14 October 1915, 1–2; *Arizona Labor Journal,* 11 June 1920, 1–2. The WFM renamed itself the International Union of Mine, Mill, and Smelter Workers, or "Mine-Mill" Union (IUMMSW) at its 1916 national convention.

5. *Miami Free Press,* 14 October 1916, 1–2; WFM/IUMMSW, *Proceedings . . . 1916,* 75.

6. *Solidarity,* 19 February 1916, 4; Dubofsky, *We Shall Be All,* 314–15.

7. Grover Perry later explained that he was unable to locate an organized IWW in Phoenix. He spoke to one Phoenix IWW member, and then convinced several IWW migratories who happened to be in town to recruit for him in the mining camps (*U.S. v Haywood et al.,* transcript of testimony dated 28 May 1918, 10970, in Box 116, Folder 3, IWW Collection, Reuther Memorial Library, Detroit).

8. Letter, from George Powell to Henry S. McCluskey, 8 February 1917, in Union Correspondence, Henry S. McCluskey Collection, Arizona State University Library, Tempe.

9. But the six-hour day had previously been proposed in Arizona. Members of the Bisbee local (WFM Local 106) had proposed a campaign for an "Arizona Six Hour Law" at the Arizona Federation of Labor convention in 1912 (Arizona Federation of Labor, "Proceedings of the State Federation of Labor," Phoenix, 1912, typescript at Library, Special Collections, Arizona State University, Tempe, 66, 71).

10. Byrkit, *Forging the Copper Collar,* 158–59.

11. Dubofsky, *We Shall Be All,* 315.

12. Salvatore Salerno, *Red November Black November: Culture and Community in the Industrial Workers of the World* (Albany: State University of New York Press, 1989), 25–26.

13. *Solidarity,* 30 September 1916, 1.

14. *Industrial Union Bulletin,* 15 July 1909, 2 (editorial).

15. Ibid., 18 January 1908, 1; *Solidarity,* 13 May 1916, 4.

16. Salerno, *Red November Black November,* 25.

17. Letter, from Grover Perry to William D. Haywood, 2 February 1917, in Maricopa County, Arizona Clerk of the Superior Court Civil Exhibits File (hereafter MCCEF), Arizona State Archives, Phoenix; letter, from George Powell to Henry S. McCluskey, 1917, in Union Correspondence, Henry S. McCluskey Collection, Arizona State University, Tempe.

18. IWW, "Minutes of First Convention, Metal Mine Workers Industrial Union 800, Bisbee, Arizona," June 15–17, 1917, in MCCEF.

19. Letter, from Press Committee [of IWW Local 800] to Grover H. Perry, date illegible but probably 6 July 1917, in MCCEF; Letter, from A. S. Embree to Grover H. Perry, 26 June 1917, in MCCEF; James C. Byrkit, "The Bisbee Deportation," in *American Labor in the Southwest: The First One Hundred Years,* ed. James C. Foster (Tucson: University of Arizona Press, 1982), 89; *Bisbee Daily Review,* 9 March 1920, 1; Lawrence W. Cheek, "A Place Called Bisbee," *Arizona Highways,* February 1989, 7. James Byrkit lists the demand for Bisbee's Mexican topmen as $5.55, rather than $5.50, for a day's wage. The various IWW activists may have written up their lists of demands differently on various occasions (*Bisbee Deportation,* 158).

20. Letter, writer's name illegible, to Grover H. Perry, from Golconda, Arizona, 1 April 1917, in MCCEF; letter from Grover H. Perry to William Haywood, Phoenix, 20 April 1917, in MCCEF; letter from Roger Culver to Grover H. Perry, 28 April 1917, in MCCEF; Metal Mine Workers Industrial Union 800 of the IWW, "Minutes of First Convention Metal Mine Workers Industrial Union 800 Bisbee Arizona June 15–June 17, 1917 [*sic*]," 15 June 1917; *U.S. v Haywood et al.,* transcript of testimony dated 28 May 1918, 8852, 8870, in Box 116, Folder 3, IWW Collection, Walter Reuther Memorial Library, Detroit. According to James Sandos, *El Rebelde* was itself a bone of contention between IWW and Partido Liberal Mexicano factional groups in Los Angeles (*Rebellion in the Borderlands,* 137). *Regeneración's* 1915 Arizona circulation, while not trivial, was so minimal as to indicate that the newspaper was seldom seen in most places in the state. *Regeneración* had 168 Arizona subscribers in late 1915 (*Rebellion in the Borderlands,* 59).

21. Miles, *Something in Common,* 492–95.

22. John MacDonald, "From Butte to Bisbee," *International Socialist Review* 17, no. 2 (August 1917):69–70.

23. Byrkit, *Forging the Copper Collar,* 183. It is impossible to state with certainty, using currently available evidence, whether or not Grover Perry moved Metal Mine Workers 800's headquarters out of Bisbee because he sought to avoid destruction of the IWW apparatus in the central western and southwestern states. However, the circumstantial evidence discussed here seems to indicate that fear of anti-IWW action caused the move.

24. Undated letter fragment from E. J. MacCosham to unknown recipient, in MCCEF; ibid., letter, Embree to Perry, 26 June 1917; ibid., letter from unknown writer to Perry, 1 April 1917; ibid., letter from Roger S. Culver to Perry, 15 April 1917; ibid., Metal Mine Industrial Workers Union 800, "Bulletin," n.d.; telegram from J. H. Donnelly to H. S. McCluskey, 9 July 1917, in Union Correspondence, Henry S. McCluskey Collection, Arizona State University Library, Tempe; IWW, "Proceedings of the Tenth Convention of the Industrial Workers of the World," 20 November–10 December 1917, 38. Surreptitious Wobbly organizing in Morenci the

previous fall had resulted in a murder, some arrests, and the forcible ejection of several IWW supporters from Morenci. The Wobblies' 1916 troubles probably convinced them to avoid Morenci in 1917 (*El Rebelde,* July–November, 1916).

25. James David McBride, "Deportation at Jerome: The Reaction to Militant Unionism in a Western Mining Camp" (Tempe, Arizona: Scottsdale Corral of the Westerners, 1978), 1, 13–15. In both "deportations," mining workers, including many men who were either IWW sympathizers or members, were forcibly detained, moved about by train, and then forced to disembark at distant points on the rail lines, far from home.

26. *Arizona Republican,* 1 November 1915, 10.

27. James R. Kluger, *The Clifton-Morenci Strike: Labor Difficulty in Arizona, 1915–1916* (Tucson: University of Arizona Press, 1970), 68–72.

28. *Arizona Republican,* March, April, May 1916; *The Copper Era and Morenci Leader,* 19 October 1917, 5.

29. *Engineering and Mining Journal* 104, no. 3 (21 July 1917):136.

30. *The Copper Era and Morenci Leader,* 9 October 1917, 5; *Engineering and Mining Journal,* 13 October 1917, 641.

31. *Engineering and Mining Journal,* 4 August 1917, 228.

32. Ibid., 21 July 1917, 136.

33. Ibid. The mine managers reported that "many of our best miners left the district," and that difficulties arose because of the "attitude" of many of the relatively inexperienced employees (Norman Carmichael, "The Wage Question in the Clifton-Morenci-Metcalf District," 1917 pamphlet, in Arizona State Archives, Phoenix, 6).

34. *Miners' Magazine,* December 1916, 3.

35. *Engineering and Mining Journal,* 21 July 1917, 136.

36. Ibid., 136–37.

37. Ibid. Only three years earlier, Superintendent John Devine of the Ray Consolidated Company (at Ray) had explained that he liked the idea of employing Mexican workers because "Mexicans are not very susceptible to agitation" (U.S. Department of Labor, "Company Towns," 14).

38. *Solidarity,* 10 March 1917, 1; 9 May 1917, 1; 9 June 1917, 1, 3.

39. Ibid., June 1917, 1, 3.

40. Ibid., 23 June 1917, 4.

41. Ibid., 26 May 1917, 3, 4.

42. Ibid., 9 June 1917, 3.

43. *Miami Daily Silver Belt,* 30 July 1917, 1.

44. John S. Goff, *George W. Hunt and His Arizona* (Pasadena, Calif: Socio-Technical Publications, 1973), 102; *Miners' Magazine,* June 1917, 3; Jensen, *Heritage of Conflict,* 391.

45. *Solidarity,* 21 July 1917, 8; Goff, *George W. Hunt,* 102; McBride, "Deportation at Jerome," 2–15.

46. McBride, "Deportation at Jerome"; *Miners' Magazine,* January 1917, 1; February 1917, 2, 5.

47. *The Copper Era and Morenci Leader,* 20 July 1917, 3.

48. Alexander M. Bing, *War-Time Strikes and Their Adjustment* (New York: E. Dutton, 1921), 217.

49. *Bingham Press-Bulletin,* 25 October 1918, 1. The Utah Copper Company had a reputation for economical, efficient operation. The decline of profitability was attributed to higher taxes, higher materials costs, and higher transportation costs.

50. However, the Miami union local had been active before the hypothetical "great spring drive" began. They sought a 50¢ daily wage increase and a union recognition agreement in December 1916 (Wilma Gray Sain, "A History of the Miami Area, Arizona" (M.A. thesis, University of Arizona, 1944), 135.

51. Jensen, *Heritage of Conflict,* 382.

52. Untitled typescript, signed by Joseph Cannon, n.d., in Arizona State Archives collection, Phoenix.

53. Mine Operators of the Globe-Miami-Superior Mining District, "Conditions and Events," 11.

54. Memorandum, typed, no name, n.d., explaining the Globe-Miami strike situation, 2, in Arizona State Archives, Phoenix. The elimination of the sliding scale (the Miami scale) would have eliminated the possibility that wages could eventually slide downward with declining copper wholesale prices. However, a "flat rate" minimum wage without the use of a binding contract during the exceptionally inflationary World War I period meant that labor and management would certainly have to renegotiate wages in the near future. That, in turn, suggested the possibility of a perpetual series of strikes over the wage issue, and may have indicated to management the truly enormous difficulties they might have had to encounter in genuine negotiations with the IWW.

Large mining corporations, including the Anaconda Corporation (Montana) and the Homestake Mining Company (South Dakota) created comprehensive card systems to track potential employees. Beginning in about 1910, these firms (and later others as well) required job seekers to report first to company employment offices, where they were screened and, if approved, issued "rustling cards" which enabled the men seeking work to approach mine foremen and request job placement. Rustling cards were extremely unpopular.

55. Jensen, *Heritage of Conflict,* 383–84, 392, 393.

56. Mine Operators of the Globe-Miami-Superior Mining District, "Conditions and Events," 19, 20, 22.

57. Ibid.; Governor Campbell had briefly replaced Governor Hunt, in a political imbroglio which was to reverse itself soon afterward, resulting in Hunt finally ousting Campbell.

58. Hunt Diaries, typescript version, 1917, 63 (dated 9 July 1917). Hunt was not the governor during most of 1917 (Kluger, *Clifton-Morenci Strike,* 73–74).

59. Hunt Diaries, typescript version, 1917, 69.

60. Ibid., 67–68.

61. *Miami Daily Silver Belt,* 14 July 1917, 1.

62. Mine Operators of the Globe-Miami-Superior Mining District, "Conditions and Events," 23; letter from Hon. George W. Hunt and Hon. John McBride, Commissioners of Conciliation, to Secretary of Labor William B. Wilson, 17 August 1917, 12, in Arizona State Archives, Phoenix.

63. Letter, from Hon. George W. Hunt, Commissioner of Conciliation, to Secretary of Labor William B. Wilson, 2 August 1917, in Arizona State Archives, Phoenix.

64. Letter, from C. E. Mills, B. Britton Gottsberger, and G. Beckett, mine managers in the Globe-Miami area, to Judge John McBride, 11 August 1917, in Arizona State Archives, Phoenix.

65. Ibid.

66. *Miami Daily Silver Belt,* 16 July 1917, 1.

67. Mine Operators of the Globe-Miami-Superior Mining District, "Conditions and Events," 21. The Austro-Hungarian Empire, of course, was one of the Central Powers, and was a declared enemy of the United States during the war.

68. *Miners' Magazine,* October 1917, 1. Most of the anticorporation testimony collected by the federal conciliators was offered by Spanish-surnamed, and especially by Slavic-surnamed workers, which suggests the extent of their participation in the strike, and the reason for the corporations' hostility toward "un-American" persons (*Miners' Magazine,* August 1917, 5).

69. *Miami Daily Silver Belt,* 21 July 1917, 1.

70. List, typewritten, headed "The Kinney House," no name, n.d., containing Globe and Miami committeemen's names, in Arizona State Archives, Phoenix.

71. *Miami Daily Silver Belt,* August 1917, passim.

72. Mine Operators of the Globe-Miami-Superior Mining District, "Conditions and Events," 9; *Solidarity,* 19 May 1917, 1; Bing, *War-Time Strikes and Their Adjustment,* 152–53.

73. Bing, *War-Time Strikes and Their Adjustment,* 152. For instance, Secretary Wilson stated that "the unions should not try to force union shop conditions during the war period where they had not been able to force them before the war" (*Miners' Magazine,* November 1917, 7).

74. Letter, from Governor George W. Hunt to Secretary of War Newton D. Baker, 9 February 1918, in Arizona State Archives, Phoenix, 1.

75. Bing, *War-Time Strikes and Their Adjustment,* 54.

76. Edward Berman, *Labor Disputes and the President of the United States* (New York: Columbia University, 1924), 126–27. Felix Frankfurter, a commission member, stated that the commission would try to "adjust outstanding controversies which touch war industries, and to leave behind such a state of feeling that no conflict involving a stoppage of work would occur for the duration of the war" (Meyer H. Fishbein, "The President's Mediation Commission and the Arizona Copper Strike, 1917," *Southwest Social Science Quarterly* 30, no. 3 [December 1949]:180).

77. Calumet and Arizona Mining Company, "Report of the Directors of the Calumet and Arizona Mining Company for the Year Ending December 31, 1917."

78. *Miners' Magazine,* November 1917, 7, 8.

79. Saul Landau, "The Bisbee Deportations: Class Conflict and Patriotism During World War I" (M.A. thesis, University of Wisconsin, 1959), 24, 25, 112.

80. *Clifton Morenci Mining Journal*, 5 July 1917, 1.

81. Ibid.

82. *Copper Era*, 13 July 1917, 1.

83. *Clifton Morenci Mining Journal*, 19 July 1917, 1.

84. Ibid., 2 August 1917, 1; *The Copper Era and Morenci Leader*, 3 August 1917, 1.

85. *Clifton Morenci Mining Journal*, 27 September 1917, 1.

86. *Copper Era*, 13 July 1917, 1.

87. *The Copper Era and Morenci Leader*, 8 September 1917, 1; 21 September 1917, 1.

88. Telegram, from seventy-three Clifton-area residents and Norman Carmichael, General Manager of the Arizona Copper Mining Company to Governor George W. Hunt, 10 November 1916, in Arizona State Archives, Phoenix.

89. *The Copper Era and Morenci Leader*, 19 October 1917, 1. There was considerable doubt as to whether these arrests were based on a genuine complaint, or whether they were part of a management-inspired antistrike effort.

90. Ibid., 1 December 1917, 1.

91. Ibid., 2 November 1917, 1.

92. IUMMSW, *Executive Board Minutes . . . 1917*, 108; *Miners' Magazine*, December 1917, 3.

93. *The Copper Era and Morenci Leader*, 9 November 1917, 1. Article also mentions that a similar agreement was signed at Jerome.

94. IUMMSW, *Proceedings . . .1918*, 12.

95. *The Copper Era and Morenci Leader*, 9 November 1917, 7.

96. *Defense News Bulletin*, 15 December 1917, 1.

97. *Miami Daily Silver Belt*, 23 October 1917, 3, 7.

98. *The Copper Era and Morenci Leader*, 23 November 1917, 1.

Chapter 11

1. *The Copper Era and Morenci Leader* carried articles throughout the summer of 1917 about the expected advent of a fixed wholesale copper price (*The Copper Era and Morenci Leader*, July–September 1917).

2. *Miami Silver Belt*, 16 August 1917, 1.

3. IUMMSW, *Proceedings . . . 1918*, 96.

4. *Engineering and Mining Journal* 106, no. 3 (20 July 1918):153.

5. Ibid., vol. 106, no. 7 (7 August 1918):324. The price ceiling was raised to 26¢ in June, 1918 (Hildebrand and Mangum, *Capital and Labor*, 112).

6. *Engineering and Mining Journal* 106, no. 9 (31 August 1918):426.

7. *Miners' Magazine*, December 1917, 1.

8. Ibid., 3; letter from H. Bronilette, Secretary, Globe Miners' Union, to Governor George W. Hunt, dated 9 February 1918, in Arizona State Archives, Phoenix.

9. IUMMSW, *Executive Board Minutes,* 80 (dated 15 January 1918).

10. IUMMSW, *Proceedings . . . 1918* (President Moyer's Report), 29.

11. DCC, "Payroll" and "Time Sheet" records, May 1903 and June 1915; ACC, "Longfellow Mine" Time Sheet records, June 1915.

12. Park, "History of Mexican Labor," 245. Park's Table 6 does not distinguish between Mexicans and Spanish Americans. Also, Park did not clearly define the occupations of the men he described in his Table 6.

13. ACC, "Longfellow Mine" Time Sheet records, June 1–15, 1918.

14. Spendlove, "History of Bingham Canyon," 66a.

15. *Engineering and Mining Journal* 106, no. 7 (16 February 1918):352; 105, no. 13 (30 March 1918):615; 105, no. 16 (20 April 1918):768; *Bingham Press-Bulletin,* 1 March 1918, 1.

16. *Engineering and Mining Journal* 106, no. 5 (3 August 1918):204.

17. Ibid. 106, no. 2 (13 July 1918):85.

18. IUMMSW, *Proceedings . . . 1918,* 12. Alexander M. Bing noted the closing of the gap between skilled and unskilled labor, the equalization of wage rates in given industries in various localities, and the standardization of wage rates for particular occupational titles, nationally. He associated these phenomena with the wartime production effort. But in the southwestern and Utah and Nevada copper mining and processing industry, these tendencies were definitely linked to prewar and wartime labor-management relations, rather than government and corporate management wartime initiatives (*War-Time Strikes and Their Adjustment,* 195–202).

19. U.S. Department of Labor, *Annual Report of the Secretary of Labor. Reports of the U.S. Department of Labor* (Washington, D.C.: U.S. Government Printing Office, 1918), 15.

20. ACC, "Payroll" and "Time Book" records, June 1915, June 1917, June 1920.

21. U.S. Department of Labor, "Transcript of the Proceedings of the President's Mediation Commission," 233.

22. Ibid.

23. Ibid., 238–39.

24. Ibid., 231–381.

25. U.S. Commission on Industrial Relations, "Alleged Deportations from Bingham Canyon," November 7–8, 118.

26. U.S. Department of Labor, "Report of the President's Mediation Commission to the President of the United States" (Washington, D.C.: U.S. Government Printing Office, 1918), 7.

27. *Miners' Magazine,* October 1917, 8; *The Copper Era and Morenci Leader,* 10 August 1917, 1. Assigning perceived ethnicity on the basis of perceived surname origins is an uncertain procedure. Perhaps as many as eleven or even twelve of the Clifton district delegates were Mexican, Spanish, or Spanish American.

28. Ibid.; IUMMSW, *Proceedings . . . 1918,* 32.

29. ACC, "Longfellow Mine" payroll, 1–16 June 1916; *The Copper Era and Morenci Leader,* 10 August 1917, 1; Philip Taft, *The AFL in the Time of Gompers,* 325; Pan-American Federation of Labor, *Report of the Proceedings of the Fifth Congress of the Pan-American Federation of Labor, 1927* (Washington, D.C.: Pan-American Federation of Labor, 1927), 19.

30. *The Copper Era and Morenci Leader,* 4 January 1918, 1.

31. Pan-American Federation of Labor, *Report on the Proceedings, Meeting of the International Labor Conference at Laredo, Texas,* 13 November 1918 (Laredo: Pan-American Federation of Labor, 1918), 18, 24–25, 41.

32. Spectacular Anglo-American career success stories were fairly well-known and are a part of the legend of the early-twentieth-century mining West. Examples appear in Clark C. Spence, *Mining Engineers and the American West* (New Haven: Yale University Press, 1970), 24, 64.

33. Personal interview with Claude Dannelly, an early-twentieth-century Hurley resident, 20 February 1975; Huginnie, "Strikitos," 173; personal interview with Bardo Juarez, an early-twentieth-century Hurley area resident, 21 February 1975; sixteen articles about retired employees from *Chinorama* (a publication of the Chino Mines Division, Kennecott Copper Mining Corporation, 1955–58; March–April 1962, 19; January–February 1965, 19; May–June 1966, 23. The same notion of employer discrimination in favor of Anglos and against Mexicans as discrimination for primarily racist social reasons, rather than for business or economic reasons, appears in a recent study of socioeconomic change in pre-1900 Texas. The authors conclude that generally, especially across south and east Texas, there was an increasingly "willful intent to discriminate against Mexicans in employment" (Kenneth L. Stewart and Arnold De León, *Not Room Enough: Mexicans, Anglos, and Socioeconomic Change in Texas, 1850–1900* [Albuquerque: University of New Mexico Press, 1993], 27–30, esp. 29).

34. George F. Leaming, "Labor and Copper in Arizona: Origin and Growth," *Arizona Review,* April 1967, 15; E. Mathewson, "History of the Ajo District," a paper read at a meeting to the Tucson Literary Club, November 1933, typescript at Arizona Room, Arizona State University Archives, Tempe; *Miners' Magazine,* January, 1917, 1, 4; February, 1917, 2, 5.

35. IUMMSW, *Proceedings . . . 1918,* 96.

36. Ibid., 32.

37. Pan-American Federation of Labor, *Report of the Proceedings of the Second Congress of the Pan-American Federation of Labor* (Washington, D.C.: Pan-American Federation of Labor, 1919), 13–14, 23; *Miami Silver Belt, Arizona Labor Journal,* 1928–30.

38. *Bingham Press-Bulletin,* 10 May 1918, 1.

39. U.S. Commission on Industrial Relations, "Alleged Deportations from Bingham Canyon," 36–37.

40. *Miners' Magazine,* November 1917, 4.

41. *Bingham Press-Bulletin,* 11 January 1918, 1.

42. Ibid., 1918, passim. Bingham was not, of course, a company town.

43. Claude Dannelly interview.

44. *Miami News,* 7 September 1912, 1, 6; *Globe Leader,* 7 May 1915, 5; *Miami Free Press,* 29 July 1915, 5; 9 September 1915, 5; 23 September 1915, 4.

45. *Miami Free Press,* 23 September 1915, 1–2; *Arizona Labor Journal,* 30 December 1915, 1; 6 January 1916, 1; 11 June 1920, 75.

46. *Miners' Magazine,* January 1917, 1.

INDEX

Acosta, Carmen, 68–69, 72, 76–77

African Americans, 6, 34, 60, 135, 137, 166, 200, 206n, 221n, 248n

Agricultural Workers' Organization: and IWW, 175–76

Ainsa, J. Y., 159, 165

Ajo (Arizona), 18, 63, 184, 198, 203

Albanian immigrants, 6, 94

Alfirevich, Matt, 108, 200

Alianza Hispano Americano, 45–46, 54, 71, 134, 159, 165

American Federation of Labor: and historiographical discussions about ethnicity, 3, 4, 5, 6, 207n, 212n; and Western Federation of Miners' 1904–07 union-building, 62; and 1907–10 Arizona labor activism, 77, 80, 86, 88; and White Pine County, Nevada, and Bingham Canyon, Utah, activism, including 1912 strike, 101–2, 121–23, 126, 237n, 238n; at 1913 El Paso ASARCO smelter strike, 130, 135–37; George Powell as convention delegate to, 151; and 1914 Ray strike, 152; and racial-ethnic exclusion, 162, 164, 166–67; and 1915–18 Arizona State Federation of Labor, 172–73; and the 1917–18 Arizona strikes, 187; and Pan-American Federation of Labor, 197; and racial-ethnic inclusion, 202

American Labor Union, 4, 62, 216n

American Smelting and Refining Company (ASARCO), 59, 63; El Paso smelter, 102, 135–38, 162; Durango, Colorado, smelter, 63

Anaconda Corporation (Montana), 192

Anaconda Mill and Smeltermen's Union (Montana), 151

Anderson, Rodney D., 64

Arizona Alien Labor Law, 144, 159–60, 172

ABOUT THE AUTHOR

Philip J. Mellinger teaches humanities and history at the University of Texas at El Paso and New Mexico State University. He received his Ph.D. in recent American social history from the University of Chicago. He has long studied and written about American urban and small-town history, western history, labor history, and social history.